Braiding Histories

Susan D. Dion

Braiding Histories

Learning from Aboriginal Peoples' Experiences and Perspectives

Including the Braiding Histories stories
co-written with Michael R. Dion

UBC Press · Vancouver · Toronto

17   16   15   14   13   12   11   10   5   4   3   2

Printed in Canada with vegetable-based inks on FSC-certified ancient-forest-free paper (100% post-consumer recycled) that is processed chlorine- and acid-free.

Library and Archives Canada Cataloguing in Publication

Dion, Susan D., 1959-
  Braiding histories : learning from Aboriginal peoples' experiences and perspectives / Susan D. Dion. Including the Braiding histories stories / co-written with Michael R. Dion.

  Includes bibliographical references and index.
  ISBN 978-0-7748-1517-8 (bound); ISBN 978-0-7748-1518-5 (pbk)

  1. Native peoples – Canada – History. 2. Native peoples – Canada – Historiography. 3. Canada – Historiography. 4. Canada – History – Study and teaching. 5. Native peoples – Canada – Ethnic identity. 6. Native peoples – Canada – Study and teaching. I. Dion, Michael R. II. Title.

E78.C2D55 2009   971.004'97   C2008-904299-9

Canadä

UBC Press gratefully acknowledges the financial support for our publishing program of the Government of Canada through the Book Publishing Industry Development Program (BPIDP), and of the Canada Council for the Arts and the British Columbia Arts Council.

This book has been published with the help of a grant from the Canadian Federation for the Humanities and Social Sciences, through the Aid to Scholarly Publications Programme, using funds provided by the Social Sciences and Humanities Research Council of Canada

UBC Press
The University of British Columbia
2029 West Mall
Vancouver, BC V6T 1Z2
604-822-5959 / Fax: 604-822-6083
www.ubcpress.ca

Dedicated to Lindy Dion

To Dad, who encouraged and supported my speaking and whose voice I continue to hear.

Always,
Susan

Contents

Acknowledgments

During the summer of 2007, I read Thomas King's book *The Truth about Stories* (2003) with my mother, Audrey Dion. It started by accident, really. I needed to read the book in preparation for a class that I was teaching, and, well, truth be told, Mom and I didn't always have a lot to talk about when I visited. It came to be our routine: we would go outside to the patio, sit at the picnic table, and Mom would listen as I read. When I finished reading, she always asked the same question: "But am I an Indian?" One day my daughter Vanessa joined us on the patio, and when I finished reading, Mom explained to her, "When I was sixteen, seventeen, eighteen years old, being Indian was not a good thing, and I didn't want to be Indian." And then Mom turned to me and asked, "Why is it that Canadians can care about the disasters around the world, why do they care about people across the oceans but they do not care about the Indians living right here in Canada?" Only then did I realize: some of my mother's questions have become my own. In many ways, this book is a response to those questions. It is informed by my hope for new and better relationships between Aboriginal and non-Aboriginal people in Canada.

Based on a PhD dissertation titled "Braiding Histories: Responding to the Problematics of Canadians Hearing a First Nations Perspective of Post-contact History," this book would not have been possible without the generous support and involvement of many people. I am thankful for the guidance offered by a committee of good teachers including Roger Simon, Kari Dehli, and Celia Haig-Brown. They offered thoughtful engagement with my work that required me to think deeply about my project and to recognize and learn from its complexities. They introduced me to theories and ways of thinking that allowed me to articulate my understanding of classroom practice. And, with compassion and patience, they supported me in the struggle to write with my own academic voice.

I offer sincere appreciation to a group of friends who talked, and listened, as I worked toward new understandings: they include Dan Bulman, Nancy Chater, Victoria Freeman, Karleen Pendleton Jimenez, Judy Patriarch, and Sid Potma. Most sincere thanks go to Lara Doan, whose love and support was especially significant during the final critical months of writing my dissertation.

Particular thanks go to my dear friend and colleague Carl E. James, who continually challenges my thoughts and ways of expressing them, who is most helpful in suggesting literatures that both inform and expand my thinking, and whose companionship and mentoring make the work of becoming an academic not only possible but a journey full of laughter and rigorous discussion.

I am deeply indebted to the three intermediate classroom teachers who participated in this project. Jenna, Diane, and Chloe, your willingness to allow me to reflect on your classroom practice provided me the space and opportunity to learn. Thanks also to the three graduate students who allowed me to include their work in Chapter 7 of this book.

Deepest thanks go to my three children, Matthew, Claire, and Vanessa, who grew up during my years in graduate school. They gave the most precious gift, which was the gift of time. They are both inspiration and perhaps my most demanding audience. I offer thanks to my mother, Audrey Angela Dion, for her wisdom and her strength, for teaching me to know who I am, and for the courage to demand responsibility and respect for a difficult history that was not always of our own making. Mom, thank you for allowing Michael and me to retell your story.

Most of all, I want to express my sincere appreciation to Michael, my brother and co-writer of the Braiding Histories Stories. Michael, your love for me, your participation in and support of my work is and always has been integral to my successes. Thank you for allowing me to reflect on our shared writing project and for permission to include our stories in the book. Our relationship is an expression of what it means to be Aboriginal.

The work that informs this book was completed during my tenure at the Ontario Institute for Studies in Education, at the University of Toronto. At that time I received generous support from both the Ontario Graduate Scholarship Program and the Southern First Nations

Secretariat (SFNS). I would like to acknowledge my counsellor at SFNS, Neil Cornelius. The financial and moral support was greatly appreciated.

Earlier versions of a few chapters were published elsewhere. I thank the following publishers for granting permission to reprint and revise this work. A version of Chapter 2 appeared under the title "(Re)telling to Disrupt: Aboriginal People and Stories of Canadian History" in *Journal of the Canadian Association for Curriculum Studies* 2, 1 (Spring 2004): 55-76. Chapter 7 was published under the title "Disrupting Molded Images: Identities, Responsibilities and Relationships – Teachers and Indigenous Subject Material" in *Teaching Education* 18, 4 (December 2007): 329-42. The Braiding Histories Stories were first published as "The Braiding Histories Stories" in *Journal of the Canadian Association for Curriculum Studies* 2, 1 (Spring 2004): 77-100.

Thank you to Vanessa Anne Fletcher for permission to use her artwork on the cover of the book.

Thanks to all for helping me to bring this project to fruition.

Braiding Histories

1

Historical Amnesia and the Discourse of the Romantic, Mythical Other

> The roots of injustice lie in history and it is there where the key to the regeneration of Aboriginal society and a new and better relationship with the rest of Canada can be found.
>
> – Georges Erasmus, *Address for the Launch of the Royal Commission on Aboriginal People*

> The dominant group in any nation state often resorts to nostalgia, to mental or cultural ellipses, and to general forgetfulness in search of meanings and definitions that serve its own ideological needs of the moment.
>
> – Amritjit Singh, Joseph T. Skerrett Jr., and Robert E. Hogan, Introduction to *Memory and Cultural Politics*

If justice for Aboriginal people lies in remembering, but forgetting serves the supposed needs of the Canadian nation, where are the possibilities for accomplishing justice to be found?

Remembering to Forget: The Discourse of the Romantic, Mythical Other

Finally, nine years after Dudley George, a member of the Stoney Point First Nation, was shot and killed by an Ontario Provincial Police officer, a public inquiry was launched. The mandate of the Ipperwash Inquiry was to investigate and report on the events surrounding his death and to make recommendations that would avoid violence in similar circumstances. The shooting of Dudley George occurred on Tuesday, 5 September 1995, during a confrontation between police and Aboriginal people occupying Ipperwash Provincial Park.[1] A burial ground is located within the park boundaries, and people from the Stoney Point band were protesting the government's unwillingness to acknowledge the ground as sacred and to treat it accordingly.

Like other Aboriginal people across Canada, those from Stoney Point were taking action in response to the Canadian government's limited action in addressing land claims, social issues, and self-determination for Aboriginal people. In the aftermath of the shooting, Mike Harris, then premier of Ontario, refused to involve the government in negotiations with people from Stoney Point, claiming that their "illegal activity" was a matter for the police.[2] Positioning Aboriginal people who have taken up arms to protect their land and their rights as mere lawbreakers and dismissing their actions as illegal is based on a particular understanding of history.

I was not surprised by the premier's response. My teaching and research practice involves sharing an Aboriginal perspective of post-contact history with non-Aboriginal teachers and students. Like the politicians, many teachers and students with whom I work resist an understanding of history that positions Aboriginal people as human agents actively resisting oppression by dominant Canadian society. Calling on images of tipis, tomahawks, furs, and feathers, teachers and students too often reveal a dehumanized representation of Aboriginal people.[3] Gail Guthrie Valaskakis (1993, 156) of the Chippewa Nation writes, "From the romantic representations ... to the marginalized Indians of historical and political process, Canadian images of Indians have worked to construct a discourse of subordination." I refer to this as the discourse of the romantic, mythical Other. In school textbooks, in movies, on television, and in all sorts of advertisements, Aboriginal people are positioned as romantic, mythical people of the past.[4]

In the *Report of the Royal Commission on Aboriginal Peoples* (Canada 1996), the authors urge Canadians to attend to the past and argue that recognizing the historical relationship is the way to accomplishing a new and just relationship. They (ibid., 27) also concluded that "most Canadians are simply unaware of the history of the Aboriginal presence in what is now Canada and that there is little understanding of the origins and evolution of the relationship between Aboriginal and non-Aboriginal people that have led us to the present moment." Like the authors, I believe that rendering non-Aboriginal people cognizant of our stories is a crucial first step in establishing fertile ground on which to cultivate an equitable relationship. Clearly, increased attention to post-contact histories is needed; we can embark on this task by including First Nations perspectives in educational forums, including schools, Canadian historical sites, cinema, and broadcast television. However, further to sharing our stories of five hundred years of resistance and replacing negative or stereotypical representations with positive diverse representations, the discourse that positions First Nations people as romantic, mythical Others needs to be altered in such a way that Canadians will be engaged in a rethinking of their understanding of Aboriginal people, their understanding of themselves, and of themselves in relationship with Aboriginal people.

Sharing our stories in a way that non-Aboriginal people will hear is problematic. The discourse of the romantic, mythical Other is premised on a "forgetting" of the past, and this forgetting of particular memories has had different consequences for different groups of people. When they (re)member the past, what Aboriginal people attempt to maintain at the centre is what many Canadians would like to forget.[5] Stories that dominate Canadian history reflect an unwillingness and inability to come to terms with the reality of Canada's relationship with Aboriginal people. Nation-to-nation treaties, forced relocation of Aboriginal people to reserve land, the policy of forced assimilation, residential schools, and the Indian Act are forgotten events of a past that does not coincide with a dominant concept of Canadian national identity. Canadians typically position themselves as defenders of human rights.[6] If they occupy a position of relative comfort, it is because they earned it through their own hard work. The long history of oppressive actions taken against Aboriginal people is a direct contradiction to that understanding. Rather than challenging the contradiction, most Canadians continue to position Aboriginal people as figures of the past, as people of a make-believe world; and possibilities for accomplishing an equitable and just relationship are jeopardized. Students with whom I speak make statements such as "real Indians lived in tipis a long time ago" and "what happened then was wrong, but in Canada today everybody is equal and should be treated the same."

Critical Events

Three events that occurred during the early 1990s both inform and explicate my understanding of the relationship between Aboriginal and non-Aboriginal people in Canada and contribute to my understanding of the complexity of teaching and learning from this shared history. In combination, these events brought to the surface a discomfort I have been wrestling with for a very long time. Currently, their chronological order seems less important than the way in which they weave together and bring to bear questions, concerns, and a basic unsettledness.

Nurturing Historical Amnesia in the Classroom

> Too many Canadians are caught in assimilationist ideology
> expecting Aboriginal people to disappear. Although initial

moves were made by design more recent moves are driven as much by ignorance.

– Celia Haig-Brown, "Healing a Fractured Circle"

During the 1980s and early 1990s, through my work as a practising teacher and as the mother of three elementary-school-aged children, I became familiar with the sequence and content of the Ontario school curriculum. As a teacher in the primary division, I observed older students from a distance as they completed their required unit of study about "People of Native Ancestry."[7] Suddenly, a totem pole constructed out of cardboard boxes would appear in the school foyer, a model of an "Indian village", would be displayed in the library, and brightly coloured, fierce-looking masks would line the hallways. These creations always left me feeling somewhat distressed about the content and methods of teaching about the First Nations. They brought back memories of my own days in elementary school. Had I not participated in the same sort of activities thirty years earlier? Although I was sure that the lessons of those days were not titled "People of Native Ancestry," I was overwhelmed by the commonality of the content. These lessons focused on Western anthropology's interpretation of material culture as it existed prior to European contact, reproduced the discourse of the romantic, mythical Other, and, as such, nurtured a kind of remembering to forget.

When my eldest child entered grade four, I was expecting him to complete a People of Native Ancestry unit. What I did not expect was the way in which his participation would bring back questions and images that had haunted me as a child. My mother was born and raised on the Moravian of the Thames Reserve near Chatham, Ontario. When my siblings and I were children, we didn't talk about being Indian; our mother had been convinced by the Canadian government's policy of forced assimilation that it was best to forget being Indian and simply act white. When I was in elementary school, lessons about "Indians" contributed to the confusion I felt regarding my mixed Aboriginal/non-Aboriginal identity. I was bewildered by the description of Indians as "noble savages," which was presented to us at school and through the media. When I was a little girl, I had a recurring dream: I would find myself in the wooded area at the back of my schoolyard, playing alone. Suddenly, I would be racing through the woods, being chased by a "bunch of wild Indians." Terrified, I turned back to see if I was getting away. Then I saw the faces underneath the war paint. They were the faces of my mother, aunts, uncles, and cousins. I grew up haunted by the images of the wild savage. My confusion lay in knowing that I was Indian but not knowing what that meant. I did not live in a tipi, hunt for my food, wear war paint, or carry a tomahawk. Yet this was the construction of "Indianness" that I was offered in my everyday life. As N. Scott Momaday of the Kiowa Apache Nation has written, an "idea of one's ancestry and posterity is really an idea of the self" (quoted in Valaskakis 1988, 268). My sense of self was in a state of conflict. As an adolescent, I buried that conflict, which did not resurface until, as a teacher and parent, I found myself confronted with the same dehumanized images of Aboriginal people. What caused my distress was the presentation of the romanticized, mythical "Indian" figure to my own child. However, it was a letter from his teachers that instigated my action.

When my son's class completed their unit of study, the two grade four teachers sent a letter home. In it, they explained that, following in the traditions of the West Coast Native people, their students would celebrate the completion of their work with a "Potlatch." The celebration would include a potluck lunch. Students would bring in food to share, dress up as Native people, and make presentations about their mask making, Indian villages, and totem poles. Some would share the "Native" legends they had written. The letter began with "Dear Parents: You probably by now have seen and heard enough about Native people." When I read that, my immediate response was anger and a kind of shock that comes from the experience of wounding. For me, the notion of "hearing enough" was an impossibility. The traditional territory of my ancestors is in what is now the state of New Jersey. Located as it was on the eastern seaboard, ours was one of the first nations to be in contact with European newcomers. As a nation, we have survived over five hundred years of colonization, but much of our knowledge and history has been destroyed. My extremely personal response to the letter was coupled with questions and concerns regarding the ways in which First Nations people were positioned by the teachers not only in the letter itself but more importantly during their lessons.

When I asked about the letter, the teachers explained that it referred to the length of the unit and the amount of work students had been asked to complete, not to the people. Yet it reflects the extent to which the unit was something other than a study of the history and culture of real people. Their approach had dehumanized the unit content for the teachers and, consequently, for the students as well. The letter went on to say that "This unit was intended to give [the students] some of the skills they would need for the next unit, Science Fair." In essence, this emphasis on skills de-emphasized the content to the point of making it irrelevant. I asked myself what conclusions the students would draw from the information they were given. What impression would it leave – that Native people must simply have disappeared, that Western society dominated and must therefore be better, that Native people were primitive savages who were not capable of defending themselves and their land? Ignoring post-contact history from First Nations perspectives promotes an image in the minds of young people that the white Euro-Canadian dominant culture is superior to other cultures and that members of that cultural group deserve advantages not provided to "inferior Others." It reinforces a belief that members of this culture occupy a place of privilege in society because they deserve it. Most importantly, I asked, "How can students begin to understand current conditions if this is what they are learning in school?" In spite of teachers' desire to generate engaging lessons and respectful images of Aboriginal people, they were reproducing a discourse that positioned First Nations people as romanticized, mythical Others. Whether in class, in the halls, or on the playground, students absorb the values, see the power relations, and hear the debates of society every day. Educators need, therefore, to take a critical look at how the image of First Nations people as romantic, mythical Others is reproduced in schools and to consider strategies to challenge it. During the past thirty years, the field of First Nations education has received increased attention. Justifiably, the focus by parents, activists, teachers, and curriculum planners has been on education by and for First Nations students. Although that work is critical and demands our continued attention and support, it is also important to question what non–First Nations students are taught about the First Nations and to investigate the challenges teachers confront in teaching this subject material.[8]

Events at and Public Responses to Kanesatake

> But even as these events unfold before us, it is clear that our
> response to them, as non-Natives, is still conditioned by the
> image of the Imaginary Indian.
>
> – Daniel Francis, *The Imaginary Indian*

During the spring of 1990, tensions increased between the Mohawk community of Kanesatake and its non-Aboriginal neighbours in the town of Oka, Quebec. A struggle concerning land located between the two communities had been intensifying for over a hundred years.[9] When the residents of Oka announced plans to expand a golf course onto the disputed land, the Mohawk set up a blockade. On 11 July, Quebec police attempted to storm it; they failed and one policeman was killed. For eleven weeks, the standoff grew steadily worse. The Canadian army was called in and applied increasing pressure. About sixty kilometres away, Kahnawake residents supported the Kanesatake Mohawk by blocking highways crossing their reserve as well as the Mercier Bridge that links non-Aboriginal residents on the south shore to their jobs in Montreal. The standoff at Kanesatake and Kahnawake lasted for seventy-eight days.

The images from Kanesatake stayed, lodged painfully in the back of my mind: images of angry white residents throwing rocks at cars carrying Aboriginal elders, mothers, and children; the absolute anger on the part of white residents at the actions taken by Aboriginal people. That anger, it seemed to me, reflected an incredulous attitude, one demanding "By what right do 'they' (Indians) inconvenience 'us' (Canadians)?" What the images represent for me is the chasm that exists between too many of us. As Noel Dyck (1991, 13) writes, "Generally speaking, Indians and non-Indians stand on opposite sides of a history of interaction and tend to be polarized further by an unequal knowledge of each other. Non-Indians are, by and large, unaware of just how little they know about Indians and of how sharply the individual and cumulative cultural experience of living on federally administered reserves departs from the experience of other Canadians." There is little knowledge or understanding of just how sharply the experiences of Aboriginal people differ from the experiences of other Canadians. In addition, there is little appreciation for the frustration that comes from the lack of response to land claims (the roots of the most recent standoff at Kanesatake date back to 1718), social issues, and the demand for the right to self-determination accomplished on our own terms.

The events at Kanesatake in the summer of 1990 dominated the media and brought international attention to the relationship between Aboriginal and non-Aboriginal people in Canada. In the years following the events at Kanesatake, the map of Canada has been altered with the establishment of the territory of Nunavut. In addition, Aboriginal people are now included during constitutional talks and have gained recognition as one of the founding peoples of Canada. These changes have not been easily accomplished, and roadblocks and other forms of confrontation continue. For many Canadians, the heightened attention to Aboriginal issues has simply increased their confusion. A five-minute media clip cannot begin to cover the complexity of the issue (LaForme 1997; Smart and Coyle 1997; Dyck 1991). Clearly, change has occurred, but this increased attention has had limited impact on the relationship of injustice. These limits serve as further evidence that the problem does not lie solely in the need for an accurate record – what we lack is the means to assimilate what is known. Without understanding the history of our relationship, how can Canadians make sense of current conditions? How is it possible to understand by what right we take a stand at the barricades? We have been speaking back to non-Aboriginal people since their arrival in our land, but what do they hear when we speak? How is justice possible in the wake of such learned ignorance?

A Letter of Thanks and the Hope of Remembrance Pedagogy

> The very hope for a just and compassionate future lies, at least in part, in working through the traumatic catastrophes we have inherited.
>
> – Roger I. Simon, Sharon Rosenberg, and
> Claudia Eppert, *Between Hope and Despair*

Theresa Alexander (Lenni Lenape–Potawatami) is my cousin. When I read statistics about social conditions affecting Aboriginal people in Canada – suicide rates, substance abuse, assault, lack of educational opportunities, and poverty – I think of Theresa. While she grew up, her life was this reality. As a young adult, she continued to be plagued with pain. She was in and out of touch with me, and in the late 1980s had cut off all contact with her extended family. The last we heard, she had moved to Vancouver. Then, early in the winter of 1991, my parents received a letter from Theresa. In it, she told us about the First Nations healing program she was involved with. It had been desperately hard, but she was getting her life on track. She was now going to school and working at a part-time job. She spoke about finally realizing that she really was worthy of the life the Creator had given her and that she deserved the happiness she had finally found. In the letter she thanked my parents for their ongoing support: "Auntie Audrey and Uncle Lindy, I want to thank you, but mostly I just want you to know how happy I am." Theresa's letter was important on a personal level, but it was more than good news about a loved one: for me, it became emblematic of the hope and possibilities of education.

Theresa's letter initiated in me what Roger Simon (1992, 9) describes as a disruptive daydream: "Education and disruptive daydreaming share a common project: the production of hopeful images. That is, the production of 'images of that which is not yet' that provoke people to consider, and inform them in considering, what would have to be done for things to be otherwise." What would it take to transform the relationship between Aboriginal and non-Aboriginal people in Canada? The hope that I found in Theresa's letter came from my realization that, if education could interrupt Theresa's concept of herself as one who deserved the pain and suffering that had been so much a part of her life, it was possible to imagine an education project capable of engaging Canadians in a process of working through the differing implications of our shared history.

The summer after she wrote the letter, I met up with Theresa at a family celebration. She talked about the difficult work of facing her past and coming to know herself. She explained how the program that she was involved with was working. It combined upgrading courses (so that she could get her high school diploma) with learning from Aboriginal elders, from history, culture, and ceremonies. She explained that through her courses she had begun to understand the Canadian policy of forced assimilation and its impact on her, on us, on our families, and on our communities. It was through this work, Theresa explained, that she was able to develop an alternative understanding of herself, her worthiness, and her place in relationship with others. She had completed her program, had found a steady job as a bookkeeper, and had made a home for herself. I told Theresa about the project I had begun, sharing a First Nations perspective of post-contact history with teachers and students. Together we talked about the change we were striving for and how (re)membering and working through the past was part of the difficult struggle to accomplish it. Theresa and I were walking on somewhat different paths, but we were headed in the same direction. We were both engaged in education projects, confronting memories of violence, investigating experiences of colonialism, understanding the impact of forced assimilation, and, importantly, we were working for the recognition of Aboriginal humanity.

Talking with Theresa affirmed my understanding of the hope of education. She also helped me to understand the complexity of the work I was wanting to accomplish. I was looking for ways of teaching that would not simply set my audience grasping for that which it had always known. Rather, I wanted to engage Canadians in a project of (re)membering, to create learning opportunities that allow Canadians to recognize their relationship with Aboriginal people, to acknowledge and understand how their own identities in the present are implicated in the history of a shared relationship. Conceptually, my project was taking form; the specifics emerged in collaboration with my brother, Michael Dion, and evolved from an incident that occurred while I was working as a special education support teacher.

Remembering, Forgetting, and the Braiding Histories Project

I was in my classroom writing report cards when Robert, a student, came to see me. He showed me his reading comprehension book and asked for help.[10] The story he had been assigned, titled "Sacagawea," featured a strong, brave Indian woman who helps keep peace between explorers and Indians.[11] Sacagawea hunts, cooks, and translates for the white explorers, and, as the story goes, many mountains, rivers, and lakes are named after her. In the account of Sacagawea, the Aboriginal woman is positioned as material wealth, stolen and traded for as if she were an inhuman object. Her goodness lies in her ability to help the white traders and explorers. Like other schoolbook references to Aboriginal people, this story focuses on the pre-contact and early contact years, contributing to the view of Aboriginal people as a people of the past.[12] One of the most frustrating things about it is that it appears in a series of stories concerning animals and inanimate objects, positioning its subjects as part of the inhuman elements of the natural world.

When I mentioned the incident of my student and his Sacagawea narrative to Michael, we began to talk about producing our own stories featuring Aboriginal people. In the Sacagawea account, we recognized the romanticized, mythical Indian figure that we had encountered in the pages of our own elementary school textbooks. During our discussion, Michael and I made a commitment to write a series of stories that would provide alternative representations of Aboriginal people; we began work on a writing project we called Braiding Histories: Learning from the Life Stories of First Nations People. In this project, we would share the stories of our ancestors in response to a need for texts that offer alternative representations of Aboriginal people as well as of their relationship with non-Aboriginal people.[13] Learning to (re)tell has been an arduous process, one that took us from producing documentary-like vignettes to what we now conceive of as (re)tellings.[14] The stories, which reflect our (re)membered past, contribute to a discourse that affirms the humanity and agency of Aboriginal people and recognizes our work as active social agents resisting ongoing conditions of injustice.

In the first part of this book, which includes the Braiding Histories Stories, I reflect on the issues and challenges involved in writing the stories as a way of unravelling the pedagogical possibilities and difficulties of presenting testimony that bears on post-contact First Nations–Canadian history. I have arranged my investigation around three thematic areas: Aboriginal conceptions of history and story, the relationship between testimony and witnessing, and questions of representation. Reflecting on the collaborative process that Michael and I undertook, looking at the work of other Aboriginal writers, and listening to their remarks on cultural production helped us comprehend the issues and challenges involved in producing texts that express the historical substance and significance of the events of colonization.

I recognize the constraints of teaching and learning within the structure of a classroom but also recognize the possibilities for, and have a desire to transform, the ways in which Aboriginal people are remembered and (re)presented in the school curriculum. In the second part of this book, I describe the Braiding Histories Project, an empirical study of how the Braiding Histories Stories, as texts offering an Aboriginal perspective of post-contact history, were taken up in the classroom. In this project, I worked with three non-Aboriginal intermediate teachers whose students were predominately non-Aboriginal to investigate how the teachers comprehended and used the stories. Their conception of their responsibilities as teachers and their approach to teaching were not atypical and offer important insights for understanding how the stories are situated in the concrete practices of classroom teaching. This project was not concerned with evaluating the teachers' capacities – instead, it was about uncovering the issues and challenges that educators confront when they take up the task of teaching and learning from Aboriginal subject material.

2
Listen Again and I'll (Re)tell You a Story

Every issue has been approached by indigenous peoples with a view to *re*writing and *re*righting our position in history. Indigenous peoples want to tell our own stories, write our own versions, in our own ways, for our own purposes. It is not simply about giving an oral account or a genealogical naming of the land and the events which raged over it, but a very powerful need to give testimony to and restore a spirit, to bring back into existence a world fragmented and dying.

– Linda Tuhiwai Smith, *Decolonizing Methodologies*

Understanding Our Project of (Re)telling

Michael and I began our project with the intention of producing a series of stories about Aboriginal people that would be appropriate for use by teachers and students in grades seven to twelve. At the time, we were aware of the need for resources that would challenge the taken-for-granted ways of knowing about Aboriginal people, but we had only an emerging awareness of the complexity of the task we were setting for ourselves. It was through the process of writing, and sharing initial drafts of our stories with friends and colleagues, that we came to understand the web of issues the content of this history surfaces and the kind of story we needed to tell to initiate the learning we wanted to provoke. Michael and I co-authored the stories, and I am deeply grateful for the opportunity to work with him. I also acknowledge his patience with my ongoing need to question, contemplate, and discuss our process. The writing of the Braiding Histories Stories was a collaborative project, but the analysis of the process is my own. What follows is the story of the writing of the stories and our approach to maintaining balance.

(Re)telling and Aboriginal Conceptions of History and Story

In preparation for writing, Michael and I made a trip to the Woodland Cultural Centre at the Six Nations community near Brantford,

Ontario. The cultural centre has an exhibit called "The First Nations Hall of Fame," a hallway lined with photographs of famous Aboriginal people. A brief description of each individual's accomplishments and contributions is included with each image. Inspired by the exhibit, Michael and I began compiling a list of individuals we wanted to write about. We thought about the impact of significant events on the lives of First Nations people. We talked about the impact of war and automatic weapons, missionaries and the spread of Christianity, disease and increasing European settlement. We decided to write about individuals whose life stories intersected with key events. We wanted students to read about the experiences of First Nations people as they dealt with changes caused by contact with Euro-Canadians.

Within Aboriginal conceptions of history and story, concern is not with a chronological telling of events; history is neither linear nor steeped in notions of social progress and evolution (Canada 1996). As Vine Deloria Jr. (1994, 100), of the Sioux Nation, has written, "The nation's stories reflect what is important to a group of people as a group. Historical events were either of the distant past and regarded as such or vivid memories of the tribe that occupied a prominent important place in the people's perspective and understanding of their situation." History is "intimately connected to the present and the future. There is a sense that there are many histories, each characterized in part by how a people see themselves, how they define their identity in relation to their environment and how they express their uniqueness as a people" (Canada 1996). As Julie Cruikshank (1990, ix) remarks, "History is woven in stories and storytelling provides a customary framework for discussing the past."

I have a faith in the power of stories that comes from my own experience and from my understanding of their use as a teaching and learning tool in First Nations cultures. Sitting around the supper table after the plates were cleared, around the campfire while on family vacations, or waiting for the clothes to dry at the laundromat, my parents told stories. They were about fond memories, difficult times, or loved ones. I appreciated listening to them as much as my parents enjoyed telling them. They were a form of entertainment, but they were much more. The stories provided me with a sense of belonging and purpose, an understanding of my connections. They taught me about who I am and about the importance of respect and responsibility to my ancestors, myself, my family, and all living things. Stories have always been valued as a means of teaching and learning within First Nations communities. They are not just entertainment but power. They reflect the deepest, the most intimate perceptions, relationships, and attitudes of a people and can be used to bring harmony and balance to all beings that inhabit the nations' universe (Keeshig-Tobias 1992b; Allen 1989).

For Michael and me, the Braiding Histories Stories are "vivid memories" of events that occupy a prominent place in our perspective and understanding of our situation. They both inform and reflect who we are. Although the stories have everything to do with us, in contrast, they call Canadians to attend to a story that many would rather forget. As we worked we had to ask ourselves, "How do we engage teachers' and students' attention in stories that tell them who they are when it is a 'who they are' that they do not want to be?" Our intention was to (re)tell the stories in such a way as to establish a scene of recognition that would invite readers to attend, to recognize that "this story has something to do with me." We asked ourselves, "On what grounds do we make a claim for the reader's attention?"

Within Aboriginal conceptions, the telling of stories is a social event. They are told for many reasons, and it is the responsibility of the listener to find meaning in them and the responsibility of the teller to tell an appropriate one. Stories are told to

> educate the listener, to communicate aspects of culture, to socialize people into a cultural tradition, or to validate the claims of a particular family to authority and prestige. There is an assumption that the teller of the story is so much a part of the event being described that it would be arrogant to presume to classify or categorize the event exactly or for all time. Those who hear the oral accounts draw their own conclusions from what they have heard, and they do so in the particular context (time, place and situation) of the telling. Thus the meaning to be drawn from an oral account depends on who is telling it, the circumstances in which the account is told, and the interpretation the listener gives to what has been heard. (Canada 1996, 33)

Within Aboriginal culture it is understood that listeners will know what is expected of them in the storyteller-listener relationship. Although these conceptions of history and storytelling inform my practice of (re)telling, I recognized that I was writing for an audience that would not necessarily share my "faith" in stories. Additionally, the school context provides its own structures of interaction between teachers, students, and texts, structures that differ from the context of traditional storytelling. As Linda Tuhiwai Smith (1999, 28) puts it, "The sense of history conveyed by [Aboriginal] approaches is not the same thing as the discipline of history, and so our accounts collide, crash into each other." In some ways, this complicates the opportunities for teaching and learning; nonetheless, the differences in approach and expectation may contribute to establishing an alternative listening position from which teachers and students can hear differently.

In response to these tensions, and drawing on the understanding that within Aboriginal traditions the power of the story resides partly in the "telling," our approach is to (re)tell in such a way that listeners hear "a compelling invitation" that claims their attention and initiates unsettling questions that require "working through" (Friedlander 1992). We wrote the stories to reflect who we are and why we are telling these particular stories. The power of the stories is situated partly in our "telling." The hope for accomplishing an alternative way of knowing lies partly in our ability to share with our readers what the stories mean to us; and a critical space/moment lies within that potential for engagement between reader and (re)teller.

Understanding the Relationship between Testimony and Witnessing

During long summer afternoons in Toronto libraries, Michael and I researched and wrote about the lives of our ancestors. We read about their struggles and triumphs, and were overwhelmed by pain, sorrow, anger, pride, and joy as we immersed ourselves in their stories. Sitting at desks piled high with books, we would frequently interrupt each other, saying, "listen to this." Our need to pass on what we were experiencing was immediate. We spoke back and forth about how these accounts of injustice and resistance weighed us down and forged our commitment to our project. We found our desire to (re)tell their stories entwined with our own story. In the moment of (re)telling, we are both witness and testifier, bearing witness to the stories of our ancestors and giving testimony as survivors of the policy of forced assimilation.

When I reflect on the writing process, I remember the First Nations Hall of Fame and the power that installation held for me. Looking at the pictures and reading the words provided positive feelings about who I am and what I am a part of. The humanity of First Nations people was produced for me as I read about the various contributions they made and continue to make as leaders in community service, medicine, law, politics, and literature. The personal affirmation I find in the Hall of Fame is significant, but something more happens there. The Hall of Fame calls me to acknowledge the contributions of First

Nations people. With this (re)membering comes an overwhelming sense of loss, in that so much of the indigenous contribution has been lost in the violence of colonization, and much of what survived is unrecognized in legitimated histories. In the hall, that which has been erased is made present. As a witness, I am called upon to listen and remember. As a witness, I have an obligation to listen and pass on that which I have heard, seen, and felt, not just as an individual but as an individual connected with others.

Like many Aboriginal people in Canada, Michael and I are survivors of the government's forced assimilation policy. We have been denied our culture and are struggling to understand how it came to be that we were deprived of the experiences of our ancestors and much of their rich traditional knowledge. In this effort, we are reclaiming our past. Gail Guthrie Valaskakis (1993, 164) writes about the move to reclaim, explaining that "For Indians, museums like art and literature are sites of re-membering, re-collecting; living locations of the contradictory articulations Indians experience in history and heritage and everyday life ... Along with land and treaty rights, Indians are laying claim to native objects and images, to museums and to history; in short, to Aboriginal heritage reconstructed, lived and imagined. In Canada, this move to transform the present by recovering the past has contributed to a new debate reclaiming memory, experience and imagination." The (re)tellings are testimony to that which we have lost. They are an expression of the historical substance and significance of the events of colonization. With our testimony, we are wanting to convey to others, to elicit in others the desire to listen and (re)member, to listen and acknowledge that which has happened. Ultimately, we hope that our stories will be a form of commemoration that will be made personal. We want them to enter into the living memory of our readers to transform how they understand themselves and their relations with First Nations people.

We (re)tell the stories of our ancestors while conscious of our pedagogical and political responsibilities. Rather than thinking only about transmitting information, we tell the stories in such a way that the power they have for us will become a part of them. Walter Benjamin (1969, 87) writes, "in every case the storyteller is a man [sic] who has counsel for his readers. The storyteller takes what he tells from experience – his own or that reported by others. And he in turn makes it the experience of those who are listening to his tale." We hoped to translate the meanings the stories had for us into a form that our readers would recognize.

As we wrote, we kept three critical questions in mind: First, could we tell the stories in such a way that our audience would have a sense of what the stories meant to us? Second, in what ways would our stories impact on the story that readers tell themselves about First Nations people? We wanted our (re)tellings to provide readers with what they needed to recognize – and take action regarding – the alterity of First Nations peoples' experiences. This prompted our third question: in giving them a sense of what the stories meant to us, would we be asking them to bear the position of witness?

Affirmation and Questions of Representation

Many First Nations writers and artists talk about their work in terms of affirmation and resistance. Elizabeth Cook-Lynn, an indigenous writer, recalls that as a child she read everything from the Sears catalogue to *Faust* but never found herself represented in any of the texts she read. She describes her response to this absence: "Wanting to write comes out of that deprivation, though, for we eventually have to ask, what happens to a reasonably intelligent child who sees himself or herself excluded from a world which is created and recreated with the obvious intent to declare him or her *'persona non grata'?* Silence is the first reaction. Then there comes the development of a mistrust of that world. And, eventually, anger. That anger is what started me writing. Writing for me, then, is an act of defiance born out of the need to survive. I am me. I exist ... I write" (quoted in Grant 1990, 124).

This statement brings me back to the question of identification and affirmation. Our (re)tellings are about affirmation. Michael and I had always questioned the legitimacy of our indigenous identity. As we read about the lives of First Nations people, we came to realize that those feelings were directly related to the government's policy of forced assimilation. It was the government's intention that we feel "not a part of" our culture. There were other connections for us. We had always felt completely deprived of our indigenous culture, but in the stories we found traces of it that our mother had passed on. As I read about Bill Reid and his desire to produce art that was "well made," I had visions of my mother sitting at her sewing machine ripping out seams in the dress she was making because they were not "just exactly right." Her sewing is her art, and she shares that desire for creating art that is well made.

Finding traces of ourselves in the stories was a source of affirmation, and our commitment to the project of (re)telling comes in part from that experience. In affirming our connections, we were responding as members of the First Nations community: asserting our collective right and our responsibility to accomplish representation. The stories of our ancestors made a claim on us, and in turn we were called upon to share them with others. We have a responsibility both to ourselves and our ancestors to take up this project.

When one examines the political struggle over representation, it is important to (re)member that Aboriginal people have always been involved with cultural production, representing ourselves and our world views in stories, art, and ceremony. It was – and is – the violence of colonization that created conditions wherein Aboriginal people were deprived of the power to control the ways in which dominant society constructed and interpreted their images. How could we represent ourselves in a way that would allow non-Aboriginal people to hear (or prevent them from not hearing, since their deafness is often voluntary)? Could we (re)tell our stories in a way that would maintain their integrity and permit non-Aboriginal people to hear them?

Work in the reconception of ethnography (Clifford 1986; Geertz 1973) has contributed to my understanding of three critical considerations in our approach to the (re)tellings. The first concerned the limits of representation. James Clifford (1986, 10) writes, "The critique of colonialism in the postwar period – an undermining of 'the West's' ability to represent other societies – has been reinforced by an important process of theorizing about the limits of representation itself." As we (re)tell the stories of our ancestors, we will in some way need to acknowledge the impossibility of representation.

Second was the understanding that, as narrators, Michael and I must include ourselves in the stories. As Clifford (1986, 8) notes, "Ethnographers are more and more like the Cree hunter who (the story goes) came to Montreal to testify in court concerning the fate of his hunting land in the new James Bay hydroelectric scheme. He would describe his way of life. But when administered the oath he hesitated: 'I'm not sure I can tell the truth ... I can only tell what I know.'" Clifford's anecdote helped us perceive that the stories were our representations, our truth, and our honesty – so how could they reflect our understanding that we were writing what we knew?

Our third concern was with recognizing the singularity of our subjects. Clifford (1986, 9) notes that "insiders studying their own cultures offer new angles of vision and depths of understanding." Michael and I challenged ourselves to be cognizant of our position not as ethnographers yet implicated in the process of representing the "alter."[1] We share a connection with our subjects, yet we acknowledge the need to recognize their singularity.

The Braiding Histories Stories

Reflections on (Re)telling Audrey's Story

> What we've learned about the theory of enunciation is that
> there's no enunciation without positionality. You have to
> position yourself somewhere in order to say anything at all
> ... The past is not only a position from which to speak, but
> it is also an absolutely necessary resource in what one has
> to say.
>
> — Stuart Hall, "Ethnicity: Identity and
>   Difference"

In part, our (re)telling project emerged from the desire to understand
and explore our position as people of Aboriginal ancestry. Thinking
about the critical initiating events (described in Chapter 1), Michael
and I recognized that our need to speak had everything to do with
our position. Yet we were uncertain about that position. In thinking
about our ancestry, we found ourselves confronted with the following
questions: Can you be Aboriginal if you didn't grow up within an
Aboriginal community? If you had no access to Aboriginal languages,
to cultural practices, are you still Aboriginal? What does it mean to
be Aboriginal, and more specifically, what does it mean to us? Many
Aboriginal people in Canada have been denied their community, and
so much Aboriginal culture has been destroyed. To a certain extent,
being Aboriginal in this country means living with that loss. How did
we live with it? What did it mean for our mother and for us? With
these questions, we turned to our mother, Audrey Dion, and began
our project with her story.

We recognized it as one of strength, pride, and respect. We learned
about loyalty, hard work, and caring from our mother and saw these
as elements of the story of Aboriginal people that we wanted to pass
on to our readers. In our mother's story, we also saw the opportunity
to explore the policy of forced assimilation and its impact on Aboriginal individuals and communities.

This story is about the impact of systemic discrimination on the
day-to-day experiences of First Nations people. Being poor is not something restricted to Aboriginal people, but the segregation on reserves
and the pervasive discrimination Aboriginal people have had to endure
is something we want our readers to be aware of. In some ways, what we

want to express here is very subtle and therefore especially difficult to put into words. In the description of home, school, work, relationship, and family, we hope to create a scene of recognition wherein readers will come to recognize what the loss of Aboriginal language and culture has meant to individuals. This story is not just about loss; it is about a woman being disconnected from her culture and her constant struggle to demonstrate to herself and others the pride that she carries. It is about her desire, and that of her children, to reconnect with Aboriginal culture and the strength that comes with that.

In its affirmation of beauty, strength, and pride, our mother's story reflects the humanity of Aboriginal people. It also presents her experience of the violence of discrimination and the shame she was made to feel. Engaging with her narrative and the contradictions of her life, Michael, Mom, and I found an understanding of complex family relationships that nurtured old wounds. The story fulfilled a healing role personally and could contribute to healing on a community level.

We recognized a significant risk in that the narrative focused on our mother's strength and her experience of discrimination. It could easily be perceived simply as an account of one woman's resilience against adversity. Fearing that readers might refuse to consider the source of that adversity and decline to wonder why it existed (and still exists), we ask them to keep the following questions in mind as they read her story:

- What does Audrey's story mean to me?
- What does it mean to my understanding of what it is to be Canadian?
- What does it mean to my understanding of Aboriginal people today?
- How does my experience of being Canadian differ from that of Aboriginal people?
- What aspect of the past are all Canadians called upon to reckon with?

The motivating question from which the story emerges is why Audrey didn't speak about her past. In contemplating it readers are asked to consider what she didn't want to tell and why she didn't want to tell it. And (drawing on Aboriginal conceptions) they are invited to consider why they are being asked to hear this particular story and what they are to learn from it. Will they recognize that it is not a request to change what happened in the past but to alter what they know and how they know the past? There is an invitation, an address offered.

Audrey, Michael, and I decided to present her narrative in the first person, feeling that this could establish a scene of recognition for our audience, enhancing the possibility of engaging the questions listed above. Writing in the first person draws readers into Audrey's world, so that they come to know her, her fortitude, her pride, and her experience of discrimination. They encounter the injustice that has permeated the relationship between Aboriginal and non-Aboriginal people. The story opens a space for initiating a "but wait, something is wrong here" response. The potential for disrupting the strength-in-the-face-of-adversity theme depends on what teachers and students do with that recognition, how it gets taken up and worked through. This theme became central to the work as it unfolded. To call attention to our role as narrators, we decided to preface Audrey's account with a section titled "We Wanted to Hear Your Stories." Here, I myself am the speaker.

We Wanted to Hear Your Stories

What is dignity?
How do you learn self-esteem?
What is the value of your history?
What happens when that history is denied?
Mom wrestles with her past
Like a pattern that would not go together,
Stitching and ripping and stitching again
Not a single garment but a multi-layered gown
That becomes a baby's frock and a son's shirt.
The comfort comes not from wearing the garment
But from remembering
The hands that did the stitching.

The blinds were open and I could feel the heat from the sun as it cast shadows on the kitchen table. Standing on the inside, I had a deceptive impression of warmth on a cold February afternoon. I had just finished lunch with Mom, and as I cleared the dishes I found myself thinking back to family meal times when I was growing up. Including Mom and Dad, there were seven of us gathered around the table, and when supper was finished we would stay there talking, listening, and telling stories. Many nights we would ask Mom and Dad to tell us about what it was like when they were little.

"How about some tea?" Mom asked, bringing me back to the present.

She started to fill the kettle. I noticed that she was leaning against the sink – for support. As if she knew my thoughts, she asked, "Do you remember, when you were little, how we would sit around the table after supper, drinking tea and talking? Sometimes we would still be sitting there at eleven o'clock."

"I was just thinking the same thing," I said, struck by the mystery of our connectedness. "You would tell stories about driving the coffee truck, and Dad would talk about people at his office. The news of the day was always a good topic to keep the conversation going longer. But the stories we liked best were the ones about what life was like when you were little. Dad was always telling us stories about his mother and growing up in Quebec." I paused for a moment to see if she would continue my thought for me, and then, with a bit of hesitation, I added, "Mom, you rarely told us about your life."

"I didn't know what to tell you kids, so I let your father do most of the talking."

I could sense from the sound of my mother's voice that this was a sensitive subject. These were not easy questions for her to answer. Feeling a need to go on, I asked, "Was it because you were so poor?"

"No, it wasn't that. Your father's family was poor too. But his family was white and I was Indian. When I was growing up, being Indian meant being poor, being called nasty names, and being made to feel as if we were worthless. What kind of after-dinner stories would those have made? Remember, I always said, 'I'm Canadian.' I didn't want to be Indian."

I paused for a moment to think back. I could hear those words again. It was a disturbing memory: "I'm a Canadian! I'm a Canadian!" There was an insistence in her voice that made me feel uncomfortable and confused. I struggled to express the feeling. Her words were not an assertion of pride but a claim for respect.

I have lived with these words all my life, and only now am I beginning to understand what motivated my mother to make this claim. She always argued, "My father joined the army during the Second World War, and we gave up our Indian status – that meant we were Canadians." I began to understand the contradiction. Being Canadian meant denying her Aboriginal identity. Other details came back to me. "I felt that you didn't want us to be Indian," I said. "Whenever anybody commented about our black hair, you insisted that our hair wasn't black – it was dark brown. I always wondered what was wrong with having black hair. It was so confusing because we knew we were 'part' Indian, but we didn't know what that meant. The Indians we learned about at school and on TV were noble chiefs and pretty princesses who lived in tipis, rode on horses, and carried bows and arrows."

"Those were not my stories."

"But, Mom, we wanted to know, we wanted to know you. We wanted to hear your stories." As I spoke these words, I felt a longing in my voice and recognized my desire to hear her story. I spoke again. "I remember you telling us a few stories about growing up on the reserve, and I remember that you took us there a couple of times. What was it like for you, Mom, when you were growing up?"

Audrey's Story

At the end of my day, I like listening to Aboriginal flute music. I turn out the electric lights, light a few candles, and sink into my favourite blue chair. It's an old but sturdy chair, re-covered more than once. I can feel the new, soft, velvety material as my hands stroke the arms. I remember, when you children were young, one or the other of you would immediately jump out of the chair, shouting "Mom's chair, Mom's chair" whenever I walked into the living room. I give the arm another soft caress and listen to the relaxing, even soothing, sounds of the flutes. The music evokes feelings of connection and I remember.

I was born on 28 March 1930 to Effie and Victor Tobias on the Moravian of the Thames Indian Reserve and was named Audrey Angela. I never could figure out why my mother couldn't have put it the other way around. I always hated my odd-sounding name. I thought Angela would have been a much better choice. It sounded pretty.

Our house was set back from the dirt road, past a
dried-out, scruffy lawn. It was a very small two-storey,
wood-frame house. The ground floor was one big open
room. There was a table and a wood stove on one side
and a bed for my parents and baby sister, Elizabeth, on
the other side. I slept upstairs with my four brothers and
sister. There was a curtain dividing the girls' side from
the boys' side. In the summer it was stuffy and hot, but
the winters were cold. Lying in bed with my sister, I
would try to ignore the cold, but the flimsy shingles
rattling in the wind made it hard to sleep. The closest
we came to insulation was the newspaper my brothers
and I stuffed into the space between the walls and the
roof. In the morning, we would push the rickety old beds
from one side of the room to the other. Stretching with
all our might, with fists full of newspaper, we tried to
remember where the gusts of wind had blown in the
night before. The floor was just as bad. In the fall, the
whole family would work at collecting dirt to pack
around the bottom of the house. This banking was
supposed to stop the wind from gusting below the
floorboards on cold winter days. But no matter how
much newspaper and mud we packed in, it was
impossible to keep the cold out of that house.

We grew most of our own food in a large vegetable
lot out behind the house. In the spring, the ground had
to be prepared and the seeds planted. One of my happy
childhood memories is playing "Peter Rabbit" in the
garden during the late summer. When the garden was in
full growth, my sister Joan, who always played the part
of Mr. McGregor, would try to catch me and my brother
Ken sneaking food out of the garden. If she caught us,
she would scare us and we would run away. In the fall,
the garden was a lot of hard work. We had to pick the
vegetables and store them in the "dugout." We would be
eating the potatoes, carrots, onions, squash, and turnips
until just after Christmas, when the vegetables would run
out and there was not much to eat. January and February
were hungry months. For supper, Mom would cook a pot
of macaroni and mix it with a can of tomatoes. At breakfast

we would sit around the table watching her mix flour and water in a big bowl. She would take a wad of the gooey mixture in her hands, roll it into little strings, and drop them into a pot of boiling water. I called this stuff "slippery mush." With canned milk and sugar it was good, but most of the time we had to eat it plain.

There were no jobs on the reserve. My father worked a few months of the year at a sawmill in town, and during the spring he fished, but there were many months when there was no work. During the winter, I remember Mom was always busy weaving baskets. Dad would go into the bush and cut down a certain kind of tree. Then came the work of preparing the wood for weaving. I remember them cutting and pounding the strips of wood. The strips had to be soaked in the washtub for a couple of days, and then there was more cutting and splitting. When the strips were the right thickness, Mom and Dad would smooth the edges with sandpaper. Sometimes they would dye the slats to make fancy patterns in the baskets. Grandma taught Mom how to weave when she was little, and Mom taught us. We made laundry baskets, waste paper baskets, and baby cradles. When we had a stack of baskets ready, Mom and Dad would go into town and sell them.

I knew that my family belonged to the Delaware Nation. What I did not know then is that Delaware is the English name given to my father's people. The original name of my father's nation is Lenni Lenape. My mother's family belongs to the Potawatami Nation, and she was from the nearby reserve on Walpole Island. I can picture my father and his friends sitting by the wood stove singing in the Lenape language, but I never learned to speak it. My father went to residential school, and when he became a parent he believed that it was best for his children not to know their own language and culture. He said that we needed to know the ways of the white world. My two older brothers went to the residential school at Muncey Town. Thankfully, by the time I was ready for school, the residential school had been closed down. We went to a small school on the reserve where the Anglican minister was the teacher. He was very strict and did not hesitate to use the strap. He taught us about the Europeans who discovered and conquered the Americas. We read stories about the white settlers who came and built a country out of nothing. The teacher and the lessons made us feel like nothing, as though we were nothing until the settlers arrived. It wasn't true. We had our own good way of living before the Europeans came. We knew how to take care of ourselves.

I was nine years old when I first moved off the reserve. Just after the Second World War began, my father and brother joined the army and were stationed in Petawawa. My mother took the rest of us kids and moved to a small town near Hamilton so that we would be closer to Dad and my brother Albert. There was work for Indians doing manual labour on the farms in the area. Mom went to work on one of the farms, and we kids went to a school in the town of Aldershot. The teachers at this school were not quite as bad as the minister on the reserve, but still we were made to feel that, because we were Indians, we were not as good as the white children. The white families owned the farms where our parents worked, and the tone of the teachers' voices let us know where we belonged on the social ladder.

When my father and brother joined the army, our whole family became enfranchised. This meant that legally we became Canadian citizens. Mom and Dad were eligible to vote, but we lost our Indian status and all treaty rights. At one point before the war had ended, we moved back to the reserve but stayed less than a year. As non-status Indians, we were not entitled to a house. We lived with Grandma for a while, but we really needed a house of our own. We moved back to Aldershot and when I was nineteen years old, I left home and moved to Hamilton, where I looked for work as a waitress.

After my family was enfranchised, I believed that I was no longer Indian. But being Indian was not something I could put on and off like a pair of shoes. Even if the government of Canada no longer considered me Indian, the people I met in my day-to-day life would not let me forget that I was. In those days, I could look for a job at certain places but couldn't even consider applying in others. I could go into some stores and restaurants, but I wouldn't even think of going into many others. Signs in storefront windows read "No Indians Allowed," and in other places a look of disgust from the clerks was enough to send me back out onto the street. I finally found a job as a waitress at a restaurant owned by a Chinese family, and I worked very hard. I was determined to make something of my life. I wanted to be a part of Canadian society, I wanted to fit in. I needed to prove that I was just as good as, or better than, the people I worked with.

I met your father, Lindy, at the restaurant where I was working. He was a regular customer. He was kind, attractive, and he was white. The waitresses were scheming, trying to match Lindy up with one of their pretty friends. But Lindy often sat in my section, and we would talk and laugh together while I served his food. I thought he was just being friendly. He was not Indian, and I never really believed that he would be interested in me. One night as I approached his table, Lindy stood up and said, "I have something to give you." When I asked "What?" he kissed me. I think our fate was sealed with that kiss. We started seeing each other regularly and before too long we were married. I remember the Catholic priest who rather reluctantly agreed to marry us. When the brief ceremony was over, he mumbled just loud enough for us to hear, "It'll never last."

But the priest was wrong. It did last. Life was not easy, but Lindy and I loved and supported each other for over fifty years. We lived in Hamilton until 1965, when your dad was offered a better job in a smaller city. We thought the move to a smaller town would be good for us, so in 1965 we moved to Sarnia. In some ways, life in Sarnia was better, but in some ways it was harder. We were the only family of mixed race living in an all-white middle-class neighbourhood. Some people were very friendly. Remember the couple who lived across the street? You kids thought they were grouchy, but they always waved and said hello to us. Not like the family who lived up the street. They had two little girls about the same age as you, but those girls were never allowed to play with you.

Looking for a job in Sarnia was horrible. When I went to apply, lots of people just told me to get out. But I needed a job and I kept on looking. Finally, I was hired to drive a coffee truck. It was hard. I felt like I was always working and always tired, but we had a home and a good life. I stayed at that job for twelve years and drove a taxi for eight years before I retired.

I grew up at a time when Indians were considered savages who had no culture and nothing of value to offer me or anyone else. I was made to feel that to be successful I had to become a non-Indian. At home, at school, or in church, I had no opportunity to learn about Aboriginal culture. I knew nothing about Lenape language, history, and ceremonies. When you and your brothers and sister asked, "What was it like when you were little?" I didn't know what to tell you. But you wouldn't be discouraged. You and your brother kept asking questions. On Sunday afternoons while I was in the kitchen baking with you kids at my elbows wanting to stir, pour, and lick the spoon, you two would start again with the questions. My hands were busy stirring, measuring, and pouring, but my mind was free to think. Maybe it was the warmth and security in that kitchen, maybe it was the civil rights movement of the sixties and the rise of the National Indian Brotherhood. Whatever it was, while I prepared the cakes, cookies, and pies that you kids would devour, I began to realize that maybe there was something I could tell, that maybe it was important for you to know a little bit about what it was like for me when I was growing up.

It was hard for me, but that was when I began to tell you a few of the stories. When I look at you today, I see a commitment to family, a joy in the telling and hearing of stories, and a deep sense of responsibility to our ancestors. This is a part of our Aboriginal culture that was not lost.

> Today I am a widow. I live in Toronto, close to some
> of my family. Each night I listen to the music of the
> flutes, and I know who I am.

Reflections on (Re)telling Shanawdithit's Story

Our responsibilities as storytellers do not begin or end with our audience. In (re)telling the stories of our ancestors, Michael and I are
responding to "a call to take up an entrusted responsibility": the narratives make a claim on us and we are charged with passing them on.
For us, being responsible meant being honest and trustworthy with
ourselves, our subjects, and our readers.

As we thought seriously about our responsibilities as storytellers, we
recognized the need to "come to know" our subjects, and so, as we
embarked on each person's story, we asked ourselves and each other
what made us want to write about that particular individual – why
did we think this person's story was important to tell, and what was
it about the story that was calling us to (re)tell? We began by researching and reading extensively about our subjects. Sometimes we did this
on our own, and sometimes we did it together. What became important were our conversations regarding our reading. Through our conversations we came to know our subjects.

Shanawdithit, the protagonist of the following narrative, was the
last-known survivor of the Beothuk, the First Nations people who lived
on the land that is now known as Newfoundland. Her family and all
those whom she recognized as her own died as a result of starvation,
disease, or murder initiated by European newcomers whose actions
were motivated by fear, greed, and a desire to control the land. Initially, we conceived of her story as one of genocide. And although we
had spent considerable time (re)telling it, our thinking about responsibility prompted us to take another look.

In our conversations about Shanawdithit, Michael kept returning to
talk about her strength, determination, and boldness of spirit, all of
which come through in what is known about her life. For example,
there is a frequently cited story about Shanawdithit in which we recognized a boldness in her spirit that we admired. She was captured
and taken prisoner by a group of well-meaning Englishmen and
-women who had decided that a few Beothuk ought to be saved so that
their culture might be studied before it was completely eradicated.
Eventually Shanawdithit was taken to live in St. John's, where her

captors would sometimes take her out for walks. She would attract the attention of the townspeople, and the children would taunt her. When this happened, she would turn and growl at the children, who would scatter, screaming as they ran to get away. Shanawdithit is said to have taken pleasure in this act. A second story is about her death. When Shanawdithit was close to death, she gave two pieces of stone as gifts to her captors. This presenting of the stones is said to have been reflective of her generous and forgiving nature. I clearly recall the moment when I heard this story differently. Michael and I were deep in conversation when I said, "It wasn't a gift. She was not meaning to say, 'I have a present for you.' She was saying, 'This is who I am, this land was ours – you stole it from us, but our presence will always be here, we will always be here.'"

The boldness we saw in Shanawdithit became our scene of recognition, and our (re)telling proceeded from that place. But this created a tension for us. We wanted to convey the horror of her experience of genocide but also to reveal her singularity. Ultimately, we made a deliberate choice to move away from the horrific details of her experiences and toward her response to and her living with the experiences. Michael spoke about the time before she was taken to St. John's, when she lived with and worked for the Peytons, a settler family. This was the last point at which she had any real control of her life, that she is said to have been happy. During this time, Shanawdithit would frequently leave the Peyton home and go into the woods; when she was taken to St. John's, she was a captive. Our fear was that setting her story at St. John's would so firmly position her as victim that it would be difficult to move our audience away from seeing her solely in that light. Considering our responsibility to her, we could not present her story in that manner. And, knowing that accounts of her time in St. John's were readily available elsewhere, we chose to tell a different story. Reading about her life with the Peyton family, we had a sense of Shanawdithit's mourning for what she had lost and simultaneously her desire to remember it. This guided our writing of her story.

In our writing there was a real move away from being guided by the question, What will the teachers and students learn about this? toward what was important about this person to us and how we could pass that on to readers. Through our process of writing, dialogue, and rewriting, we saw a change in our sense of responsibility to our readers: it was not about giving them details about the name of the river or dates or number of deaths inflicted. It was about coming to know our subject and establishing a relationship with her.[2]

Her Solitary Place: Shanawdithit's Story

For five of the last years of her life,
Shanawdithit lived with a family.
Was it her family?
Shanawdithit wore clothes.
Were they her clothes?
Shanawdithit learned a new language.
Whose language was it?
Shanawdithit was buried.
Was her body painted with red ochre?
Was she wrapped in birchbark?

Shanawdithit spent the whole afternoon cleaning the
Peytons' house. A couple of times she walked out the
front door and sat on the steps, resting. Her energy was
not what it used to be, and now there was this annoying
cough that just would not go away. She had heard this
kind of cough many times before; both her mother and
sister had suffered with it until they died. Shanawdithit
looked up to the sun; there was not a cloud in sight. She
stared directly into the shining ball of fire and was
momentarily blinded, but she found some pleasure in
this forced darkness. She could see herself in a canoe,
paddling upriver, with her father in front. The banks
of the river were lined with beautiful trees, interrupted
only by grassy meadows. It was in one of these grassy
meadows that Shanawdithit once lived with her family.
The vision disappeared as quickly as it had come. As
Shanawdithit stood up, perhaps too quickly, she felt a little unsteady. Her unfinished chores waited for her inside.

Back in the house, Shanawdithit used all her strength
to squeeze the rag dry; she watched closely as the dirty
water slowly dripped into the rusted basin. The lye soap
she used to scrub the floor made her hands burn and
turned her skin to an ugly, blotchy mess. It was not the
same colour as the beautiful red ochre that had once
been used deliberately to coat her skin.

When she had finished her cleaning, Shanawdithit took
one more long look around the house to be certain
everything was in its proper place. She noticed the wood

she had placed beside the fireplace had been toppled.
Probably a mouse had disturbed the delicately balanced
stack. It was a trick she had learned from her father
when she was a little girl. He taught her how to pile
wood awkwardly; if the wrong piece were chosen first,
the entire pile would fall. This trick would tell you if
some animal had been to your campsite while you
were gone. It was a game she enjoyed playing with the
children of the house. As she bent over to straighten the
stack, the comb from her hair fell to the floor. She stared
at it for a moment, remembering her mother, Demasduit,
who had given it to her the first time she had braided
Shanawdithit's hair. She picked it up and tenderly pushed
it back into place.

Satisfied that her chores were complete, she left again,
out the front door, down the steps, not stopping to rest.
She walked around the house to the back. The clearing
behind the house stretched at least thirty feet.
Shanawdithit walked to the edge of it, gently pushed
through bushes, and stepped into the woods beyond.

Although she did not know the names of the months,
she did know that it was late summer. The cranberry
bush that she knelt beside was full and ripe. Some of the
berries had already fallen from its branches. Picking a
few, she rolled them in the palm of her hand, feeling
their plumpness. She popped them into her mouth one
by one, savouring the flavour. As she tasted the burst of
fresh juice, she remembered the life from which she had
been separated. She was picking berries with her mother,
little sister, aunt, and small cousins. They were searching
for the ripe blueberries, partridge berries, and marsh
berries that grew in the fields. Together they worked to
fill their birchbark containers to the brim. As they
worked, Shanawdithit grabbed a handful of berries and,
as quietly and carefully as possible, placed her full container down. She sneaked through the brush and, quiet
like a fox, pounced on her little sister, squishing the
berries into her hair. Shanawdithit looked to her mother,
expecting a scolding for playing when she was supposed
to be working, and although she got the scolding, she
also caught a glimpse of a smile. Demasduit had enjoyed

watching the childish prank, but her protective spirit was constantly on guard. Listening to the scolding, Shanawdithit recognized fear in her mother's voice. Demasduit feared that the noise of children playing might attract the attention of a white hunter. An encounter with the whites could mean capture or even death. Demasduit spoke to the children of the need to complete their work. Others in the village were depending on them to bring back an abundant collection of berries. While Demasduit spoke, she slyly took a single berry from her container. Turning back to her work, with a smile she tossed the berry to Shanawdithit, who caught it, rolled it around the palm of her hand, and popped it into her mouth.

Startled out of her daydream by the loud snap of a branch breaking under her foot, Shanawdithit had to think for a moment about where she was. The time of berry picking with her family was gone and she was alone. Even so, the pleasant memory of her childhood brought a small smile to her lips. It also came with an ache in her heart. Who would listen to her story of berry picking with her mother? Who would remember? This story, like many she had heard from her mother and father, would soon be lost, remembered by no one. Shanawdithit looked back at the Peyton house and decided to move on in search of her special place. The sun was beginning to set, but she didn't feel fear; she began to feel more at ease.

Reaching a clearing, Shanawdithit could see the fallen tree, its huge trunk covered in a blanket of moss. Moving closer to the tree, she sat down, relieved to be in her favourite place. She felt the damp coolness of the moss and then pulled it away to reveal the tree's bark. In her mind, everything still seemed so clear. She missed collecting the bark from trees and the work of moulding it into utensils and containers. Her hands were always busy. She had especially enjoyed watching her father use the bark to build canoes. She had an eye for detail, and her father would smile as she stood watching the canoes take shape. She peeled off a piece of bark but stopped, feeling tired. Maybe tomorrow she would collect more and make a small canoe for the Peyton children to play with.

It was almost completely dark now. On a previous visit to this place, she had dug a deep trench beside the trunk and had covered it with leaves and branches. Guided by the light of the moon, she removed them to reveal her precious sleeping spot, a space just big enough for her to lie in. She curled up and pulled a blanket of leaves over her body to keep warm. The coughing started again and she could not sleep. As she lay thinking, her eyes grew heavy and closed. She dreamt that she felt the squirming of her little sister, asleep beside her. She heard the soft breathing of her parents and the buzzing of insects. She opened her eyes and saw the mamateek where her family slept. It was big and round, with long wooden poles bound together, covered with birchbark and deerskin. There was a fire pit in the centre. She shivered again and watched the curl of smoke from the fire rise to the opening at the top.

Shanawdithit awoke, heard the branches creak, and felt a gust of wind blow through the trees. She closed her eyes and waited a little anxiously for the voice of her mother to come back to her. When Shanawdithit woke with the morning sun, she was hungry. Wearily, she raised herself and found the spot on the tree where she had peeled the bark the night before. This time she dug a little deeper to get at the inner bark; she tore off a piece, put it in her mouth, and chewed. The flavour of the bark was familiar and comforting to her.

As she sat quietly, Shanawdithit thought about the painful nightmares that had disrupted her dreaming. Her father, her uncle, there were no men asleep in the mamateek. There was no food. She saw herself with her mother and sister, weak from hunger. They had left their camp and were walking toward the coast in search of food. Shanawdithit saw the terror in her mother's eyes. What was the price of survival? They had resisted with nearly every ounce of their energy, but sensing it was their last hope for survival, they gave themselves over to the white hunters.

Shanawdithit could not escape her memories. She saw the faces of her aunts, uncles, and cousins. She recognized the face of hunger and disease and death. The newcomers had made these faces familiar to Shanawdithit. The stories

that Shanawdithit heard around the fire changed from
stories about her people to stories about the newcomers
and the grief, hardship, and revenge they had brought.
The men spoke about being robbed of their
ability to move freely around their land in search of
food. They talked about how the newcomers used their
powerful weapons and hunted for more than was needed,
stealing food from the Beothuk. The newcomers even
used their weapons to kill the Beothuk. Shanawdithit
remembered the blast of gunfire and rubbed her leg. She
could sometimes still feel the pain from her own wound.

She dug for another piece of bark and remembered that
when she was a little girl, there had always been food to
eat. During the summer, they had spent time on the seacoast. In a canoe her father had built, she and her
mother would paddle to nearby islands to collect eggs
from the wild birds nesting there. Her father and uncle
fished for salmon that would be dried on racks in the hot
summer sun. In the fall after the hunt, the caribou meat
was hung to cure. She remembered visiting the storage
mamateeks that stood along the riverbanks. Everyone
worked together all summer, filling them with food for
the long winter season. There was even time for playing
in the river.

The sun's heat was becoming intense. Shanawdithit got
up and covered her dugout with leaves. It was these trips
to the woods, to her special place, that helped her live in
a world that was not her own. Shanawdithit knew she
would go back to the Peytons' house. She understood
that it was not hers. She would return to the family that
was not hers, to a language that was not hers.

Reflections on (Re)telling Mistahimaskwa's Story

Each (re)telling is a copy but not a carbon copy. Retelling, like translation, must be done "so that it gives voice to the *intentio* of the original not as reproduction but as harmony, as a supplement to the
language in which it expresses itself, as its own kind of *intentio* ... A
real translation is transparent; it does not cover the original, does not
block its light, but allows the pure language, as though reinforced by
its own medium, to shine upon the original all the more fully" (Benjamin 1969, 79). We can never be sure that we know the intentions

of our subjects. Our hope is to portray the singularity of individuals and to do so in such a way that they would recognize themselves in our narratives. Wherever possible, we have included details of what they said and did, and we attend to the expressive, emotive aspects of these details as we have imagined them.[3] We must always be conscious that, in the act of writing, we ourselves are constructing the story. Thus, we have exercised caution in attributing intentions to our subjects and have chosen not to focus on generalized characteristics such as "strength" or "bravery." We want to reflect the complexities of our subjects as they responded to the events of colonization.

Mistahimaskwa's story addresses the transition period – wanting to answer for the students what happened between the time before contact, when Aboriginal people lived their own ways on the land, to the time when Europeans came and "settled" an "empty" land. We begin with Mistahimaskwa's trial as a setting of the stage. The trial is a reflection of the dominant story. There was a massacre, he was the leader, he was responsible, he was guilty, he would be punished.

In my encounter with Mistahimaskwa's story, I was surprised by the depth of wisdom and commitment that this man demonstrated in his efforts to maintain control of Cree land, language, and culture. The Euro-Canadian newcomers were there to stay, but his hope was for a relationship based on respect. Somehow, that seemed like a possibility within his grasp. He challenged the system – his work was not only about personal survival or even that of his immediate followers. He had a vision of the totality of what was at stake. The very existence of the Cree as a nation, as a people, was under attack. He recognized and challenged the systemic injustice being perpetrated against Aboriginal people of the plains. The clarity of his actions in response to the purposeful intentions of the Canadian government called me to bear witness to his story. It is particularly useful in its potential to disrupt the dominant version of Canadian history that positions "settlers" as coming to an empty land and building a nation out of nothing. The land was not empty; it was national territory, and it was forcibly emptied of buffalo and people.

Mistahimaskwa's story spoke to Michael and me in a way that we felt unable to completely enunciate. In responding to the violence perpetrated against a people for the purposes of land acquisition, we give readers access to our anger, pride, and sorrow. We felt the need to reflect the violence, pain, and loss in a way that they would recognize as a call to bear the weight of the burden of loss. The details of the devastation are carefully told. The intent of the Canadian government was so clearly to destroy a nation that, for us, Mistahimaskwa's story easily leant itself to speaking directly about oppression. However, we feared that non-Aboriginal readers might perceive this as a personal attack on them and thus resist our message. Therefore, we offered them a listening position that provides some distance between themselves and the events of the narrative. In the opening address we ask, "Mistahimaskwa was not in my history book. Why did I not hear his story?" This offer is followed up by a request to those who have inherited the land to hear the account. Thus, having been denied access to it, they are now being asked to accept responsibility for hearing it.

One of the challenges of (re)telling Mistahimaskwa's account was dealing with the amount of content. This story, of the long and painful process of starving a nation into submission, spanned many years. Deciding what must be included and what could be omitted became a major task. For example, after he was first asked to sign a treaty, Mistahimaskwa waited for ten years before doing so, choosing instead to observe how living on a reserve would affect those who had already signed. We felt that the details of what he did during these years were less important than his decision to wait. Thus, we concentrated on it and excluded the details. His decision to defer signing a treaty angered many of his followers, who held him responsible for the starvation they endured. Although we could understand his reasons for waiting, we could also appreciate their anger.

When the story was presented to students, we added a map of Canada marked with the original territory of the Plains Cree.[4] Students immediately recognized the physical space represented in the map of Canada, and as such it provided a visual connection to the story. It also provided a visual confrontation with the knowledge that this land belonged to someone else. In our (re)telling, we deliberately placed the events of the story in relation to Confederation, as a means of locating it within the time frame of legitimized history that students are taught in school.

I Shared Their Anger

The charge was treason-felony and the verdict was "guilty."
Mistahimaskwa, chief of the Plains Cree, was sentenced
To three years in the Stony Mountain Penitentiary.
Mistahimaskwa spoke in his own defence:
"I always believed that by being the friend of the white man,

I and my people would be helped by those of them who had wealth.
I always thought it paid to do all the good I could.
Now my heart is on the ground."
Mistahimaskwa fought for the rights of his people.
Why was he sent to prison?
Mistahimaskwa was not in my history book.
Why did I not hear his story?

On the morning of 2 April 1885, members of Mistahimaskwa's band
went into the white settlement at Frog Lake and killed nine people.
They then travelled to Fort Pitt and, after evacuating the fort, burned
it to the ground. At his trial, Mistahimaskwa accepted responsibility
for the actions of his warriors, saying, "Even as they rallied I called
to them Tesqua! Tesqua! (Stop! Stop!). But they would not be stopped.
They were angry and although I did not share their desire to shed the
blood of the intruders on our land I share their anger."

When Mistahimaskwa spoke at his trial, he was not able to tell his
story, but now, speaking to you, to Canadians who have come to
inherit the land that once gave life to the Cree Nation, I will pass his
story on to you. It is the story that I hear Mistahimaskwa tell about
his life and the events that led to the 1885 attack at Frog Lake.

Mistahimaskwa's Story

Before going out on a hunt, I
would go with my spiritual
leaders to make an offering at
the Iron Stone. At this sacred
monument, we would pray for
a successful hunt, a hunt that
would give life to our people.
The Iron Stone was a protector of the buffalo and a
guardian of the Cree because
as long as there were buffalo,
there would be food, clothing,
and shelter for our people. But in 1866 the Iron Stone
was taken away. Christian missionaries, who had no
respect for our spiritual practices, loaded it on a cart and
moved it 160 kilometres north to Victoria Mission. When

I saw that the stone was taken away, I was angry. I heeded the words of my Holy Men, who recognized the removal of the stone as a sign of impending danger. They warned that, without the protection of the stone, disease, starvation, and war would overtake our people. The prophecy of our Holy Men came true. Each year more and more white people came to our territory, and their presence became a threat to our lifeways.

We were a hunting people and our lives were tied to the buffalo. The buffalo was a gift from Manitou to the Cree, and we praised its spirit. We made use of every part of the buffalo: the hides became our clothing, the stomachs were used as bags, the bones and horns were made into tools, and the meat fed our people. I was a young chief but I had many lodges, and people looked to me for leadership. I spoke with our head chief, Wihaskokiseyin, about the prophecy and the declining buffalo herds. We talked about the white hunters with their automatic rifles, who killed hundreds of buffalo, taking only the hides and leaving the carcasses to rot. Without the buffalo we could not survive, but for many of the white hunters, killing was nothing more than a sport.

Four years after the Iron Stone was taken, smallpox erupted in the Cree camps and spread like a prairie fire across the plains. Hundreds of our people died, and those who did survive were too weak to hunt. I was afflicted with smallpox when I was a child, and this time I did not get sick, but many people in my band died. When the worst was over, I sent scouts out in search of buffalo. When the scouts returned, they described what they had witnessed. Our land was desolate, entire families had been eliminated. They saw abandoned camps where the only signs of life were the wolves gnawing on the corpses of men, women, and children. I listened in horror to the stories of my scouts, and the prophecy echoed in their words.

Fall came and we thought the worst was over, but because we had not been hunting through the summer we could not move north to the protection of the woods.

We were forced to spend the winter on the prairies in search of food. That winter, the herds did not come north and we had to travel far to the south. There were a few scattered herds around the Hand Hills, and a large gathering of Cree had assembled there. Many council fires were held and we talked about our conditions. We heard reports that the Hudson's Bay Company had sold Cree land to the Canadian government and there was a lot of talk about what we would do. I met with Chiefs Little Pine, Wihaskokiseyin, and Kehiwin. We did not know who or what the Canadian government was, but they must have heard about our meetings. They sent Missionary George McDougall with a message of friendship and goodwill. Our head chief, Wihaskokiseyin, expressed our response, saying, "We heard our lands were sold and we did not like it, we don't want to sell our lands; it is our property, and no one has the right to sell them." He asked McDougall to tell the Canadians to come and meet with us. They refused and our concern turned to anger. We were being ignored and our lands stolen from us.

In the fall of 1872, the buffalo disappeared and we were once again forced to spend the winter on the plains enduring harsh conditions with insufficient food to sustain our people. Some members of my band left in search of buffalo, hoping to kill a stray. Others returned to hunt and fish in the lakes north of the North Saskatchewan River. I moved the remaining members of my band into the South Saskatchewan River Valley where we found some protection from the winter and a few buffalo. That year, there was a frantic search for food. I can still see the thin, wasted bodies of my people, who were forced to eat their horses and dogs. There were times when we were so hungry that we tore our tipis and boiled the bits of hide to make a watery soup. I thought again about the prophecy of our Holy Men. We had known starvation before the white people came to our territory, but never before had the buffalo been so scarce.

We had lived side by side with the missionaries and the Hudson's Bay Company men for many years. But this thing called the Canadian government was a mystery to us. Some of the younger Cree warriors wanted to fight. Many times, I had to speak to my warriors. I told them that we would not win against the white soldiers with their automatic weapons and that fighting with the newcomers would not solve our problems. Each year more settlers were moving west, occupying our lands, killing our game, and burning the woods and prairies. We needed an agreement with the newcomers that would protect our land and the remaining herds of buffalo for our people. Again, George McDougall came to speak with us, and this time he had gifts to distribute. He told us that the government would meet with us the following summer and that in the meantime they wanted us to accept gifts of food, blankets, and ammunition. My people were starving, but I told McDougall, "We want none of the government's presents! When we set a fox trap we scatter pieces of meat all around but when the fox gets into the trap we knock him on the head. We want no baits! Let your chiefs come like men and talk to us." It was not easy for me to walk away from food when my people were starving, but I would not be bought off with a few pounds of meat when our land and our freedom were at stake.

The following year, agents representing the Canadian government came to meet with us. But they had no intention of listening to our demands. They came with promises of food and medicine to those of us who would sign away our land and agree to live on what they called an Indian reserve. The agents said that the buffalo were disappearing and that Indians would have to give up hunting and make the change to an agricultural way of life. Our chief, Wihaskokiseyin, had come under the influence of the missionaries, and he agreed to sign a treaty, but Chief Poundmaker was unmoved by the offers. He spoke for those of us who would not sign. He told the government agents that "The government mentions how much land is to be given to us. He says 640 acres, one square mile for each family, he will give us. This is our land! It isn't a piece of pemmican to be cut off and given in little pieces back to us. It is ours and we will take what we want." Conditions were desperate, but I was not prepared to accept the government's deal. I wanted a treaty that would protect the land and the remaining buffalo for the Cree. The treaty that the Canadians were offering was no more than a rope around our necks. It would be the end of our freedom and would turn us into prisoners in our own land.

My band was growing. I had sixty-five lodges, more than five hundred men, women, and children. Wihaskokiseyin was still considered the head chief, and even though I had a larger following, I deferred to him. We were close friends and often consulted one another. He would say that I was a dynamic and effective leader and that my band was destined to do great things. But the white newcomers had a different impression of me. The missionaries saw me as a pagan because I would not convert to Christianity. Government officials saw me as a troublemaker because I would not accept their gifts and sign a treaty. They were angry when I spoke to the Cree and warned them not to sign their treaties, but I was not afraid to voice my opposition to the Canadian treaty system. The treaties did not provide a fair exchange for surrendering our land and our freedom. We had no guarantees that we would escape starvation if we could not adjust to farming. I wanted something better. The buffalo were almost gone and I knew that eventually I would have to deal with the Canadians, but as long as there were buffalo on the plains, I would not sign away our freedom. At the summer gathering, I told the government agents that I would wait four years and during that time, "I would watch to see whether the government would faithfully carry out its promises to the Indians who had signed their treaties."

I met with the leaders in my band and told them that we would travel south in search of the remaining herds. We would wait four years and watch what happened with those bands that had signed treaties. I was not willing to give up our land until we had assurances that our conditions would improve. Again, I had to argue for peace. My war chief, Wihaskokiseyin, was anxious to fight. I had

gained the reputation as a leader who would not give in
to the whites and had attracted many young rebels to my
band. My son Imasees was one of the most rebellious.
He, like Wihaskokiseyin, was anxious to show the Canadians that the Cree would not give up easily. I managed
to persuade my followers to hold back. I told them about
a battle in my younger days when we were at war with
our traditional enemies the Blackfoot and the Peigans.
Our enemies had been armed with automatic rifles given
to them by white traders. And again the prophecy came
back to me. War was the third element of the prophecy.
It had been a warning. We had suffered great losses in
our last battle with the Blackfoot, and I did not want to
go up against the rifles of the Canadians. My warriors listened and we moved south.

Four years later, when the last of the buffalo were gone,
pressure to sign a treaty was great. My people were starving and many families had left my band and signed a
treaty under other chiefs. I travelled north to see for
myself what conditions were like for the treaty Indians.
What I saw sickened me. Thousands of our people were
camped near Cypress Lake. Their skin tipis were rotting
and falling apart; some of our families were living in
shelters of cloth and tree branches. Our people were
starving and in rags, their moccasins worn out, their
horses sold, and even their dogs gone to make stew. The
transition from hunting to farming was not made easily,
and the Canadian government had not kept its promises,
yet, as chief, I had to make a decision. Those bands that
had signed a treaty received some support, but because I
had refused to sign, my band received nothing. Tensions
were rising and still the consequences of signing weighed
heavily. I was haunted by the words of the prophecy. I
had taken its warning seriously and worked to prevent
the loss of our freedom, but my people were dying and
they were my first priority. I signed my adhesion to
Treaty Six on 8 December 1882.

Signing the treaty increased the tension within my band.
Many of my warriors were angry. They were angry at me
for not signing earlier and for not arranging a

better deal. They wanted to know why they were still starving. Again, many of my young followers wanted to fight. I knew that we could never win a war against the newcomers and believed that the only way to pressure the Canadians into honouring their promises was to unite. I believed it would take the power of a united Aboriginal assembly to force the Canadians to keep their promises. I travelled to other reserves, met with their chiefs, and organized a Grand Council at Poundmaker's Reserve near Battleford. During this council, the leaders of twelve bands sent a message to the Canadian government protesting its failure to keep its promises. But the government continued to ignore us. We had agreed to sign treaties and live on the reserves, but we were not willing to sit by and watch our people die from starvation. After the failure of the gathering at Battleford, many of my followers dispersed. I was left with a hostile core of young warriors, and their resentment smouldered through the winter.

In the spring of 1885, my people rebelled. I was away from the reserve on a hunting trip and returned late on 1 April 1885. Word had arrived only that day that Louis Riel and the Métis had been successful in a battle at Duck Lake. I knew nothing about the Frog Lake attack until after the first shots were fired, and although I counselled for peace, my war chief was in command and I was unable to stop my warriors.

Even after the Iron Stone was taken, I always hoped that we could live in peace. We were not put here by the Great Spirit to shed each other's blood; nor were we meant to control each other's lives. I believed that one day Canadians would recognize our rights to the land and respect our traditional lifeways. Did my faith in the newcomers cost me the trust of my people?

Remembrance Storytelling

As a form of remembrance storytelling, our (re)telling practice draws on a discursive tradition in which history is something more than a chronology of events. In our approach, the study of history is concerned with understanding who we are, our relationships with others, and the kind of world we want to create. I describe our stories as (re)tellings to signal that I am telling again – but telling differently – stories that have been narrated before. Thus, I mark them as significant and the present time as significant for their telling. With my testimony, I want to convey to others, to elicit in others, the desire to listen and (re)member, to listen and acknowledge that which has happened. Our practice is sustained by an understanding that "not to remember is to accede to the erasure or distortion of collective experience; to repress memory is to reenact and perpetuate oppression" (Couser 1996, 107).

Gesturing toward the Messianic Horizon

Michael and I understand our (re)tellings as grounded in the hope for justice. We consider the need for these (re)tellings within a situation where ongoing conditions of injustice mean that First Nations people continue to experience pain and loss; they are greatly needed. As Stó:lō writer Lee Maracle (quoted in Grant 1990, 129) explains, "Racism is for us, not an ideology in the abstract, but a very real and practical part of our lives – the pain, the effect, the shame are all real."

Our stories are offered as part of a healing process. Janice Acoose (1993) and Marie Annharte Baker (1994) both comment on the healing power of stories and the need to affirm the beauty and strength of First Nations people. Baker (ibid., 114) writes, "The story is a helper, a guide, and becomes also a personal friend. I think of the stories as healing because they help us connect to some part of the earth." Shoshana Felman (1992) echoes this understanding of the healing nature of narration in her discussion of Albert Camus' *The Plague*. Felman (ibid., 4, 5) considers that Camus' positioning of the physician as privileged narrator "might suggest that the capacity to witness and the act of bearing witness in themselves embody some remedial quality and belong already, in obscure ways, to the healing process." She goes on to say that what necessitates the testimony may be "the scandal of an illness." This understanding of the healing potential of stories and of acts of injustice as an illness is referenced by Rupert Ross' (1992, 168) discussion of indigenous philosophy: "Wrongdoings are viewed as misbehavior that requires teaching or an illness that requires healing." The stories were certainly a source of healing for Michael and me. We also consider them to serve healing in the public sphere of the classroom.

We wrote the stories with all Canadians in mind, hoping that they would contribute to healing by accomplishing change in the relationship between First Nations and non-First Nations people. We intended them as an acknowledgment of the pain of the past and a hope for things to be different today and in the future. In this we are not alone. As Gerald McMaster (Plains Cree) and Lee-Ann Martin (Mohawk) (1992, 18, 20, 21) comment, "Indigenous artists in all fields across the Americas are seizing this opportunity to reflect upon the past, depict contemporary realities and present a vision for the future ... Recognition of the truths of recent history and contemporary life is essential in providing a clarity and vision for the future ... The indigenous nations of North America were once considered 'vanishing.' Indeed several indigenous nations were obliterated by ethnocide and genocide. Yet we endure. That is worth celebrating. Our struggles against programs of enforced assimilation are testimony to our powers of cultural tenacity. That is worth celebrating." Recognizing injustice and celebrating resistance are first steps toward accomplishing justice. The purpose of our stories is not to assign blame or guilt. They are about healing and recovery.

The understanding of narrative as a source of harmony and balance is a recurring theme within Aboriginal conceptions of storytelling and history. Responding to testimony about the Wounded Knee Massacre, Marie Not Help Him, a Lakota woman, replied, "I think it is important for history to be brought out" (quoted in Josephy and Alvin 1994, 6). Her statement resonates with my sense that our history is part of our being and that we have a need and a purpose to speak it. To maintain, or more accurately, to re-establish harmony and balance, it must be spoken. Mohawk writer Beth Brant (1994) explains that the imbalance that exists within Aboriginal people and in their relationship with non-Aboriginal people is created by racism and poverty.

The understanding and appreciation of harmony and balance shared by many Aboriginal people may come in part from their relationship with land and their environment. Josephy and Alvin (1994, 11) explain, "There was a symbiosis between the land and the people. Because of their spiritual attachment, one gave life to the other, and it behooved humans to keep that attachment in balance and harmony by proper conduct and thoughts, lest it harm the people's well being." The demand for balance and harmony exists not only between people and the earth: as Paula Gunn Allen (1986, 56) states, it involves all beings that inhabit the tribes' universe.

How can our (re)tellings contribute to establishing balance and harmony between peoples? Creating balance for Aboriginal people and in their relationship with non-Aboriginal people necessarily requires that I consider how and from what position the latter will interpret our stories. So I ask, will our stories be traumatic for our readers? Will our stories wound? Is it possible to (re)tell these stories with a concern for both Aboriginal and non-Aboriginal people?

Intimacy

In *Our Chiefs and Elders,* David Neel (1992) of the Kwagiutl Nation bears witness to and shares testimony of leaders from West Coast First Nations. His book is an extraordinary collection of photographs presented with statements from the chiefs and elders themselves. Neel (ibid., 12) describes his approach to a photography session: "When I photograph people I set up my equipment, we talk, I take pictures, and it is a relaxed, shared experience." His effort has resulted in images that reflect the humanity of his subjects. For me, Neel's photographs call forth positive feelings of existence. I see them not only as demonstrations but as celebrations of our existence, our power, our strength, and our wisdom. For Neel (ibid., 11), "The photographs are my interpretation, my vision, of these human beings."

The stories that Michael and I wrote are our interpretations of the lives of specific First Nations people. Writing about translation, Gayatri Spivak (1993, 183) states that "Unless the translator has earned the right to become the intimate reader, she cannot surrender to the text, cannot respond to the special call of the text." In researching our narratives, we found ourselves relying on texts that, for the most part, were written by non-Aboriginal people. Basing our stories on this material was risky work. As Smith (1999, 36) warns, "Writing can be dangerous because, by building on previous texts written about indigenous peoples, we might continue to legitimate views about ourselves which are hostile to us." We had to step back from the sources and imagine our subjects. We worked at establishing an intimacy with the people whose life stories we were (re)telling, a practice that enabled us to get beyond the research texts and speak from our own perspective. At these times, we felt the voices of our ancestors very clearly. Spivak (1993, 191) remarks that, "If you want to make the translated text accessible, try doing it for the person who wrote it." First and foremost, Michael and I wrote for the individuals whose life stories we were (re)telling.

Relationship

In an effort to more fully understand the process of storytelling, we looked to Aboriginal writers for insight and guidance. Discussing the importance of relationship in the storytelling experience, Jo-ann Archibald (1997, 40) of the Stó:lō First Nation writes, "The oral tradition implicates the 'listener' [reader] into becoming an active participant in the experience of the story. An inter-relationship between the story/storyteller/listener is a critical principle of storytelling." Through the process of establishing relationship, we saw the possibility of reflecting the power the stories had for us. Archibald (ibid., 42) adds, "The power of the storyteller to make the listeners/readers visualize and feel like they are part of the story is a part of ... the mystery, magic and truth/respect/trust relationship between the speaker/storyteller and listener/reader." Michael and I realized that our relationship with each other had enabled to us to build a relationship with our subjects; thus, we began to see the importance of relationship to our process. Archibald (ibid.) writes that "Inter-relating between story/ listener and the text/reader invites the reader to interact with his many stories to provide a framework for thinking critically about one's own historical, cultural, and current context in relation to the story being told." As we worked, we became conscious of the connection we hoped to establish among and between ourselves, our subjects, and our readers. And this awareness became a central principle in how we came to (re)tell our stories. We recognized that, in the act of (re)telling, much of who we were would be integrated into the stories, and we wanted to make our presence felt. In fact, we deliberately attempted to make our presence explicit. Thus, we prefaced each of our (re)tellings with a mixture of statements and questions through which we addressed our readers directly, because, as Paula Gunn Allen (1989, 1) of the Laguna, Pueblo, and Sioux nations writes, "to hear our stories as we tell them, a non-Indian reader needs to know where they come from, how we compose them, and something of their meaning for us."

We used a variety of narrative techniques for establishing relationship. Our opening statements are a direct "speaking to," and, as such, they serve as a form of address, but they also provide information about why we are passing on this story and what in particular we are requesting that the readers attend to. For example, "Her Solitary Place: Shanawdithit's Story" begins with a series of comments and questions directed to the reader (see page 33). It is our way of "speaking across the table" with a request to "listen to this." Through the questions we want to pass on to the reader a sense of why we are telling this particular story. In some instances, we included an introductory section that further contextualizes our connection with the subject and begins to create relationship between him or her, ourselves, and our readers. Wherever possible we quote subjects directly and include details of their thoughts and feelings. This contributes to a sense of intimacy within the stories. I believe that the ability to establish relationship between ourselves, subjects, and readers offers an opportunity to confront denial. Through the process of establishing a bond with subjects, the readers' need to deny is replaced with a need to know and understand what occurred and why it unfolded as it did.

By taking this approach, we draw readers into an encounter with the human repercussions of colonization. Their attachment to and implication in the stories, both as individuals and as Canadians, are integral parts of the reading/listening experience. Readers find themselves engaged with stories that demand both (re)membering and thoughtful response.

Attention to Details

(Re)telling our stories without describing the intimate connection between First Nations people and the land would be impossible; however, we have taken care to describe that relationship in such a way that human existence is affirmed. Our stories reflect Aboriginal knowledge of, relationship with, and respect for the land in a way that does not deny the human existence of First Nations people. We were similarly careful in our portrayal of Aboriginal spirituality and have made a determined effort to address its nuances and critical role without creating an image of the mythical Other. To capture readers' attention, we request that they focus on details that will support their recognition of difference and show the significance of that difference. In our Mistahimaskwa narrative, for example, we recognized that readers could not appreciate the impact of the loss of the buffalo without understanding the spiritual relationship between the Cree, the buffalo, and the land. Thus, we balanced detailed descriptions of spiritual practices with those concerning everyday experiences.

In and of themselves, details are not enough to point up and expose difference. They can be seen as filler in a story that is familiar, glossed over on the basis of a "yes, yes, I know that already" response. It is only when a story is approached as being unfamiliar that details have the potential to surprise, unsettle, and astonish, and thus to work as disruption, calling what we know and how we know into question (Simon et al. 2000). The opening questions in Shanawdithit's story draw attention to the specificity of her experience. They serve as a way of passing on the priority of attending to the details. In our stories, we ask readers to see what they have not seen before, what they have not been called upon to see before. If we can (re)tell in such a way that they perceive the story as unfamiliar, the attention to detail will be effective. Rather than developing a false sense of knowing how it is, we hope to activate the attention to detail as a way of disrupting the way in which Canadians hear and respond to stories of First Nations–Canadian relations.

We want readers to attend to what they find surprising or astonishing about the stories – surprise being those elements in the story that were not known before. As a starting point for discussion, teachers might ask both their students and themselves, "What did I not know before? Why didn't I know? What is the significance of not knowing?" Astonishment is that which they already know to be true but in which they find a certain unbelievability. Many who read Mistahimaskwa's narrative will already know that the near extinction of the buffalo brought death and starvation to the First Nations. However, our detailed description of the impact on the day-to-day lives of communities of people evokes astonishment and offers a way of looking at one's own psychic numbness and how that can be broken.

Attending to the Suffering of Others

As previously noted, we began our writing project firmly committed to representing the humanity of First Nations people. As we proceeded, the issue of how to address the pain, suffering, and tragic loss that repeatedly surfaced in their lives became a critical concern. In "Desperately Seeking Absolution: Native Agency as Colonialist Alibi?" Robin Brownlie and Mary-Ellen Kelm (1996, 211) describe the way in which some writers, attempting to represent the agentic power of First Nations, actually "use evidence of Native resilience and strength to soften, and at times to deny, the impact of colonialism and thus implicitly to absolve its perpetrators." We were writing conscious of this concern yet were also aware that a story that focused detailed attention on suffering and loss would be taken up as the all-too-familiar story of the "poor, pitiful Indian." Thus, we had to interrogate ourselves as to our purpose in asking our readers to look toward the suffering of others. Out of respect for both our subjects and ourselves we had to seriously consider the extent to which – and the way in which – we would tell about the suffering of First Nations people. Was it possible to describe the details of this while guarding the dignity of the subject?

The salience of this issue became clear during a moment of reciprocal witnessing. One of the first (re)tellings we completed was that of our mother, Audrey Angela Dion. Michael and I interviewed her and worked collaboratively on writing her narrative. She was born and raised in the reserve community at Moravian Town. Hers is a story of strength and determination. It is also one of forced assimilation, poverty, and discrimination. Sitting at her dining room table with my own three children as witness, I read our (re)telling aloud. As I spoke, I became overwhelmed with concern. Our story reflected the treatment Mom received from white society. Would hearing it be humiliating for her? Although I felt this uncertainty, I had made a commitment to read the story, so did not stop. When I finished, I looked immediately toward Mom and asked, "Is it okay to tell?" Clearly, it had been a difficult listening experience for her, but Mom's immediate response was, "That tells how bad it was and people will finally know what it was like for me."

I recount this incident to explicate my understanding of the propriety of our telling and of the reasons for asking readers to attend to the detailed suffering of others. Our mother's reply echoed the words of Dori Laub (1992a, 71), who wrote, "Testimonies are not monologues; they can not take place in solitude. The witnesses are telling to somebody; to somebody they have been waiting for for a long time." Michael and I were surprised by the force of our mother's response. We felt that we had been intimately connected with the testimony-witnessing relationship but had been unaware of the "waiting to tell" element of testimony.

Speaking of the suffering that was, and in many ways still is, a part of the life experiences of First Nations people cannot efface the loss. Yet, as Laub (1992b, 91) puts it, "the testimony in its commitment to truth is a passage through, and an exploration of, differences." Through our mother's response, I understood her to be saying that we were able to capture, at least for her or, rather, most importantly for her, a telling that reflected the singularity of her experiences. For me, this was personally affirming; more importantly, it signalled the possibility that, as testimony, our (re)tellings did reflect the alterity of First Nations experiences and could potentially initiate a consideration of that alterity in the minds of our readers. Telling our mother's story and excluding the details of suffering would have made it incomplete, erasing the significance and reproducing the oppression. Laub (ibid.) writes, "testimony is inherently a process of facing loss – of going through the pain of the act of witnessing." The one who testifies is waiting to tell – and our listening is a reciprocal act through which we accept our responsibility to attend to that which someone else has lived and is now asking us to hear.

Yet, I was right to be concerned. Exposing the wounds of Others is not something to be done without serious consideration. In our role as (re)tellers, Michael and I faced the double responsibility of witnessing: to hear and then pass on what we had heard in a way that would invoke a respectful listening. Keeping in mind our understanding of the ease with which our intended audience could so easily look away, or look inappropriately as spectator or voyeur, we spent a considerable amount of time working out how to deal with this challenge. How would we accomplish a renewed attentiveness to a story of which the readers could quite possibly be extremely weary? We understood that, if, in our (re)telling, we allowed the suffering to dominate a story, the singularity of its subject would be lost. We approached each (re)telling cognizant of the need to establish a scene of recognition for readers. The space in which they can recognize our subjects as individuals differs from story to story and is carefully woven from the various threads that we uncovered.

Responding to the Call to Witness

As we wrote, we were confronted with critical issues that challenged our thinking and guided our process. Establishing relationship, attending to details, and working through how to tell about the suffering of others emerged as challenges in each account. Deborah Britzman (1998, 117) notes that the study of traumatic historical events "requires educators to think carefully about their own theories of learning and how the stuff of such difficult knowledge becomes pedagogical." In (re)telling the Braiding Histories Stories, Michael and I have taken our responsibilities seriously. The voices, actions, and experiences of First Nations people claimed our attention, and we made a commitment to the project. Through it, we are claiming a space within which we call Canadians to begin the necessary work required to face a shared history that demands responsible attention. Our project is sustained by our understanding that a new and better relationship between Aboriginal people and Canadians requires that we must all attend differently to our shared history.

Exploring ways to provoke within teachers and students an awareness of their own involvement in, and desire to maintain, a version of history that supports the "forgetting" of injustice (both past and continuing) is an ongoing struggle. The need to deny history in an attempt to maintain an honourable sense of self is powerful, and the methods are deeply embedded in the dominant versions of Canadian historiography. By relying on a series of mechanisms, including confrontation and naming, and by working through and with relationship, the Braiding Histories Stories engage readers in difficult learning. They invoke a commitment to, and participation in, a practice that binds remembrance and learning. These bonds are intended to enable readers not only to recognize the limits of their knowledge, but to recognize what of themselves is tied up with their understanding of the history and contemporary substance of Canadian–First Nations relationships.

Sometimes, when I speak with groups of teachers and students about the relationship between Aboriginal people and Canadians, I am overwhelmed by a respectful silence – but it is a silence that is grounded in uncertainty regarding what to say, and in this it pre-empts the possibility of working through the difficult learning in which they are called upon to participate. I recognize and share their concerns. Talking about traumatic events and one's connection to the suffering of Others is "dangerous" work. However, we cannot use our fear of saying the wrong thing as an excuse for not doing the work. In the following chapter, I investigate the problematics of hearing and describe the prevailing classroom discourses that structure teaching and learning contexts in schools.

3
Listening – But What Is Being Heard?

> Ignorance ... is not a passive state of absence – a simple lack
> of information: it is an active dynamic of negation, an active
> refusal of information.
>
> – Shoshana Felman, "Psychoanalysis
> and Education"

While exploring the challenges associated with our project of
(re)telling, I found myself entangled in the tensions that emerge in
the intersection of speaking and hearing across difference. As I wrote,
I was confronted and guided by the following questions: What do
non-Aboriginal people hear when we speak? What is the appeal, the
enticing nature, of the discourse of the romantic, mythical Other?
What is the source of the refusal to hear? Edward Said (1994, xi) dis-
cusses the way in which colonizing governments made use of stereotypes and notions about bringing civilization to primitive or barbaric
minds as a means of justifying their actions: "They were not like us
and for that reason deserved to be ruled." Said (ibid.) argued that cultural forms "were immensely important in the formation of imperial
attitudes, references, and experiences." I argue that non-Aboriginal
Canadians continue to rely on misrepresentation as a mechanism to
defend against attending to the post-contact experiences of First
Nations people in Canada. The failure to listen is sustained through
various mechanisms, including

- challenging the narrative's relevance to one's life in the present
- locking the events in a history that has no present
- dehumanizing Aboriginal people
- claiming "there is nothing I can do, therefore I don't have to listen"
- asserting that the stories are too hard to listen to.

Canadians "refuse to know" that the racism that fuelled colonization
sprang from a system that benefits all non-Aboriginal people, not just
the European settlers of long ago. This refusal to know is comforting:

it supports an understanding of racism as an act of individuals, not of a system. It creates a barrier allowing Canadians to resist confronting the country's racist past and the extent to which that past lives inside its present, deep in the national psyche. The need to deny racism in Canada's past resurfaces again and again in its present.

Difficult Learning

There is something repulsive about having to ask why this should be the case. Why is it so difficult for Canadians to look toward our reality, to hear our stories? When I shared initial drafts of the Braiding Histories Stories in classrooms, teachers and students would tell me that the stories were too hard to listen to. In response I wanted to tell them, "Hard to listen to? Try surviving them." Yet, as an educator, if I hope to tell the stories in a way that engages listeners in hearing, I have to be willing to interrogate and respond to their resistance to hearing. Thus, Michael and I proceeded with our (re)tellings only after thoughtful consideration of what was at stake for readers as they were called upon to attend to and learn from a First Nations perspective of post-contact history. We have come to understand that the knowledge we offer will "provoke a crisis within the self – it will be felt as interference or as a critique of the self's coherence or view of itself in the world" (Britzman 1998, 118).

In "Signs of Silence, Lines of Listening," history of English culture professor Iain Chambers (1996, 51) addresses the difficult task of attending to stories of indigenous Others:

Other stories, memories and identities cause [Western] authority to stumble. For they talk back to it, take the language elsewhere, and then return with it to interrupt the nation-narration at its very "centre." An earlier imaginary unity is challenged and complicated by other traditions, other voices, other histories, now seeking a home and looking for an accommodation in this state ... The emergence and insistence of an elsewhere in the heart of the languages, cultures and cities we presume to be our own forces us to relocate ourselves, and with it our sense of individual and national identity. The links that previously positioned us in our privileges, and located the others elsewhere, are loosened. They become disturbing even threatening in their fluidity.

Engaging stories of First Nations post-contact experiences draws attention to the place of Aboriginal people in Canada and their relationship

with Canadians. Our stories offer a disruption to Canadians' understanding of themselves and, as such, require a process of "learning from."
  Deborah Britzman (1998, 117, 118) delineates the meaning of "learning from":

> Whereas learning about an event or experience focuses upon the acquisition of qualities, attributes, and facts, so that it presupposes a distance (or, one might even say, a detachment) between the learner and what is to be learned, learning from an event or experience is of a different order, that of insight ... But precisely because insight concerns the acknowledgment of discontinuity from the persistence of the status quo, and hence asks something intimate from the learner, learning from requires the learner's attachment to and implication in knowledge ... Learning from demands both a patience with the incommensurability of understanding and an interest in tolerating the ways meaning becomes, for the learner, fractured, broken, and lost, exceeding the affirmations of rationality, consciousness, and consolation.

For Canadians, learning about Aboriginal people, history, and culture from the position of respectful admirer or patronizing helper is easy and familiar. Learning that requires recognition of implication in the relationship and a responsible response is not easily accomplished.
  Learning from the events of colonization is "made more fragile" than learning about them because it involves difficult knowledge. Britzman (1998, 117) defines difficult knowledge as the study of "experiences and the traumatic residuals of genocide, ethnic hatred, aggression, and forms of state-sanctioned – and hence legal – social violence." It concerns the study of "another's painful encounter with victimization, aggression, and the desire to live on one's own terms." The Braiding Histories Stories require readers to engage with difficult knowledge and as such comprise difficult learning, that is, learning that will hold open the present to its insufficiency. Understanding the demands of "learning from" further clarifies the challenge that teachers and students confront when reading the Braiding Histories Stories.

Investigating the Dynamics of Denial
Drawing on a Kantian conception of the self, artist-philosopher Adrian Piper (1993, 25) argues that "we instinctively resist the challenge of cognitive discrimination by confining our range of judgments to those objects and properties that conform to pre-existing categories and concepts that structure not only our experience, but thereby our

selves."[1] I find her work particularly useful in my attempts to both understand and respond to the dynamics of denial that are set in motion when Canadians encounter post-contact stories of First Nations–Canadian relations. In this section of the chapter, I explicate the salient points of her thesis that contribute to that understanding.

Piper (1993, 26) writes, "Kant tells us repeatedly that if a perception does not conform to the fundamental categories of thought that ensure the unity and coherence of the self, they cannot be part of our experience at all." According to Piper, Kant is saying that, if we are to maintain ourselves as rationally unified subjects, we must employ consistent and coherent rules to organize the data supplied by our senses. From this, Piper (ibid., 29) asserts that "the resistance to integrating anomaly is a general feature of human intellection that attempts to satisfy a Kantian requirement of rational self-preservation."

Canadians entertain a firmly established sense of themselves as defenders of equity, justice, and human rights. Relying on Piper's thesis, I argue that Canadians do not register the details of the post-contact experiences of First Nations people, because those details do not conform to their self-concept. The refusal to hear our stories can be seen as, in Piper's (1993, 29) words, "a perfectly general disposition to defend the self against anomalous informational assaults on its internal coherence." Piper (ibid., 30, emphasis in original) explains that "*pseudorationality* is an attempt to make sense of such data under duress, i.e., to preserve the internal rational coherence of the self, when we are baldly confronted by anomaly but are not yet prepared to revise or jettison our conceptual scheme accordingly. It is in the attempt to make sense of anomalous data in terms of empirically inadequate concepts that the mechanisms of *pseudorationality* – rationalization, dissociation and denial – kick in to secure self-preservation." These pseudorational mechanisms provide the means to erase anomalous data from one's domain of awareness, sustaining the appearance of rational coherence.

Piper (1993, 30) employs this model to define the phenomenon of xenophobia and xenophobia to explain discrimination. For her, xenophobia is the fear "of what is experientially unfamiliar, of individuals who violate one's empirical conception of persons and so one's self-conception." She regards discrimination as a type of xenophobia, and she distinguishes between first-order discrimination and higher-order discrimination. The former is "a conscious contempt for and dismissal of persons simply because they bear a primary disvalued attribute. Higher-order discrimination is nonconscious prejudice" (ibid., 32).

Through the use of rationalization and dissociation, xenophobia produces various forms of stereotyping. Piper (1993) remarks that "It selects certain perceptually familiar properties of the person for primary disvalue, and distorts or obliterates those which remain. It thereby reduces the complex singularity of the other's properties to an oversimplified but conceptually manageable subset, and this in turn diminishes one's full conception of personhood. For the xenophobe, this results in a provincial self-conception and conception of the world, from which significant available data are excluded." This provincial theory is sustained with the aid of denial. Piper's thesis is that political discrimination is a response to xenophobia.

Piper (1993, 39, 42) believes that discriminatory actions can be self-corrected by a well-intentioned individual: "It is possible for someone to have xenophobic reactions without being a full-blown xenophobe, in the event that she views them as causes for concern rather than celebration." By contrast, a first-order political discriminator is identified by his "personal investment" in his provincial conception of people: "His sense of self-preservation requires his conception to be veridical and is threatened when it is disconfirmed." This, Piper explains, is what "motivates the imposition of politically discriminatory stereotypes." Stereotypes allow for the sorting of people according to valued and disvalued properties. A first-order political discriminator's personal investment in "honorific" stereotypes demands that he apply the same approach to his own self-image: "This means that that self-conception is a source of personal satisfaction or security to him; that to revise or disconfirm it would elicit in him feelings of dejection, deprivation, or anxiety; and that these feelings are to be explained by his identification with this self-conception."

To maintain an honorific stereotype, a first-order political discriminator must assess not only particular groups of ethnic or gendered others but everyone, including himself, for valued and disvalued properties. Someone with a deep and personal investment in such a stereotype is obliged to mould his personality to fit the imposed expectations. A first-order political discriminator who fails to fully conform to them views himself as inherently defective, damaging his self-esteem and also his capacity for self-knowledge. As Piper (1993, 43) remarks, "A sign that a person's self-conception is formed by an honorific stereotype is that revelation of the deviant, primary disvalued properties provokes shame and denial rather than a reformulation of that self-conception in such a way as to accommodate them."

These two reactions (shame and denial) are reciprocal expressions of the same dispositions:

> Shame involves the pain of feeling publicly exposed as defective, and denial is the psychological antidote to such exposure ... So a person whose self-conception is defined by an honorific stereotype will feel shame at having primary disvalued properties that deviate from it, and will attempt to deny their existence to herself and to others ... The properties regarded as anomalous relative to the stereotype in question are experienced by the first-order political discriminator as an assault on the rational coherence of his theory of the world – and so, according to Kant, on the rational coherence of his self. (1993, 44)

In light of Piper's thesis, it follows that for many Canadians the stories of First Nations post-contact experiences initiate feelings of shame and guilt, and are therefore denied. After years of working in the field of education, I am intensely aware of the extent to which teachers and students value their concept of themselves as defenders of human rights. Teachers with whom I speak find it necessary to remind me that, though there have been some problems in the past, Canada is by far one of the best places in the world to live, and that Canadians guard the values of liberal democracy. Freedom, equity, and justice are not only protected in Canada: Canadians travel the world as peacekeepers to defend these rights for unfortunate others. In their history books, through television advertisements, including Heritage Minutes, and daily news highlighting Canada's peacekeeping role around the globe, students are constantly inundated with the message that Canadians are committed to upholding the values of equity and justice. In a myriad of ways, their concept of themselves as honorary global citizens is confirmed.

Thinking critically about these relationships and interrelationships, I realized the extent to which the dehumanized representation of Aboriginal people and the denial and erosion of their culture and histories are produced and reproduced to comply with the needs of non-Aboriginal people. I began to understand the ways in which non-Aboriginal people use various forms of defence to protect themselves from having to face the events of the past and from questioning their own resistance to hearing. For me, understanding the dynamics of denial clarified the complexity of the task of (re)telling. Teachers often say to me, almost pleadingly, that they don't know what to teach. Recognizing that their position of ignorance is complicated by "the incapacity – or the refusal – to acknowledge *one's own implication* in the information" (Felman 1982, 30, emphasis in original) makes simply providing material about First Nations post-contact experiences an insufficient response. Drawing on the work of Lacan, Felman writes, "Teaching, thus, is not the transmission of ready made knowledge; it is rather the creation of a new condition of knowledge – the creation of an original learning – disposition" (31).

Pedagogical Considerations

> Pedagogy is a practice within which one acts with the intent
> of provoking experience that will simultaneously organize
> and disorganize a variety of understandings of our natural
> and social world.
>
> – Roger Simon, *Teaching against the Grain*

What Michael and I hope to accomplish is entangled in a complex web of interconnecting threads. The Braiding Histories Project encompasses a double agenda: our need to (re)member and (re)tell in a way that affirms the strength and humanity of First Nations people is complicated by our need to (re)tell in a way that will engage Canadians in a rethinking of their current understanding. Thus, the stories were written in such a way as to confront the motivated denial of Canadians. The extent to which we have concerned ourselves with the needs of non-Aboriginal listeners may imply that, yet again, Canadians are controlling the representation of First Nations people. However, our work is not about non-Aboriginal people controlling how we tell our stories – it is a case of Michael and I, as individuals of Aboriginal ancestry, writing for a specific audience with a specific purpose in mind. There is a time and a place for the unabridged telling of one's stories, but we have accepted a pedagogical responsibility and are committed to telling them with consideration for the position of our audience. We take seriously Britzman's (1998, 19) admonishment that "the teacher is ethically obligated to formulate theories of learning that can tolerate the human's capacity for its own extremes and its mistakes, resistance, belatedness, demands, and loss without creating more harm. The work of education must be a working through of education."

As writers, Michael and I recognize meaning making as a fraught and complex site of interactions between authors/texts and readers/hearers

– a site that is ultimately not controlled by what is said/remembered or how. How teachers and students understand the stories and the meanings they make are influenced by their prior comprehensions, experiences, codes, beliefs, and knowledge. Yet, because meanings are not fixed, centred, and unchanging, we hope that by in some ways pre-empting and in other ways confronting their need to deny, we will be providing readers an opportunity to learn from the life stories of First Nations people.

So, though we (re)tell the stories with consideration for the needs of our audience, we are aware that, as David Lusted (1986, 4) so clearly articulates,

> Knowledge is not produced in the intentions of those who believe they hold it, whether in the pen or in the voice. It is not the matter that is offered so much as the matter that is understood. Knowledge needs to be conceived as produced in exchange. Knowledge is produced in the process of interaction, between writer and reader at the moment of reading, and between teacher and learner at the moment of classroom engagement. Knowledge is produced in the consciousness, through the process of thought, discussion, writing, debate, exchange; in the social and internal, collective and isolated struggle for control of understanding from engagement in the unfamiliar idea.

Through the (re)tellings, we offer teachers and students the "unfamiliar" in the hope of engaging their attention. Lusted adds further direction, explaining that an attempt at critical knowledge production aimed at changes in understanding must include proper attention to the conditions necessary to maximizing the opportunities to effect those changes. According to Lusted (1986, 5, 9, 10), the "necessary conditions" include

> a mode of address which is sensitive to the actual social positioning of its respondents and an acknowledgement of different contexts in which they perform ... What was, and remains, required [is] an effective pedagogy that precisely work[s] on changing the consciousness of the students ... For such relations to be worked towards requires a constellation of pedagogies addressed to the complexity of experience constituting any learner's and learner group's gendered, raced, classed, aged and discrete biographical social and historical identity. What is required, therefore, is attention to open-ended and specific pedagogies,

sensitive to context and difference, addressed to the social position of any learning group and the positions of the individuals within it. Pedagogy in general is always inevitably tied to a historical moment defined within the then current state of knowledge.

We agree with Lusted's assertion that the needs of the audience and the context of teaching be taken into consideration but add that this effort must be balanced with maintaining the integrity of our purpose.

The Braiding Histories Project: A Pedagogy of Possibility

When teachers take up the task of teaching about Aboriginal people, they are enacting historically structured social forms that organize, regulate, and legitimate specific ways of thinking and communicating. The discourse of the romantic, mythical Other is enacted through the teachers. How and what teachers communicate about Aboriginal people is based not on an arbitrary decision but is established on a long history of how Aboriginal people have been positioned in relation to non-Aboriginal people. Aware that the discourse of the romanticized, mythical Other is embedded in a teacher's understanding of what it means to teach First Nations subject material but simultaneously holding a somewhat contradictory faith in the transformative power of education, I realize that accomplishing change calls for a project that will interrupt the dominant discourse and offer teachers and students alternative ways of knowing.

Writing about indigenous approaches to research and theory, Linda Tuhiwai Smith (1999, 39) of the Maori Nation explains that decolonization "is about centering our concerns and world view and then coming to know and understand theory and research from our own perspectives and for our own purposes." Although the discourse that positions Aboriginal people as romanticized Others is firmly ensconced in Canada's school curriculum, many educators have become aware of its limitations and inadequacy. Many teachers with whom I speak feel constrained by their own lack of knowledge and the lack of appropriate resources available to them. The Braiding Histories Project was completed in response to the needs of a broadly defined community of teachers who were concerned with their own practice and the ways in which it reproduced conditions of injustice. The project is situated within a field of theoretical work concerned with relations of pedagogy, relations of power, and how people come to know what they know within the constraints of specific cultural and social forms. In practice, this involves educators in learning to investigate the multiple and contradictory ways in which what they teach and how they teach are deeply implicated in both producing various forms of domination and constructing active practices of resistance and struggle.

Critical Pedagogy

An amalgam of educational philosophies, critical pedagogy supports a belief in the centrality of education in determining political and social relations (David Trend, cited in Giroux 1992). Henry Giroux (1992, 98-99) writes that critical pedagogy "focuses on the production of knowledge and identities within the specificity of educational contexts and the broader institutional locations in which they are located. Critical pedagogy refers to a deliberate attempt to construct specific conditions through which educators and students can think critically about how knowledge is produced and transformed in relation to the construction of social experiences informed by a particular relationship between the self, others, and the larger world." The application of questions, concerns, and perspectives drawn from critical pedagogy focuses attention on specific ways in which the discourse of the romantic, mythical Other perpetuates and legitimates the reproduction of unjust social relations. The approach to First Nations subject material that emphasizes the transmission of content knowledge avoids a discussion of the relationship between Aboriginal and non-Aboriginal people. For example, teaching the Bering Strait theory dismisses as myth Aboriginal conceptions of creation and delegitimizes land claims based on the presence of Aboriginal people on this land since time immemorial. Teaching that focuses on furs and feathers, tipis and longhouses, canoes and snowshoes positions Aboriginal people as primitive inhabitants of the past.

Teaching about Aboriginal people that confines itself to Aboriginal interactions with European settlers suggests that the value of Aboriginal people lies in their ability to assist European settlers in the building of a new nation as opposed to the recognition of the existence of fully established, self-reliant, and self-governing nations prior to European invasion.[2] Teaching about Aboriginal people in ways that continue to reflect a Eurocentric ideology positions descendants of European settlers as superior to the inferior Aboriginal Other. The increased attention to Aboriginal issues in the news media has raised the concerns of many teachers regarding their approach to First Nations subject material; however, though they may have engaged with multiculturalism and anti-racism, the majority of teachers have not yet taken active steps toward transforming their practice. Critical pedagogy makes clear the need for an investigation of the extent to which belief systems have become internalized to the point that many teachers unsuspectingly rely on dominant discourses to give structure to their approach to teaching without recognizing the inadequacy or questioning the effects of those discourses. Thus, to its task of identifying the existence of the discourse of the romantic, mythical Other, the Braiding Histories Project adds that of uncovering the conditions that keep discourses in place. The project entails more than introducing our stories of Aboriginal people to the curriculum: "It means understanding and rendering visible how Western knowledge is encased in historical and institutional structures that both privilege and exclude particular readings, voices, aesthetics, authority, representations and forms of sociality" (Giroux 1992, 27). I bring a sense of crisis to the representation of Aboriginal people in education in an attempt to examine not only what we choose to say and do, but what structures what we say and do (Cherryholmes 1988, 14).

Decolonizing Education

In questioning the legitimacy of master narratives that position Aboriginal people as romanticized, mythical Others, the Braiding Histories Project calls for the recognition of the situated nature of knowledge. Describing the prevailing curriculum in schools and universities, Marie Battiste, a Mi'kmaq scholar, explains that traditional academic studies ignore indigenous world views, knowledge, and thought, claiming superiority for the Eurocentric history, literature, and philosophy in which they are grounded. Describing this situation as cognitive imperialism, Battiste (1998, 20) writes that "cognitive imperialism is a form of cognitive manipulation used to discredit other knowledge basis and values and seeks to validate one source of knowledge and empower it through public education. It has been the means by which the rich diversity of peoples have been denied inclusion in public education while only a privileged group have defined themselves as inclusive, normative, and ideal. Cognitive imperialism denies many groups of people their language and cultural integrity and maintains legitimacy of only one language, one culture, and one frame of reference." The concept of cognitive imperialism draws attention to the relationship between power, knowledge, ideology, and schooling. It raises the question of "how knowledge is constructed and translated within and between different communities located within asymmetrical relations of power" (Giroux 1992, 26). Teaching and learning are social and political in nature; they are both a product and a process of history.

Battiste calls for a decolonizing of the curriculum, a process that will require Aboriginal educators to be actively part of the transformation of knowledge. Quoting Elizabeth Minnich, Battiste (1998, 24) remarks, "it is not just knowledge and thought that need to be changed but also 'preconscious cultural assumptions and habits that are fraught with emotion and reflect not only the ignorance but the systemically created and reinforced prejudices of the dominant culture.'" The Braiding Histories Project is my attempt to unravel the allure of current practices and then contribute to constructing an alternative approach to teaching First Nations subject material: an approach that nurtures forms of understanding that allow teachers and students to see the connections between the meanings they make, societal parameters, and their own positions, desires, previous knowledge, and experiences.

Discussing the relationship between history and power and writing about the experiences of indigenous peoples in New Zealand, Linda Tuhiwai Smith (1999, 33) comments, "Our orientation to the world was already being redefined as we were being excluded systematically from the writing of the history of our own lands. This on its own may not have worked were it not for the actual material redefinition of our world which was occurring simultaneously through such things as the renaming and 'breaking in' of the land, the alienation and fragmentation of lands through legislation, the forced movement of people off their lands, and the social consequences which resulted in high sickness and mortality rates." These reflections on the legacy of colonialism begin to make visible various exclusions and repressions that have resulted in certain forms of privilege existing unacknowledged within a Western view of history. Linda Tuhiwai Smith makes clear the need for an investigation of conditions that have allowed those privileged by virtue of the legacy of colonialism to claim the authority to speak for indigenous people, defining not only our histories but our very selves. The Braiding Histories Project is my response to the important questions, Who is speaking for whom, under what conditions, and with what consequences?

Transforming Unjust Social Relations

Exploring ways to provoke within teachers and students an investigation of the extent to which prevailing classroom discourses contribute to the reproduction of unjust social relations is an ongoing struggle. In an effort to contribute to it, the Braiding Histories Project involves working in cooperation with teachers to reveal what they are teaching, why they teach the way they do, and how they can make use of the Braiding Histories Stories to create possible and desirable change. It is about creating a pedagogy of possibility.

I am working with a concept of pedagogy as explained by David Lusted (1986, 2, 3, emphasis in original): "As a concept, it draws attention to the *process* through which knowledge is produced ... Pedagogy addresses the process of production and exchange, the transformation of consciousness that takes place in the interaction of three agencies – the teacher, the learner and the knowledge they together produce." This understanding of knowledge production signifies the importance of attending to the conditions of engagement. As Lusted writes, the teacher is not a neutral transmitter of knowledge, the learner is not an "empty vessel," and knowledge is not immutable material to be imparted. Thus, as we act in the hope of transforming practice, it is not enough to (re)tell the stories and pass them on to teachers, expecting "transformation" to miraculously take place. The Braiding Histories Project is directly concerned with producing texts that might initiate such learning and with identifying the kinds of classroom conditions that support transformative practice.

Recognizing the multiple subject positions of teachers and students, and that time and place are not static, this research aims at uncovering shared questions, issues, and concerns in the hope of providing direction to teachers who want to transform their teaching practice. Such a pedagogy, as Roger Simon (1992, 57) explains, "will require forms of teaching and learning linked to the goal of educating students to take risks, to struggle with ongoing relations of power, to critically appropriate forms of knowledge that exist outside their immediate experience, and to envisage versions of a world that is 'not yet' – in order to be able to alter the grounds upon which life is lived."

Prevailing Classroom Discourses

Multiculturalism and the *People of Native Ancestry* Documents
In 1972, the National Indian Brotherhood published its policy paper *Indian Control of Indian Education* (ICIE), which was adopted as policy at the Canadian federal level in 1973. The policy focused on education for First Nations students but also contributed to accomplishing change in the representation of First Nations people in the Ontario school curriculum. In 1975 and 1977, the Ontario Ministry of Education (OME) published the *People of Native Ancestry* (PONA) guidelines and the *Multiculturalism in Action* support document (OME 1975, 1975b, 1977). A brief review of these publications will illustrate how, in

combination, they contributed to establishing an alternative representation of First Nations people in the curriculum.

The concept of multicultural education grew out of the activism of the civil rights movement of the 1960s. African Americans in the United States led the movement for the recognition of minority rights. Joined by other ethnic and minority groups, the civil rights movement had a significant impact on educational institutions. Minority groups demanded that schools reform their curricula to reflect the experiences, histories, cultures, and perspectives of the diverse populations they served. Demands included the hiring of more teachers of colour, the push for community control of schools, and the revision of textbooks to make them reflect the diversity of peoples in the United States (McCarthy 1993).

The policy paper titled *Indian Control of Indian Education* (National Indian Brotherhood 1972) originated in the concern of First Nations parents about the continued academic failure and sense of alienation experienced by their children in federal and provincial schools (Kirkness and Bowman 1992, 15). Authors of the policy were critical of existing curricula: "Where the Indian contribution is not entirely ignored it is often cast in an unfavorable light ... Courses in Indian history and culture should promote pride in the Indian child and respect in the non-Indian students" (ibid., 34). The policy paper put out a clearly stated request for materials that would more accurately represent First Nations people, culture, and contributions to Canadian history, for both First Nations and non–First Nations students.

Change in education for and about First Nations people came at a time when calls for reform were heard within the field of curriculum studies. A shift from the technical approach taken by traditional theorists occurred during the 1960s with the advance of the discipline-based conceptual-empiricists.[3] The early 1970s saw the emergence of a group of educators, known as reconceptualists, who were dissatisfied with the apolitical, ahistorical, and technological orientation of the curriculum field. These theorists, including William Pinar (1975) and Michael Apple (1979), expressed concern regarding the socio-political function of the curriculum and the role of the school in reproducing social inequality. They played a significant part in "reconceptualizing" the major issues, concerns, and modes of educational inquiry that provided a focus for curriculum theory and practice. It is a mode of theorizing whose supporters rejected the positivist and conservative nature of existing curriculum theory and practice. Reconceptualists recognized the need for a "fundamental reconceptualization of what curriculum is, how it functions, and how it might function in emancipatory ways" (Giroux, Penna, and Pinar 1981, 94). They began the work of examining the ways in which schools legitimize certain forms of knowledge and cultural interests. By the late 1970s, "earlier modes of reconceptualizing were being further developed to include perspectives drawn from the Frankfurt School version of critical theory and ethnographic school studies grounded in a neo-Marxist perspective" (ibid.). The work of Henry Giroux and Jean Anyon focused primarily on how schools function to reproduce, in both the hidden and the formal curricula, the cultural beliefs and economic relationships that support the larger social order. A second focus was on how the very texture of day-to-day classroom relationships generates various meanings, restraints, cultural values, and social relationships. Reconceptualists share a deep-seated interest in the connection between meaning and social control.[4]

A recognition of the school as an agent of social change and of the demands that education be relevant both to the students' interests and society's needs produced conditions conducive to the creation of the PONA documents.[5] Produced for teachers of Native students, they were also of interest to those educators teaching about Native people. Teachers of non-Native students were to use the PONA documents to assist with developing awareness and appreciation for the heritage and distinctive traditional and contemporary cultures of the original people as well as for their continuing contribution to Canadian society. The guide for intermediate classes advised teachers to identify and work to overcome stereotypes and prejudices: "We must move beyond the mere toleration of different heritages and perspectives towards an active commitment on the part of both the original people of our land and other Canadians to foster an understanding of the integrity of each ethnic group's cultural inheritance" (OME 1977, 3). Teachers were directed to achieve an appropriate balance between heritage and issues of conflict. The PONA guides were premised on an understanding that "Schools can play a vital role in transmitting current and valid information about Native people to the non-Native community" (ibid., 5).

The PONA documents are part of a multicultural discourse that focuses on knowledge and appreciation of cultural difference. In *Multiculturalism in Action* (OME 1975a), students are expected to become aware of their own culture and to know about and respect that of others. Within the rubric of multicultural education, festivals, religious celebrations, language, and customs become the object of dialogue, writing, and research. Students might be asked to participate in a multicultural feast or in dancing, singing, or other culture-specific activities. The multicultural discourse sets the culture of First Nations people apart as something distinct, something to be respected. It offers non–First Nations students the position of respectful admirer. Even if students have not actually considered First Nations history within a multicultural discourse, they have already learned how they are expected to respond to teaching about another culture. During my speaking sessions in classrooms, students tell me, "Oh! I just love the dancing; it's so mystical," or, "How come you couldn't teach us how to chant?" These students are responding within a previously learned structure that calls for a demonstration of respectful admiration.

The celebration of diversity advocated by multiculturalists provides an alternative to the representation of Aboriginal people as savage Others and is now firmly established within both teachers' and students' frames of reference for responding to First Nations subject material. In response to ongoing concerns regarding marginalized students and the representation of difference in the school curriculum, a group of radical multiculturalist and anti-racism scholars introduced additional questions and concerns, and advocated for the implementation of anti-racism education.

Anti-racism Education and the 1991 Native Studies Guide
Developed by community groups and social activists in Great Britain, the United States, and Canada, the primary objective of anti-racism education is to transform schooling and education by eliminating racism in all its various forms. Responding to growing evidence that racial discrimination permeates the education system, many Canadian school boards adopted anti-racism directives. Although its main focus is on discriminatory behaviour, anti-racism education challenges the Eurocentric nature of the curriculum, calling for the inclusion of alternative perspectives.

In 1993, the OME published a document titled *Antiracism and Ethnocultural Equity in School Boards*. It was a response to the 1992 New Democratic government's amendment to the Education Act, which required all school boards to develop and implement anti-racism and ethnocultural equity policies. The goals of anti-racism education, as described by the OME (1993, 5), are to achieve "equitable treatment of members of all racial and ethnocultural groups and the elimination of institutional and individual barriers to equity."

An overall objective of anti-racism education is a conscious examination of and challenge to the Eurocentric nature of the school curriculum and the inclusion of a balance of perspectives. This translates into specific directives for teaching, such as confronting stereotypes and racist ideas, providing opportunities for students to question the information they receive, encouraging them to seek out alternative and missing information, and addressing "the historical and current reasons for the continued unequal social status of different groupings" (Thomas 1984, 22). During the late 1980s and through the 1990s, teachers were inundated with materials that stressed a zero tolerance level for overt discriminatory practices. In its application, anti-racism education has begun to achieve some success in teaching students that judging others on the basis of racial difference is wrong, unfair, and unacceptable. However, the call to challenge the Eurocentric nature of the curriculum has resulted in only minor attempts at change. Although teachers are comfortable in presenting racism constituted as individual acts of discrimination, they are less able to confront the ways in which racism permeates the school curriculum and classroom practices.[6]

In response to both the anti-racism and the multicultural discourses, many post-1990 history textbooks include in the requisite chapter on Native people a section dealing with current issues. Residential schools, reserves, and the Indian Act are introduced as aspects of the policy of assimilation, and publishers have made an initial effort to combat stereotypes. For example, Prentice Hall, which publishes Angus Scully et al.'s *Canada through Time* (1992), has included photo essays that introduce students to contemporary First Nations people who occupy professional roles such as teachers, writers, and lawyers. The influence of the anti-racism discourse is also evident in the *Curriculum Guideline: Native Studies Intermediate Division* issued by the OME in 1991. Similar to the PONA documents, it is designed for schools with significant First Nations populations but is also recommended as an appropriate resource for teaching non-Aboriginal students about First Nations history, culture, and issues. It begins with a typical focus on the pre-contact period but also includes sample units with such titles as "Legislating Change" and "Forces of Assimilation." This guide offers teachers and students directions for investigating the process of colonization and its effects on First Nations people. It includes "Attitude and Value Objectives" such as "willingness to analyze assumptions and attitudes underlying judgment of cultural superiority and cultural equality, appreciation of the effects of the interaction between Native societies and European settlers" (OME 1991, 24).

This document provides an excellent starting point for teachers who are interested in offering an alternative perspective on Canadian history. However, my observations of classroom practice and discussions with school-board history consultants have revealed that it is not being used by teachers of non-Aboriginal students. When I asked the administrator in my own child's school about the document, I was told, "We are under no obligation to make use of that guideline in our schools." During the 1998-99 school year, I spoke with a number of experienced history teachers from grades seven and eight who expressed their concerns regarding the place of Aboriginal material in the curriculum. They explained that "if there is not an explicit unit of study addressing First Nations subject matter, the issues pertaining to Aboriginal people will not be addressed."[7]

Recognizing Limitations

The traditional social studies discourse that involves students in cultural dissection continues to be at the core of the Native peoples unit. Students are still required to study the clothing, type of shelter, religious beliefs, recreation, music, and dance of the various First Nations. Textbook publishers have expanded their chapters, but the survey approach to pre-contact material culture remains strong.[8] Casual mention is made of what happened to the people and their culture after European contact. The difficult issues surrounding post-contact history are addressed in passing, as if to say, "The settlers didn't know any better, and what occurred in the past was sad. But everything is better now and we all truly value and appreciate the Aboriginal contribution to Canadian culture." Within the majority of Canadian history classes, First Nations people continue to be relegated to historical footnotes. They may be considered, but only so far as they relate to European exploration, settlement, and nation building. The progress of European settlers remains the focus of study.

This perspective suggests that the Europeans were stronger and more advanced and therefore capable of making progress, whereas the First Nations people are depicted as victims of that progress. A discourse of sympathy is developed, evoking in the non-Aboriginal students feelings of pity for people of the First Nations. The elimination of First Nations people and culture, presented as the inevitable result of progress, promotes the idea in the minds of students that the white Euro-Canadian dominant culture is superior to others and deserves advantages not provided to the "inferior Other." This view of the First Nations is constructed from a Eurocentric perspective and perpetuates the myth of superiority. In order for students to become involved in an investigation of the impact of colonization on First Nations communities in Canada and its implications for today, they require the opportunity to hear the story of conquest and resistance, of invasion, violence, and destruction. If they are to learn how the relationship between Aboriginal people and Canadians developed, they need opportunities to investigate how the attitude of superiority and the desire for power and control motivated the actions of the European settlers.

The multicultural discourse, with an emphasis on "celebrating our differences" as an approach to teaching about First Nations people, is supported by teachers, administrators, and publishers of curriculum resources. Students are encouraged to participate in activities such as mask making, totem pole constructing, and building replicas of Indian villages. These hands-on activities are attractive for students, but they do little to promote any true appreciation for the complexities of First Nations culture. Teaching about material culture without attention to the values, concepts, beliefs, and world views of First Nations people reproduces stereotypical representations. It reflects what Cameron McCarthy (1993, 292) refers to as the cultural competence approach, suggesting that cultural diversity is a valuable resource that should be preserved and extended.

Influenced by the multicultural discourse, the PONA guidelines offered a new and positive approach to teaching about First Nations people but did little to address issues of equality and justice. An in-depth study of various Aboriginal cultures is a crucial part of the story. However, if students are to understand the destruction wrought by European colonization, they must progress beyond examining material culture. They must also develop an awareness that, prior to contact, the First Nations were independent, with well-developed social, cultural, political, and economic practices. Although strategies for investigating a First Nations perspective of post-contact history lie within the parameters of anti-racism discourses, and the *Curriculum Guideline: Native Studies Intermediate Division* (OME 1991) provides useful unit outlines and resource lists, my observation of classroom practice and my frequent discussions with history consultants have shown that the Eurocentric nature of the curriculum has not yet been examined and challenged. The anti-racism discourse was taken up by teachers and students in such a way that the emphasis on eliminating discrimination, or what McCarthy calls the "prejudiceless goal," overshadowed the need to investigate the Eurocentric nature of the curriculum.

A host of scholars working in faculties of education, both in Canada and internationally, have expressed concerns regarding how anti-racism education is taken up by teachers and students in schools. George Dei (1996, 25) writes that "Anti-racism education may be defined as an action-oriented strategy for institutional, systemic change to address racism and the interlocking systems of social oppression." However, in the vast majority of Canadian classrooms, teachers and students are not yet confronting questions that will unravel the knotted interconnections of knowledge and power; who is speaking to whom, on whose behalf, and in what context (Godard 1990, 185)? Like many recent scholars, Schick and St. Denis (2005, 296) argue that "the celebration of 'cultural difference' and the narrative of the nation as raceless, benevolent, and innocent has implications for the reproduction of racial privilege."[9] They also assert that practices that fail to address the effects of racism are counter-productive and write, "Without acknowledging racism and race privilege in curricular practices, the effects of colonization continue" (296).

The PONA documents and the 1991 *Curriculum Guideline: Native Studies Intermediate Division* reflect attempts to alter the ways in which First Nations content is represented in the school curriculum. The multicultural and anti-racism discourses, combined with the actions of First Nations political activists and artists, have provoked many teachers to question their own pedagogy. However, though it is important to acknowledge this shift, neither the multicultural, the anti-racism (as practised by teachers), nor the traditional social studies discourse offer teachers and students an opportunity to investigate the ongoing implications of the colonial relationship between First Nations people and Canadians.

In "After the Canon," Cameron McCarthy (1993) provides critical insights into the limitations of the multicultural and anti-racism approaches. He argues that multicultural education has been appropriated by dominant humanism and is now limited to specific debates regarding content, texts, and attitudes and values. McCarthy (ibid., 290) writes, "As Departments of Education, textbook publishers and intellectual entrepreneurs push more normative themes of cultural understanding and sensitivity training, the actual implementation of a critical emancipatory multiculturalism in the school curriculum and in pedagogical and teacher-education practices in the university has been effectively deferred." Cultural understanding and sensitivity training are safe and offer a non-controversial approach to teaching First Nations content. Many teachers, like many Canadians, resist a discussion of the past that stirs up dissension.

In response, McCarthy (1993) advocates for the implementation of a "critical emancipatory multiculturalism," which he describes as "the radical redefinition of school knowledge – it is a process that goes beyond the language of 'inclusivity' and emphasizes relationality and multivocality as the central intellectual forces in the production of knowledge." Critical educators are concerned with transforming the curriculum from one that reproduces inequality to one that supports equality and justice. Giroux (1992) describes critical education as a particular kind of practice that operates on two basic assumptions: a language of critique or a questioning of presuppositions and a language of possibility. Critical theory, and McCarthy's work in particular, is useful in explicating my ongoing concerns with the presentation of First Nations content in the school curriculum. It is not enough to replace negative, stereotypical representations with positive and diverse alternatives. If, as critical educators, we are concerned with accomplishing change that will contribute to transforming the relationship of injustice, teachers and students require ways of engaging with and speaking to the legacy of three hundred years of oppression, the ongoing inequitable distribution of power and resources, and the relations that sustain those inequities.

In the following two chapters, I tell the story of the issues and challenges teachers confronted when they took the Braiding Histories Stories into their classrooms.

4
The Braiding Histories Project

As I explained in Chapter 1, (re)telling the stories was central to the work of the Braiding Histories Project, but understanding and learning from how teachers would use the stories in their classrooms were equally important. In this part of the book, I investigate how, in the context of two intermediate history classes, teachers and students comprehended and made use of the Braiding Histories Stories. Exploring the problematics of teaching and learning from the stories, the project was initiated by questions about why teachers teach the way they do, what supports their teaching practices, and how the stories both disrupt and affirm dominant approaches to teaching about Aboriginal people and Canadians. Is it possible to create and support teaching practices that will support the establishment of a renewed relationship premised on equity and justice? My work on this project was grounded in my belief that when a community of teachers and learners comes to understand how events of the past impact on current conditions, it can use that understanding to begin to take active steps toward accomplishing justice by participating in new forms of interaction that honour the dignity of the Other.

Critical Ethnography
Constructing a critical ethnography, I begin with an organizing problematic that addresses how ordered sets of social practices operating on and through teachers contribute to the reproduction of dominant ways of knowing about Aboriginal people. The work is situated, in part, within the history class, allowing for critique and potential transformation of teaching practices involving Aboriginal material. Recognizing the implicitly ideological and subjective nature of research, I work conscious of the limits of its claims and with consideration of

how, as a form of social practice, it, too, is constituted and regulated through historical relations of power and existing material conditions (Simon and Dippo 1986).

I have immense respect and appreciation for the three teachers, Diane Carr, Jenna Marsh, and Chloe Bell, who participated in the project. Their honest efforts and commitment made it not only possible, but an exciting and positive experience as well.[1] They demonstrated a clear commitment to me personally and to accomplishing understanding. Their involvement in the project was premised on their understanding that the work of the project was directed toward responding to the needs of classroom teachers who, in their daily practices, struggle with the challenge of teaching Aboriginal subject material.

Working with the three teachers, I intended to examine the cultural and historical production that teachers are caught up in when they teach Aboriginal subject material. As Jo-anne Dillabough (1996, 143) explains, "Teachers, like other agents in the educative process, are bound by cultural location, history and experience when formulating notions about what counts as First Nations knowledge in schools." How and what teachers communicate about Aboriginal peoples is not based on an arbitrary decision, but on a long and established history. The purpose of my study was not to find fault with how the teachers taught or to measure the effectiveness of the Braiding Histories Stories. It was about working in cooperation with the teachers to create knowledge and understanding with the potential of informing a pedagogy of possibility.

The Braiding Histories Stories were written with the intention of disrupting narratives that position Aboriginal people as romantic, mythical Others. Investigating what happened when teachers took them into their classrooms, with a focus on the ordered sets of social practices of the intermediate history class, I examined how these practices led to the construction of particular ways of knowing about Aboriginal people. How do the structure of the history class and the teachers' understanding of their responsibilities as teachers legitimate certain responses to the stories but suppress others? How do teaching practices accomplish and regulate how teachers and students construct their understanding of the stories? I investigated the complex ways in which ideas, attitudes, and perceptions regarding Aboriginal peoples are constructed and translated through the various representations and practices that name, legitimate, marginalize, and in some ways exclude the experiences of Aboriginal peoples in intermediate history classes. The project brings into focus questions concerning how teachers understand and negotiate their "responsibilities for teaching" Aboriginal subject material.

The teachers who participated in the Braiding Histories Project allowed me to ask questions and to look in on their own questioning of themselves and their pedagogy. In investigating how they comprehended and used the Braiding Histories Stories, I examined the kinds of questions they asked and those they refrained from asking, as well as the issues they were comfortable taking up and those they were unable to address. I looked in detail at how the teachers positioned Aboriginal people, and I attended to the ways in which their directions structured specific responses from their students. In analyzing the interaction between teachers, students, and texts, I considered the following questions:

- How do the teachers respond to the alternative positioning of Aboriginal people offered in the Braiding Histories Stories?
- In what ways do teachers draw on the stories to reinforce the humanity of Aboriginal people?
- In their efforts to make sense of the stories, what discursive practices do teachers rely on?
- How do they assist students in renegotiating their concept of Aboriginal people, or is it the students who help the teachers?
- What are the constraints teachers operate within, and how do they resist those constraints?
- What do the teachers emphasize in the stories, and what do they overlook?

I asked these questions as a way of uncovering and understanding how what teachers do in their everyday practice of teaching regulates the production of meaning about Aboriginal people for them and their students.

Questions of Power, Knowledge, and Teaching

This project was initiated by my concerns with representation and power. The absence of Aboriginal texts in schools is not inconsequential. As Linda Tuhiwai Smith (1999, 150) notes, "Indigenous communities have struggled since colonization to be able to exercise what is viewed as a fundamental right, that is to represent ourselves. Representation of indigenous peoples by indigenous people is about countering the dominant society's image of indigenous peoples, their lifestyles and belief systems." The Braiding Histories Stories were written to reflect the complexities of being Aboriginal and of the relationship between Aboriginal people and Canadians. We do have the right to tell our own stories, to insist that materials used in schools representing Aboriginal people be produced by Aboriginal people. My work, which started with this struggle, led to questions about how pedagogical practices function in ways that reproduce/reposition Aboriginal people as romantic, mythical, and Other. This transition in my project did not come easily and was informed by a range of critical research in education.

My initial written analysis of the interactions that transpired between teachers, stories, and students focused on the teachers. In my writing of the teachers' stories, I was determined not to "blame" them, yet my first drafts constituted little more than descriptions of their "failure" to teach the stories properly. After struggling with multiple drafts, speaking with colleagues, and sharing drafts with the teachers themselves, I continued to wrestle with how to tell the story of what had happened when the teachers took the stories into their classrooms. It was through the process of presenting drafts of my analysis with a broader audience of teachers that I came to understand what I was missing in the data.[2] When I shared my initial interpretations with groups of teachers, I heard a response from the audience that sounded something like, "Those teachers got it wrong. But I'd do it differently. I'd do it right." For me, these responses suggested that what had played out in the classrooms arose entirely from "mistakes" made by the three teachers. These responses made me intensely uncomfortable and informed my rethinking of the work of the Braiding Histories Project.

In my initial analysis of the data, I was working with a "sovereign notion of power" (Popkewitz 1998). In my telling of their stories, teachers had the power to determine whether or not to use the stories, which ones to employ, and how to present them. Premised on this understanding, "power was treated as 'something' that was owned, a sovereign-owned power like in the days when kings ruled. Modern sovereign-owned power belonged to bureaucracies of the schools" (ibid., 4). This thinking about power placed responsibility for what had occurred in their classes with the individual teachers, and though I do not discount the agentic power of individuals, the Braiding Histories Project points to questions about what structures the teachers' approach to the stories. Rereading the transcripts of the audiotaped class lessons with a focus on teachers' questions and responses to students, I recognized that I needed to consider the "systems of reasoning" that inform teachers' practice. As Thomas Popkewitz (ibid., 6) explains, "There is a system of reasoning that historically circulates in schools about [Aboriginal people], and that reasoning is the 'culprit' that needs to be investigated." With this in mind, I re-examined the data, but now I looked at how systems of reasoning had structured the teachers' approach to the stories, enabling them to engage with certain issues the stories introduce while disabling engagement with others.

My questions about teaching Aboriginal subject material derive from a range of readings in critical theory in education. Most specifically, this reading contributed to my questions regarding why and how teachers, who had an expressed commitment to teaching an alternative perspective of post-contact history, continue to teach in ways that reproduce dominant discourses. This literature pointed me to an investigation of how the institution of the school determines and constrains the specific uses of texts. Although "texts test and contest the limits of a genre or discursive practice" (Godard 1990, 185), I needed to attend to the power of the systems of reasoning that circulate in schools and the ways through which those systems work to reproduce the status quo. As much as I considered the Braiding Histories Stories to be offering a deliberate disruption to dominant discourses, I needed to attend to how they were complicit in the reproduction of dominant discourses. The work of the project required that I reconsider the classroom as a site of struggle where the questions of "who is speaking to whom, on whose behalf and in *what context*" (ibid., emphasis added) are crucial.

How was power working in the context of the history class? What are the "systems of reasoning" that structure the teachers' approaches to the Braiding Histories Stories? Where did the systems derive from? How could I understand the relationship between the knowledge teachers seemed to draw on and the power of that knowledge to structure teachers' practice? How were the teachers able to negotiate the complex and contradictory demands made of them? These questions point to the knotted interconnections between knowledge and power. Drawing on a "productive notion of power," Popkewitz (1998, 5) explicates his understanding of the knowledge-power relationship:

> Much of modern life is ordered through expert systems of knowledge that discipline how people participate and act. In a commonsense way, expert knowledge shapes and fashions "our" thinking and acting about the calories in our diet as contributing to our personal health; about the pollution in our environment as affecting our lives;

about our body and mind as having stages of development, personality, and processes of self-realization; and about our children as having intelligence, growth, and a normal childhood. These thoughts that are assumed as natural are not natural thoughts; they are thoughts built from expert systems of knowledge. The power of such expert knowledge is that it is not only knowledge. Ideas function to shape and fashion how we participate as active, responsible individuals.

Listening again to the taped dialogue between myself and the teachers during our interviews and planning sessions, I asked what expert systems of knowledge they were drawing on that structured their approach to teaching Aboriginal subject material and the Braiding Histories Stories.

During the interviews and the planning sessions, the teachers spoke about a variety of issues, including, for example, developing skills, covering the content, celebrating diversity, and encouraging respect for difference. Looking in detail at the teachers' comments, questions, and concerns, I was able to begin to identify the expert systems of knowledge that informed their practice. Their actions, and how they understood those actions, "do not occur from a single set of distinctions but are forged through a grid by which intelligibility is given to actions. I call this grid a scaffolding. The scaffolding focuses on the different trajectories of ideas that come together to construct the 'reasoning' and the actions of teaching" (Popkewitz 1998, 30).

In this study, I am concerned with a complex grid of ideas and practices that teachers take up and with how that grid produces particular ways of knowing about Aboriginal people. As Popkewitz (1998, 31) comments, "The consequence of the scaffolding is not the sum of the different ideas but the result of the grid deployed in the concrete practices of classroom teaching. Further, the normalization produced includes and excludes – not by the categorical privileging of groups ... but through generating principles by which individuals construct themselves as active, self-motivated persons." The project reflects my work toward understanding how different discourses of pedagogy operate, generating principles for participation and action – that is, to understand the system of reasoning that has historically circulated in schools around teaching about Aboriginal people. In listening to the teachers talk about the stories, I heard their effort to work through how to present the Braiding Histories Stories *and* to teach well, how to address issues *and* to meet the needs of their students, and how to recognize injustice *and* to nurture the development of good citizens.

Understanding the teachers' approach to the stories required attention to the scaffolding that structured their approach and how that structure enabled teachers to take up certain issues and disabled their ability to respond to others.

The teachers did not talk or think about their approach to the stories as being structured by a grid or a scaffolding. Conscious of their "responsibilities" as teachers, they were aware that, in multiple ways, the stories challenged their ability to meet those responsibilities. After lengthy deliberations, I recognized that the teachers who participated in the Braiding Histories Project did not "get it wrong." They were doing the work of teaching. The attention to issues called for by the stories collided with their understanding of what was required of them. By this, I do not suggest that they occupied a single coherent position. The work of teaching is riddled with contradictions, and teachers' responses to them depend on a multitude of factors. In significant ways, the Braiding Histories Stories challenge teachers' understanding of what is expected of them as history teachers. As I contemplated what had happened to the stories, my analysis shifted from focusing on the teachers as individually responsible for their approach to a recognition of the ways in which the stories challenged their concept of their responsibilities as teachers. In many ways, the stories created a crisis for them, so that, in their classrooms, they were engaged in a constant struggle. If they took up the work of the stories, how could they maintain their position as teachers? My focus on the story of the stories shifts the analysis from my initial concerns with the meaning constructed through the actions of individual teachers when they talked about Aboriginal people to the "rules and standards by which that meaning is constructed" (Popkewitz 1998, 2).

Reflexive Considerations

> Subjectivity is not something that we wear like a badge of honour that can be taken out and paraded around. It is constantly with us, a garment that cannot be removed.
>
> – Alan Peshkin, "In Search of Subjectivity"

My own place in the world is tightly woven into the Braiding Histories Project and amplifies my need to be especially vigilant in questioning and acknowledging how what I see and hear is filtered through my multiple subjectivities. What I write is my interpretation. I came to this research project seeking knowledge and with the intent of contributing to the understanding of what it means to teach Aboriginal subject material in intermediate history classes. I did not come from the position of knowing "how it is" or "what it means" to non-Aboriginal teachers to teach the stories. I recognize the complexity of my relationship to the project, and though I struggle to be ever conscious I am cognizant of the impossibility of recognizing the multiple ways in which my subjectivity infiltrates my work.

The teachers brought to the project a deep sense of commitment to address the oppression of Aboriginal people. Each of the teachers had a desire to learn more. They looked to me as the "expert" who would provide them with new resources that would allow them to integrate a First Nations perspective into their curriculum. From the start, I resisted this position and worked at maintaining the position of participant observer. My purpose was to learn from what the teachers did with the stories. My struggle to respectfully represent what transpired in their classrooms has been an arduous one. How could I write about approaches to the stories that were problematic for me but were considered by the teachers to be "some of the best lessons I ever taught"? In writing about what had happened to the stories, how could I respectfully acknowledge the work of the teachers while addressing the problematics of their teaching? In addition, I was accountable not only to the teachers but to Michael and myself as (re)tellers, to our subjects, and to the hopes that we had for the stories.

My telling of what happened to the stories is constructed from my reinterpretation of the words and experiences of the teachers and their pupils. Drawing on our dialogue during the planning sessions and interviews, and on the classroom interactions between teachers and students, I constructed my knowledge and understanding. The story of the stories reflects the meaning I made from the data and what was important to me. It represents a partial retelling bound by my own perspective. What I had access to through the data were the more private struggles of the three teachers.

In my writing, I am concerned with understanding how teaching practices and institutional structures serve to support the reproduction of dominant ways of knowing. The extent to which the discourses of professionalism dominate teaching practices cannot be explained solely by the actions and intentions of individual teachers. I pay full attention to the social and institutional context in order to reveal the tensions and demands teachers confront in their teaching of the Braiding Histories Stories. As educators, we enter the institution and learn its modes of operation as well as the values that it seeks to maintain as true. As subjects who are shaped by the institutions, we are agents of change rather than its authors – change that may either serve hegemonic interests or challenge existing power relations (Weedon 1997, 25).

The meaning that teachers took from the stories was influenced by their relationship with me. The students themselves read them within the frame structured by the teachers. In my telling of the story of the stories, I stress the interactions between teachers, students, and texts. It is in these interactions that meaning is produced. It was important not to ask if teachers provided students with a "true" or "correct" reading of the stories because there are always multiple possible readings (Davies 1993, 151). Equally, it was important for me to understand and question what each of the teachers brought to the stories and what discourses they took up in their teaching of the stories. I found it necessary to look carefully at the differences between what teachers and students said during the presentation of the story and during the follow-up class dialogue and at how the teachers presented student assignments and how students responded to those assignments. The purpose of my analysis of interactions between teachers, students, and stories was to understand the possibilities teachers offered students as they worked through and constructed meaning from their engagement with the texts.

I audiotaped the interviews and planning sessions in which the teachers and I participated, gave them transcripts of these, and asked for their comments. Initially, I was frustrated by their lack of feedback. Reflecting on moments of frustration led to important realizations. I recognized how my investment in the project was colliding with their needs and desires. As much as I hoped for participation from the teachers, ultimately, this was my project. I wanted to involve them, but their purpose differed from mine. They had legitimate practical concerns regarding time constraints, parents, administration, and the needs of students. Although they were genuinely interested in the content, their plan was to teach this unit and move on to the next one.

As I reviewed the transcripts and reflected on the process, including that of writing my initial drafts of what had transpired in the classrooms, I had the sense of something being subverted. I realized that tension and struggle had underlain every step of the project, and that, to some extent, they had subverted its purpose. Although I couldn't positively identify their source, I concluded that they were at least partly grounded in our differing expectations. The teachers' ideas regarding what constituted teaching differently collided with my vision of alternative representation. At the time, none of us were aware of the conflict between us; nor were we prepared for the collision. They got more than they bargained for in the stories and in me.

The Research Problem

My research concentrated on how the teachers would use the Braiding Histories Stories to initiate a rethinking of post-contact history and its implication for present actions and future possibilities. Given their particular understanding of the past, how would they negotiate stories that positioned Aboriginal people not as romantic, mythical Others but as human agents actively resisting oppression by non-Aboriginal people in Canada? Through dialogue and reflection, would they recognize how the stories they brought and their understanding of their responsibilities as teachers mediated their interpretation of the texts? Would they recognize the possibility to disrupt current perceptions and find something new?

The Participating Teachers

My first step was to identify teachers who were concerned with and interested in interrogating their teaching about Aboriginal people. I had worked with a number of teachers in the past who had demonstrated an interest in investigating and making changes to current approaches to teaching Aboriginal subject material. I felt it was important to work with teachers who recognized an existing problem with the ways of teaching about Aboriginal people and who were concerned with accomplishing change. What was most important was the teachers' recognition of the problem and desire to make a contribution to change. Two of the three teachers who participated in the project joined through a personal invitation from me. The third teacher was referred to me by the history consultant at her school board.

Data Collection

Initial Interview

At the beginning of the project, I conducted semi-structured interviews with each teacher at her home or school. During these interviews, the teachers spoke about their understanding of their current teaching practices as related to First Nations subject material, their understanding of what was wrong, inadequate, or missing in them, and of the kind of change they hoped to accomplish. A list of initiating questions can be found in Appendix B. I also conducted at least one midpoint interview with each teacher, in which she could talk about how her lessons were proceeding and ask questions about the work. Finally, I conducted a debriefing interview with each of the teachers.

The interviews allowed me to develop an interpretive understanding of the meanings, values, and motives held by the teachers concerning their presentation of First Nations subject material. At the conclusion of the initial interview, I gave them copies of the Braiding Histories Stories and explained why and how we wrote them and what we hoped they would achieve. (See Appendix A for copies of the stories as they were formatted for classroom use.) I asked them to read the stories, to think about how they would use them in class, and to participate in a series of collaborative planning sessions with the other teachers to develop ideas for their lessons. I added that, if, after reading the stories, they chose to opt out of the project, I would appreciate the opportunity for a short interview to discuss the decision.

My data included the transcribed audio recordings of the interviews and planning sessions, as well as of lessons taught and small-group discussions among students. I received copies of the students' work, with comments added by the teachers. One of the teachers provided me with copies of the unit test completed by her pupils. I also kept notes of my telephone conversations with the teachers.

Planning Sessions
Before they taught the stories, the teachers participated in three planning sessions; at the conclusion of the project, they took part in a fourth one. During these sessions, they were able to speak with each other regarding their interpretation of the stories and their ideas about using them in class. (A copy of the agendas for each planning session can be found in Appendix C.) I was present as both participant and observer, as I worked collaboratively with the teachers, exploring their responses to the narratives and the development of their lesson plans.

The fourth planning session enabled teachers to talk about what had transpired when they shared the stories with their pupils. They brought samples of work that students completed in response to the stories. During this session, teachers shared what they had learned from working with the stories in their classrooms.

Classroom Recordings and Samples of Student Work
The teachers themselves made the audio recordings of their classes. I asked them to record introductory lessons, small-group discussions,

and any other sessions related to the teaching of the stories. I also asked for copies of student notebooks and of any follow-up activities students completed in response to the stories.

An Introduction to the Participating Teachers

Diane Carr is a soft-spoken, mature woman with a gentle and professional manner. Before we worked together on the Braiding Histories Project, she and I were professional acquaintances. I asked her to participate when a colleague told me of her interest in using stories in history teaching. Diane responded enthusiastically to my June 1998 invitation to join the project, remarking that it offered an excellent opportunity for her to "learn something new and to be inspired."

Jenna Marsh is a small dynamic woman. Prior to the study, she and I were casual acquaintances. We belonged to the same recreation club and often shared stories of our teaching experiences. She told me that she enjoyed camping and canoeing, and spent much of her time in northern Ontario. Concerned with wildlife protection and the natural environment, she has a keen interest in Aboriginal conceptions of earth-human relationships and believes that Western society has a lot to learn about living in harmony with the natural world. Her time in northern Ontario had heightened her awareness of and concern with issues affecting Aboriginal people. When I was looking for people to participate in the Braiding Histories Project, I remembered Jenna's interest in Aboriginal issues. I called her, told her about the project, and asked if she would like to be involved. (For more details regarding these two teachers, see Table 4.1.)

Chloe Bell is an extremely hard-working and involved educator. She is both exuberant and assertive, and describes herself as ambitious. The mother of two young children, she was just beginning a master of education program at the time of the study. In addition, Chloe is an associate teacher responsible for supervising the practicums of six pre-service teachers each year. She also participates in a variety of professional development workshops and conferences. Chloe's commitment to the project equalled that of Diane and Jenna, but, for two reasons, the data from her work with the stories are not included here. First, due to technical difficulties, the tape recordings of her interviews and classroom lessons were unclear and much of the dialogue was inaudible. Second, Chloe's participation in the project was interrupted. During the first semester, she began teaching the stories as part of her language program but was obliged to stop when she temporarily assumed the position of vice-principal at her school. Although she did

Table 4.1

Teachers' academic and teaching experience

	Diane Carr	Jenna Marsh
University degree	BA (English and psychology) BEd	BA (music and French) BEd
Teaching experience	11 years teaching grade 1 12 years teaching grades 7 and 8	20 years teaching a variety of grades and subjects. No previous experience teaching grade 7 or 8 history
Subject focus	History	Music, French, English, and phys. ed.
Teaching assignment	Grade 8 class with history on rotary	Grade 7 class with history on rotary
Interest in the project	Particular interest in teaching history through story. Special interest in teaching about Native people	An interest in learning more about Aboriginal philosophy, particularly earth-human relationships
Current concerns	Learning more about post-contact and contemporary situations confronting Native people in Canada	Teaching something other than stereotypical representations of the pre-contact period
School location	St. Bridget's in Purple Grove, a suburbanizing rural community of 10,000 located 60 kilometres from a large metropolitan centre	Brighton Public School in Greenfield, a suburban community of 67,000 located 60 kilometres from a large metropolitan centre
Student population	The students were Catholic and the class was not racially or culturally diverse	A school with racial and class diversity

return to teaching the stories in her second-semester history class, the interruption and the technical problems made it difficult for me to acquire a coherent sense of what had transpired in her work. Thus, I excluded her data from this book.

Context: Moral and Material Conditions
None of the schools from which I collected data were near an Aboriginal community, and the majority of students had few prior experiences with Aboriginal people. During the time of the study, the Mansfield

District School Board, where Jenna taught, undertook an active program to advance anti-racism practices in all of its schools. Teachers were asked to take part in various workshops and presentations, curriculum support materials were sent to the schools, and posters announcing a zero tolerance of racism were displayed at the entrance to all schools. Teachers were encouraged to include multicultural and anti-racism themes in all their units of study. In her role as an English instructor, Jenna began teaching a multicultural literature unit each year. At the time of the first interview, she was teaching grade eight at Woodland Public School, but her timetable did not include history. Jenna planned to teach the Braiding Histories Stories as part of the multicultural literature unit in her English class. In June, Jenna transferred to Brighton Public School and found that her teaching assignment included grade seven history. This would enable her to teach the stories as part of a history unit.

My project was carried out during an extremely antagonistic period in Ontario's educational environment. Never before had there been such widespread disruption in the province's schools. In 1997, the school year before I began collecting data, there was a province-wide political protest that included a three-week withdrawal of services. While my project was under way, all three teachers were involved in either strikes or lockouts. This was a time of immense change, including curriculum revision, the introduction of standardized testing, and reductions to special education and English as a Second Language programs. These changes increased the workload for teachers and had a negative effect on morale in all areas of education.

In the spring of 1998, when I started looking for project participants, teachers were already feeling the cumulative effects of these various tensions. When I contacted the history consultant from the local school board, he gave me a list of fifteen teachers who were interested in the topic and in professional development projects generally. I contacted all fifteen, but thirteen declined involvement, stating that, considering the current climate, they were unable, unwilling, or simply uninterested in taking on extra work. Of the other two, one underwent the initial interview but later withdrew when her teaching assignment was changed from intermediate to kindergarten. The sole remaining teacher from this list was Chloe Bell. Another teacher whom I had contacted through a recommendation from a personal acquaintance withdrew, remarking that, given the tenuous state of his position as teacher-librarian, he did not want to commit the extra time.

Locating participants was not my only difficulty: the negative atmosphere permeating all levels of school life created a general malaise that infiltrated the planning sessions. The teachers complained of exhaustion and had little time to review transcripts or prepare questions. Additionally, each session typically began with a considerable amount of venting by the teachers, who were frustrated with the negative media representation of their profession, the increased workloads, the lack of support for students with special needs, and so on. Finally, the project went ahead with three participating teachers. As stated above, one was suggested by the history consultant; the other two came to the project via personal invitations from me.

Experiences with Aboriginal People

Diane Carr described herself as having had little or no contact with Aboriginal people. Nonetheless, during the interviews and planning sessions, she described a series of personal experiences that played a key role in shaping her knowledge of and interest in the relationship between Aboriginal people and Canadians.

During her high school years, she had worked at a historic site commemorating the work of Jesuit martyrs who, as she put it, "brought Christianity to the Huron Indians." Diane explained that the story of the missionaries who "sacrificed everything to 'save' the lives of the Indians" was an important part of her knowledge of Native history. In the mid-1980s, she spent a summer in northern Ontario. During this trip she became conscious of the desperate socio-economic conditions confronting Aboriginal people and the lack of interest expressed by many non-Aboriginal people living in northern communities.

When the events at Kanesatake made the headlines during the summer of 1990, Diane found herself drawn to the news stories; she read newspaper and magazine articles in an effort to learn what was happening. At about this time, she became friends with a young Aboriginal woman from Kahnawake. She visited this woman's home on the reserve south of Montreal and was struck by the contrast between this community and what she had seen in northern Ontario. It was much bigger, offered people many more opportunities, and showed fewer visible signs of poverty. Diane's personal experience, in combination with the events occurring in the broader society, led her to question the role played by the Canadian government in the lives of Aboriginal people. Diane felt that Canada "has not always been in the right place" in the relationship: "The Canadian government took control of the lives of these people – Native people were 'set up' for a life of poverty and failure" (June 1999).

Jenna Marsh emigrated from Holland with her family when she was ten years old and grew up in a small southern Alberta town. Her early memories of family experiences positioned Aboriginal people as victims who required help. She understood that, in comparison to the Aboriginal people she saw and felt "sorry" for, she enjoyed a comfortable life. She described herself as having had almost no personal contact with them and had no memory of learning about them in either elementary or secondary school. As an adult, she made an effort to read newspaper and magazine articles about them. Her knowledge and understanding of contemporary issues were derived from popular media representations, including what she heard on CBC radio and television and what she read in newspapers and magazines. Angry regarding injustices such as residential schools, she was concerned with ongoing conditions of suffering and asked who was to blame, why such injustices had been allowed to occur, and who would defend Aboriginal people now.

Jenna recognized the limitations of her knowledge about the history of Aboriginal people and their relationship with dominant Canadian society. Like many Canadians, she had adopted a discourse of pity that positioned Aboriginal people as poor victims of injustice, and she expressed an obscure sense of obligation to defend them. She had no interest in the study of history. She had not enjoyed it as a student and was not especially interested in teaching the subject, yet she believed that it was important for understanding why current circumstances existed. Once assigned responsibility for teaching intermediate history, she perceived this to include informing students that Aboriginal people were and are victims of injustice, and she hoped that the Braiding Histories Stories would provide a solution to this "mess."

My objective was to investigate the scaffolding that structured the teachers' approaches to the stories. Like Jo-anne Dillabough, I conceived of the teachers as neither deliberate perpetrators of injustice nor powerless victims of a pre-ordained teaching process. Given their existing position, their understanding of their responsibilities as teachers, how would they respond to the Braiding Histories Stories? How would this engagement disturb their understanding and manner of teaching about Aboriginal people? What kinds of questions would the stories initiate for them? How would they reconcile competing tensions? In the next section of this chapter, to reveal the scaffolding that structured their approach to the stories, I investigate their initial ideas for teaching them.

Teaching and Responsibility

Dialogue during the planning sessions was never easy, as teachers struggled to work through how they would respond to the issues that the stories called for while still meeting their responsibilities as teachers. "What do I think about the stories? How do I feel about working with them? What will students learn from them?" As the teachers wrestled with these and other questions, particular themes emerged as central to the grid that gave intelligibility to their practice. The scaffolding of ideas that teachers drew on to frame students' engagement with the stories was not named as such: it was buried in the discourses of teaching. Teachers introduced and explored ideas having to do with their understanding of what it meant to "teach well." This included questions about engaging student attention by ensuring the relevancy of content, meeting curriculum expectations, and providing students with opportunities to develop their skills and master new vocabulary. Their desire to "take care" of their pupils became especially salient as teachers discussed questions about the details of oppression introduced in the stories – how could they attend to the suffering but not "upset" their students? In addition, they needed to maintain order and to ask questions they would be able to answer. As history teachers, Diane and Jenna were especially concerned with how they could nurture citizenship in light of the actions perpetrated by the Canadian government. Given its response to Mistahimaskwa and the Cree Nation, and the effects of the assimilation policy on Audrey's life, how could they nurture pride in being Canadian?

Teaching Well

During the planning sessions, the question of how to make the stories relevant was an ongoing concern. Teachers talked back and forth about what constituted relevance and how to establish it. They drew a link between engaging student attention, making content "real," and accomplishing understanding. As Diane explained, "I still maintain the only way I can have anyone understand is to relate it a little to them and to now. Can you think of a circumstance ... like I would start ... where people have been forced to give in to the ways of others? Well, issues of ... the kids will talk about government issues, maybe the welfare, the single mom and the welfare cuts. Or maybe they'll talk about the cuts to hospital services or they may talk about their educational extra-curricular activities. Then, without being too political, they have to go from now" (October 1998).

The teachers understood "making it relevant" to mean revealing connections between the stories and the students' lives. Here Diane suggested that beginning the lesson with an event or issue that was familiar to students could provide a starting point to explain the story itself. Alternatively, the teachers planned to focus the discussion on an incident in the story with which their pupils could identify. For example, Jenna suggested that her students could "relate" to the experience of Native students who were not allowed "to use their own language when they got beyond grade six." In their discussions about how to approach the stories, the teachers worked from the position that, in order for the students to learn from the story, they had to be engaged, and in order to engage student attention, it was the teachers' responsibility to establish relevance between the stories and the students' lives in the present.

The challenge of teaching the stories became one of making the content relevant, and the question of how to establish connections between the stories and the lives of the students was an ongoing concern. During the second planning session, Diane stated, "that brings up another issue ... that you can address with kids because they understand not being heard." Later, Jenna added, "I feel that the more you can, to a degree, identify with a situation, the more sort of global understanding you have of what's going on" (October 1998).

The teachers also discussed an approach to the stories that would position the Aboriginal subjects as heroes or role models. Diane considered focusing on Mistahimaskwa as the man who was willing to take a stand against those in power. She considered asking students, "How do you take that stand? That is, how do you have the strength to stand up for what you believe in? And that is what Mistahimaskwa did" (September 1998). This approach draws attention to the individual and away from the socio-political context. Students learn about the power of the individual, but it is a power enacted in isolation. The purpose of the lesson becomes learning about the admirable qualities of the individual, and students are expected to learn how to be like the hero.

With this move into a "professional register about pedagogy, teaching is an analytic task or a task of organizing the classroom around something seen as 'real' or the reality of teaching" (Popkewitz 1998, 6). The need to attend to the students and their experiences began to dominate the planning sessions as the teachers talked about what "would work" and what "was necessary" for students to learn from the stories. In these discussions, concern with establishing the grounds on which students could relate became more important than the content of the stories. The scaffolding structured the teachers' planning in such a way that students' learning about themselves became the focus of the lessons.

Teaching History and Taking Care of Students

Ontario's intermediate history program begins with an introduction to the discipline. Both the ministry documents and the textbooks advise teachers to start by having students investigate their own family histories. Diane hoped that this would spark their interest in studying history:

> I tend to spend a lot more time telling the stories because I've gathered them myself over the years, and I think that's the way we have to get kids to appreciate the past, their past. And then know that their story is important as well, to tell their story ... It is cool in grade seven and eight to still talk about what you can do and who you are and where you came from. And so, some of these family timelines, or these personal timelines, they [the students] get up and they talk about them. So I do a tremendous amount of work at that point. (August 1998)

During the first planning session, Diane shared her approach to the intermediate history program, and Jenna agreed that having students begin with their own narratives "made sense" as an introduction to the Braiding Histories Stories. The teachers' desire to make the stories relevant was reinforced by the curriculum content that called for attention to students' individual histories. Following the curriculum allowed Diane and Jenna to address their concerns with "caring for" and nurturing student self-concepts.

During the second planning session, Jenna described how her class was completely absorbed in sharing their individual histories: "I was really surprised last Friday at how well they received one another's presentations and I felt that there was a lot of respect and there was a lot of dignity celebrated and so on ... Because there's those other themes like self-identity, self-esteem, ridicule, all those sorts of things; I'm sort of hoping that I can go to those themes" (October 1998). The content of the history class was reformulated as Diane and Jenna took up the psychologically derived discourses that position teachers as responsible for taking care of students.

Thomas Popkewitz (1998, 64, 69) describes this concern with "caring for the soul" of the child as a discourse of "pastoral care." As a discursive practice, pastoral care entails the double tasks of "instilling the correct habits and attitudes" and "enhancing subjectivity through making children 'self-motivated,' 'self-disciplined,' and possessed of a 'positive self-image.'" Popkewitz suggests that "the pastoral care of the child is now part of the doxa of schooling itself; that is, the unquestioned assumptions through which practice is organized. School instruction is dominated by concerns regarding children's dispositions,, attitudes, and feelings. Emphasis is placed on developing social behaviors and psychological attitudes." Diane and Jenna relied heavily on a discourse of pastoral care in their approach to the Braiding Histories Stories. Concerns with developing student self-esteem broadened to include teaching respect for difference and the "right moral attitudes" regarding the suffering of indigenous Others.

Nurturing Good Citizenship
By the end of the nineteenth century, schooling was promoted as a form to "'rescue' the child from the moral and economic evils of industrialization as well as to produce the citizen who participated in a liberal democratic society ... Historical discourses about the redemptive character of schooling are inscribed in contemporary education ... There is a continual theme of education saving the nation through the saving of the soul" (Popkewitz 1998, 59).

When asked why history is taught, Diane and Jenna spoke about the social purposes of teaching. Both explained that, primarily, teaching history is about developing good citizens and learning from the mistakes of the past. As Diane put it, "I'm fortunate to teach it [history] every day, and it's my subject, and then many children take it in grade nine, and then that's it, and they don't want to take it any more. But I think what it helps them to do, the main reason why we should teach our history is, what did we do in the past? How is it affecting us? And then how do I not repeat it in the future?" (August 1998).

With a strong emphasis on content details, Diane teaches about the ordinary people of Canada's past. She wants her pupils to recognize that they have much in common with the historical figures they study: "It is about learning how people handled it. History is filled with culture and values and it provides the opportunity to teach kids about culture and values. I can identify and students can know that there were people who worked hard and struggled and it's only what we're doing. It's humbling, it's not ancient" (June 1999). Drawing on these ideas that frame her approach to teaching, Diane encourages students to identify with people from history: "The people we study are just like us; they worked hard and struggled just like us; we attend to their stories so that we can learn from their hard work and struggle."

When asked what constituted a good history teacher, Jenna explained that he or she inspires students to think deeply about social issues and to develop an awareness regarding the world around them. For Jenna, the study of history enables us to perceive how the past has shaped the present; it also conveys morals, values, and the elements of good citizenship. She remarked that "students need to be taught to respect peoples' rights and dignity and to have compassion for those less fortunate." Believing in education for social action, Jenna expected students to take a stand against injustice. She explained her position: "We study history so that we can learn from our mistakes. Students need an issues approach to history that requires them to learn about the implications of the past and to understand who has power and control in our society." Jenna envisioned using the Braiding Histories Stories to show her pupils "what history can teach us about our own situations, specifically, why Canada is in such a mess in its relations with Aboriginal people" (June 1998). In the teachers' discussions of how to present the stories, the idea of learning from past mistakes loomed large.

Looking to the stories for "lessons" to be learned, teachers took up the discourses of multiculturalism and anti-racism. In her struggle to work through how to approach teaching the stories, Diane referred to her "usual" approach to the Native peoples unit. Drawing on her prior experience, she shared her ideas for teaching the stories with the other teachers. She explained that she understood the unit to be about developing a sense of pride in learning about the cultural traditions of Native people, approaching it as a celebration of cultural difference. She considered it an opportunity to encourage in students an appreciation of the ongoing presence of Native people in Canada and the contributions of our Native people to Canadian culture.

When asked about their relationship with Aboriginal people, both Diane and Jenna described experiences from their past:

Diane: On Saturday you would see them come to town to do their shopping. Two girls were in my class in high school. They were very quiet. They lived in town, with relatives I think, during the winter because they couldn't get back and forth to home. The fishing camp where we lived was an exclusive spot where affluent Americans would come for their holidays. When you went into town you had to step over the Indians passed out in the streets. It was very, very bad. I had never seen it so bad. When I tried to talk to the owners at the camp who lived up there, they weren't interested in talking about it. [They] just brushed it aside. (August 1998)

Jenna: My parents were very racist about black people but they were not racist toward Native people. My dad would often pick up Indians that were hitchhiking and give them a ride home to their reserve. There were lots of reserves around, and I knew that the reserves were rundown and poor. I would see them [Indians] living on the streets of Calgary when we went to the city. And I would feel sorry for them because they seemed to be the underdogs in society, but I didn't know why they became that way. Indians in Calgary were drunk and unemployed. (June 1999)

These personal stories, which reflect the hardship Aboriginal people have suffered, inform the teachers' reasoning about the responsibilities of good Canadian citizens to take action to end the hardship and suffering of Aboriginal people. Thus, the lessons to be learned from the Braiding Histories Stories have to do with the responsibilities of good citizens. The teachers expanded their redemptive role to include a sense of responsibility for saving Aboriginal people. Teaching the stories becomes a way of sharing that commitment with their students. This discourse of social care becomes a central piece of the scaffolding that structures their approach to the stories.

Fissures in the Scaffolding

When planning their lessons, Diane and Jenna voiced concern that students would find some elements difficult to deal with. Although they were committed to addressing questions of injustice and were determined to attend to the history of oppression detailed in the Braiding Histories Stories, they knew that these issues might create conflict in the classroom. Diane was especially worried that the conflict would spill into the broader school community and that she would be held accountable.

Avoiding Conflict

During her initial interview, Diane explained how she addressed teaching about issues of social justice:

There's one particular text, and there needs to be more of these, but it has bios on famous Aboriginal people, and I think that's wonderful. And I try to talk about Buffy Sainte Marie, and I try to bring in some of her music, I try to deal with whatever I see as current. Then I also take that, after that, I try to deal with the injustices in terms of, okay, however we did have reservations, we still do, and we did have residential schools, and what happened? And I also talk about where are those reservations? I have some children who say that they grew up near one, and I also had people who I went to high school with who came in from the reservation, and had to board for the winter in town. So I tell my personal stories. How would we like to do that? And you couldn't go home because the water [was frozen and] there was no way home until spring. And how sad you'd be, and how you'd handle that to get an education. So then I say let's talk about that. Where have you been? Where have you seen a reservation sign? Well they start their limited knowledge. They were on holidays, they know there's one over ... they know there's one when they travelled there. And I say where and what does it look like to you? Then I say okay, that's when the treaty side came in. I think I'm fortunate being able to teach in a separate school where social justice can be taught. (August 1998)

Drawing on her own memories and asking students to describe what they had seen, Diane relied on discourses of social care and pity to teach about the oppression of Aboriginal people. Encouraging students to empathize with Aboriginal people, she asked, "How would you like it if?" and "How sad would you be?" This approach to teaching about Aboriginal people and Canadians, which includes a didactic recounting of factual events and a nurturing of an empathetic response from students, limits engagement with difficult knowledge and avoids conflict.

During our third planning session, Jenna and Chloe discussed the challenge of talking with students about oppression and how to deal with students' feeling that they were being blamed for conditions over which they had no control. Diane joined the conversation, expressing her fear (I reproduce her words verbatim, including the starts and stops in her speech, because they reveal her difficulty with this issue):

My biggest fear in teaching, and when I was even thinking, my planning ... where I have to come down to. Okay, where am I going? Why am I using these stories? Is it to gain respect for the Aboriginal people? My biggest fear, and I really think ... I liked where you were going with Audrey's story and the things you were going to bring out and I liked the idea that maybe you thought you would ... We started to talk and I gave you that suggestion about the other story ... because my fear is, if we talk about ... and that would be injustices so that would be the theme of that story, because, as I was even thinking last night, am I using these stories for a whole year? This could be, as I was working, as I dug through things I already had, this could be a whole year's worth of work but I still am working with grade eight or grade seven. They do not have all of that mentality of that discussion going for them, so what key do I have to get into? (October 1998)

Struggling to articulate her response to the challenge of teaching the narratives, Diane went on to ask, "Where am I going? Why am I using these stories? Is it to gain respect? If we talk about injustice?" Diane's scaffolding supports an approach to the study of Native people that focuses on celebrating cultural difference and encouraging students to appreciate the contributions of Native people to Canadian society. Before she took part in this project, Diane's teaching about injustice meant informing students about reserves and residential schools, and focusing on the hardship and sorrow in the lives of Aboriginal people.

Thinking about the Braiding Histories Stories and how to teach them, Diane found herself confronted with questions about what it means to teach about injustice. How would she accomplish her goals of celebration and appreciation if she were to teach about injustice? In the group planning and her individual planning, Diane struggled with meeting her responsibilities as teacher. Although she saw teaching about injustice as part of her role in developing good citizens, the issues raised in the stories position Canadians as the perpetrators of injustice. She asked the group and herself, "Where do I take my different cultural groups? Where do I place them in my Canadian history?" For the teachers, attending to the oppressive actions of the Canadian government, as the stories required, exposed cracks in their scaffolding.

In discussing the current relationship between Aboriginal people and Canadians, Jenna identified potential problems involving responsibility and guilt. She explained what she expected her students to know and not know regarding the oppressive social conditions experienced by Aboriginals:

They [the students] are aware of homelessness, especially because a lot of these guys get into the city and that's very evident. But I don't think it is very clear about who is homeless, like, I think it is sort of across the board. I don't think it is fairly clear. However, I think they will hear stories, I think a lot, like, that whole thing in the North about substance abuse, and some of them may be aware of that type of thing and they may say "Oh why?" and "How come?" and "Why are we all to blame?"[3] They will have some difficulties with that. Like, I think those things will be sensitive. (June 1998)

Jenna's concerns applied not only to students but to herself as well. As we continued to talk, Jenna added, "And as a teacher I think it is important to recognize that there'll be difficulties for me too" (June 1998). Aware that questions of guilt and responsibility weave through the study of First Nations topics, she realized that these issues were inherent and acknowledged that guilt could initiate resistance from students and teachers.

Fearing that she might challenge parents on this controversial issue, Diane was especially worried about their responses and that of school administration.[4] During our follow-up interview, she explained, "I was worried about what parents would say when their children came home challenging the actions of the Canadian government and the Catholic church and [I] was reluctant to appear critical" (June 1999). Both Diane and Jenna wrestled with issues that their scaffolding did not support. In the past, Diane had limited her teaching about injustice, and her ability to address the issues introduced in the stories was constrained by her fear of upsetting parents and administrators. Jenna was unsure of how to deal with questions regarding guilt and responsibility. Considering the ways in which discourses of "pastoral care" permeate teachers' practice, introducing difficult knowledge upsets the order of things and triggers the need to move away from that which is disruptive back to that which is familiar and orderly. The discourse of pastoral care directs teachers toward a more traditional approach to teaching Aboriginal subject material.

During the planning sessions, both Jenna and Diane spoke about the need to justify the time spent on the narratives. Diane explained that, because the Native peoples unit had been discontinued, other teachers had excluded it from their lessons; nonetheless, teaching it remained optional because the overall objective of conveying its content remained within the curriculum. She argued that she could still justify its inclusion to parents and to her principal. Ultimately, however, devoting time to hearing and responding to Aboriginal voices was widely perceived as interfering with the "legitimate" curriculum.

The details of the post-contact relationship were positioned as marginal to Canadian history as represented in the textbooks and curriculum guidelines. Addressing them became an "extra" and, because they were perceived as not counting, as consuming time better spent on the required subjects. The teachers felt the need to justify teaching the stories. They could also cite lack of time as a basis for avoiding the difficult issues they raised. They argued that, in presenting the stories at all, they were already doing more than their colleagues. Taking care of their students meant that teachers were responsible for covering the content and avoiding content that would be disruptive for students and their community.

Teacher Ignorance

During our initial interview, I asked Jenna what she thought students needed to know regarding the First Nations:

Jenna: I don't think I know for a fact anything about the treaties that they [students] might hear kind of in their [incidental] hearing of the news media about land claims, land settlements, what's going on in Algonquin Park. They don't even know anything about that. So any resources that I could lay my hands on would be really good for me to share with them. I'm not sure where I would go for that. The Internet may be one resource but, if you had any access to any of that stuff from either history teachers, or ... That's kind of nice where you're saying we may get together and talk about it. Perhaps they [Diane and Chloe] would have some resources and information that we could access and then it would be integrated. That's what everybody is talking about now anyway. That would be good because they [students] don't know anything about that.

Susan: And do you think it is important?

Jenna: Well, I think it is important. Well, I think it is important for them to see why this is becoming such a big issue right now. Actually, personally I lose track of who is sitting on which roadway to protest and for what reason. Like, is the clear-cutting being done up in Temagami by Aboriginal people so that they can harvest the forest, or is it being done by big corporations to make money? Like, I'm not really one hundred percent sure.

Susan: Yes, it's hard to keep track, isn't it?

Jenna: And you know the big thing out in BC [*Delgamuukw v. British Columbia,* the 1997 Supreme Court case that acknowledged Aboriginal title], all of that stuff, I don't really have a clear idea of that, and yet when students want to understand ... Where I gain most of my understanding that I have at present ... They seem to speak out a fair amount. I think we seem to be getting information. And then when all this mess [the events at Kanesatake] was going on in Quebec, I read some articles in the *Maclean's* magazine about where the Native people would be, and then I actually became quite interested, thinking that perhaps they'd have a whole lot more sense than all the rest of us had.

Susan: Right.

Jenna: And, what are the Québécois going to do with the Native population? If they say sorry we don't want you because we are on the road with the federal government and you guys are going to just ...

Susan: Yes.

Jenna: But there's not a whole lot out there to get, you know. I think it is very complex and very complicated. (June 1998)

Jenna's words raise questions about teachers' knowledge of the content. Jenna began by expressing her need for resources to support her lessons on Aboriginal topics. As she continued to speak, her frustration surfaced. She received her university education and teaching certificate at a time when First Nations subjects were absent from the curriculum. Like many teachers, she found herself relying on the mainstream media for her understanding of issues, including land claims and struggles over resource management. As Jenna reported, this resulted in a limited understanding and ultimately much confusion. She was beginning to recognize that Aboriginal peoples and Canadians face multiple and complex problems. At the same time, she was becoming increasingly aware that she knew little about either current issues or the history of the relationship. Thus, the lack of knowledge itself becomes a part of the scaffolding that shapes the teachers' approach and a way of avoiding the difficult issues introduced in the stories. Teachers cannot teach what they do not know.

The scaffolding of ideas that normalizes teachers' approaches to teaching Aboriginal subject material in schools gives intelligibility to their teaching practice. This scaffolding or overlapping of different discourses functions to construct students' understanding of themselves, of Aboriginal people, and of themselves in relationship with Aboriginal people. Some knowledge becomes lost in the scaffolding, and some knowledge the scaffolding cannot support.

In Chapters 5 and 6, keeping in mind the teachers' understanding of their responsibilities, I investigate how they responded to the Braiding Histories Stories. I asked how their engagement with the stories would "bother" their understanding of and ways of teaching about Aboriginal people. What questions would the stories initiate for them? How would they reconcile competing tensions?

5
"Her Solitary Place": Teaching and Learning from Shanawdithit's Story

When they took Shanawdithit's story into the classroom, Diane and Jenna were confronted with the task of responding to the call for rethinking history offered through the story while continuing to meet their responsibilities as teachers. Wanting to understand how the scaffolding that gave structure to the teachers' practice affected how students heard the story and what they learned from it, I investigated three elements of the teaching process: how the teachers introduced the story, the discussions that followed the reading of the story, and the written work completed in response to it. I examined how the teachers used Shanawdithit's story to discuss the loss of Beothuk culture, to nurture empathy for the suffering of Aboriginal people, and to convey lessons in citizenship. Their approach to Shanawdithit's story revealed how their understanding of the function of narrative structured their lessons in ways that repositioned Aboriginal people as objects of investigation and suffering victims.

Offering an Alternative Listening Position

My interpretation of what transpired between the teachers, the students, and Shanawdithit's story is determined in part by my understanding of what the story has to offer. In contrast to information about the "Native People of Newfoundland" that students find in their history textbook, "Her Solitary Place: Shanawdithit's Story" is the story of a young woman with a family, a home, and memories. Shanawdithit's response to the eradication of everyone whom she recognized as her own reflects her power, strength, and humanity. The (re)telling offers teachers and students opportunities to hear of loss, strength, and enduring presence. I hoped that, in the detailed account of Shanawdithit's experience of colonization, teachers would find ways of engaging students in an investigation of how Shanawdithit became "the last of the Beothuk" and her reaction to being the last.

The story begins with an opening address in which Shanawdithit's present is contrasted with her vanished past:

> For five of the last years of her life,
> Shanawdithit lived with a family.
> Was it her family?
> Shanawdithit wore clothes.
> Were they her clothes?
> Shanawdithit learned a new language.
> Whose language was it?
> Shanawdithit was buried.
> Was her body painted with red ochre?
> Was she wrapped in birchbark?

The life Shanawdithit remembers is dramatically different from her life at the time of the story. This detailed naming of Shanawdithit's loss was intended to establish a starting point for reading the story. If teachers and students read the story conscious of the depth of Shanawdithit's loss, would they be compelled to ask the following questions? What happened? Why did it happen? Why was Shanawdithit living this experience? What does this story mean to me?

Rather than relying on a telling of the story that offers listeners positions of guilt, shame, and pity, I hoped to offer teachers and students alternative listening positions. I hoped that (re)telling a detailed story of how people actually lived the conflict would initiate questions. I wanted students to question the power relationships at work and to perceive how the search for wealth motivated the actions of the colonizers that resulted in the eradication of a nation. I believe that accomplishing justice includes hearing and learning from the stories of our shared relationship and that bearing witness to the testament of Aboriginal lives is a part of reparations. Shanawdithit's story calls for the recognition that Beothuk claims to the land were not erased by their deaths. Her story is testimony to the enduring presence of Aboriginal peoples on the land. Much of what the world knows about the Beothuk originates from Shanawdithit's stories, and in Newfoundland today extensive archeological work continues in an effort to learn more about both her and the Beothuk Nation.

Shanawdithit's story does not offer a customary framework for discussing the past. (Re)telling a detailed story of how people actually lived the conflict, it is meant to disrupt the concept of history as evidence and to engage readers in investigating the complexity of their relationships with Aboriginal peoples.

Shanawdithit's Story in the Classroom

In different ways, Diane and Jenna took up discourses that allowed them to organize intelligible approaches to their teaching of the story. Concerned with teaching well and taking care of the needs of their students, the teachers used the story to teach about what happened. Wanting her students to appreciate cultural difference, Diane used the story to teach about the details of Beothuk culture and the loss of culture. Jenna, framing the story as a story about genocide, assigned students research and asked them to present their findings. Drawing on her experience and understanding of the function of the narrative, Diane encouraged students to empathize with Shanawdithit. For both Diane and Jenna, the story called students to empathize with the suffering of Aboriginal people and offered lessons in citizenship.

Students are less constrained by structures of teaching. In their engagement with the story, they heard Shanawdithit's struggle with the knowledge of her impending death and her knowledge that she was the last. For some students, this (re)telling initiated questions about their understanding of the larger story of Canada. Students wanted to talk about Shanawdithit's response to suffering and to investigate the cause of her suffering.[1]

Diane, who integrated the Braiding Histories Stories into her Native peoples unit, taught Shanawdithit's narrative at the unit's beginning. She enjoyed it and considered it very useful for informing students of cultural practices and extent of loss. Jenna, who did not find the story appealing, presented it at the end of her unit, after having taught Audrey's story and Mistahimaskwa's story. Her approach focused on covering the content and conveying the importance of respecting difference. Table 5.1 shows the lesson sequence followed by each teacher.

Introducing the Story and Establishing a Frame

Through their introductory questions and activities, the teachers began to structure students' engagement with the story. Framing the story as a story about loss, Diane asked her pupils to attend to the loss of culture; Jenna, less concerned with details, wanted students to hear the story as focused on the eradication of a nation.

Table 5.1

Lesson sequence for Shanawdithit's story

	Diane Carr	Jenna Marsh
Lesson 1	Opening discussion, reading the story, follow-up discussion	Small-group independent research assignment
Lesson 2	Ongoing follow-up discussion	Reading the story, follow-up question sheet
Lesson 3	Written assignment	Whole class discussion of questions
Lesson 4	Small-group discussion	Continued discussion

Learning about Culture

Diane introduced the story by reviewing concepts and terms students had learned during previous lessons. She began with the following questions:

Question One: What is meant by the term "culture"? Looking at the definition that we have developed cooperatively, what is meant by the term "culture"?

Students respond: It is the total way of life of a group of people. You look at everything they did, the way they built their houses, their clothing.

Question Two: Okay, good. All right, based on that, what do you think influences the development of a people's culture?

Students respond: Things that happen in the past. Their habitat. The climate.

Question Three: When we were studying our own cultural background or talking a little bit about it, what were some of the things that you found very significant about your culture?

Students respond: What our parents do for a living. Things that happened during their lifetime, for example, war, immigration. (November 1998)

Diane, familiar with a particular use of stories in her history classes, relied on storytelling to teach the details of historical events in a way that students would find interesting. Drawing on this familiar approach, Diane's questions prepared students to pay attention for details of cultural practices that they would hear about in the story.

Through this approach, Diane was able to make the past and the strange familiar for students. Taking care of the needs of her students, Diane reinforced a connection between prior lessons, during which they had learned about themselves and their own culture, and this story in which they would learn about Shanawdithit and Beothuk culture. With her questions, Diane was able to affirm her position as teacher and make students feel capable as they approached the story confident in what they knew. The curriculum frame, established by the teacher, encourages students to attend to details of cultural practices. In this lesson, Diane began by drawing student attention to the concept of shared humanity.

Diane's approach to teaching intermediate history gave form to her introductory questions, but the story itself is complicit in this approach. Diane's opening questions mirror its introductory address, which draws attention to elements of culture, including clothing, language, and burial practices. Inadvertently, I had provided teachers with an opening that supported an approach to the story premised on a review of the material aspects of culture. Working through the grid of ideas that structured her understanding of what it means to teach history, and in response to the opening address, Diane's questions nurtured learning about the details of culture. Framing the story in this way, she sought responses to factual questions and a demonstration of student skills. Her practice was linked to a search for mastery and the performance of achievement. It did not require, nor did it easily accommodate, the asking of disruptive questions. Diane's approach worked to foreclose engagement with the story as a testimony of loss, pain, and agency, and tended, therefore, to avoid questions of responsibility in the present or the past. Shanawdithit became fixed in the past as a victim. Her actions vanished, and the acts of white colonial settlers were not investigated. One consequence of this was that Diane was able to secure her position as teacher in the classroom.

Whereas Diane was concerned with students learning the details of Beothuk cultural practices prior to engaging with the story, Jenna was less preoccupied with the details of culture. Instead, she initially asked students to hear the story of genocide. She took up questions about the details of culture during the follow-up discussion. Prior to reading the story, Jenna asked students to do some research about Shanawdithit and the Beothuk:

Okay, on the Shanawdithit [story], I had about ten kids do some research on the Beothuk and they helped me pronounce it a hundred times. They kept correcting me, it was very interesting. They found that a lot of the information was duplicated and that sort of annoyed some of them because, as they found stuff on the Internet, that's exactly what somebody else found in a textbook and that's what someone else found in the encyclopedia. But they [students] certainly gained the idea that they [Beothuk] were on Newfoundland and then they were driven to the interior, this Exploits River. I think they were sort of sent along there. And they missed the migration of the caribou and their food was taken away and blah, blah, blah. Then they [students] presented to the class, so even though some of it was repetitive, I said it doesn't really matter, so they presented to my other class and then to this one, to my own. I wasn't really too worried about everybody getting exactly the same story or the same background. I wanted them to have kind of a general idea that the whole nation was wiped out, and in their reading, they found out very quickly that she was the last one. I think that had an impact on them. (January 1999)

Taking care of the needs of her students, Jenna provided them with opportunities to develop their research and presentation skills. She was not particularly concerned with the details of the story, nor did she consider the implications of the limited information available to students. For her, the significance of the story lay in knowing that the nation was wiped out and that Shanawdithit was the last. This, as Jenna explained, had an "impact" on the students, establishing the frame within which the story would be understood.

Working with Narrative

Writing about his experience of sharing stories with non-Aboriginal students, Kashaya Pomo scholar Greg Sarris (1993, 151), explains, "Students see narrative and context of production as extricable, independent from one another, and draw lines governed by preconceived notions of narrative." But, as Paula Gunn Allen (1989, 1) of Laguna, Pueblo, and Sioux ancestry, writes, "to hear our stories as we tell them, a non-Indian reader needs to know where they come from, how we compose them, and something of their meaning for us." Within the Aboriginal tradition of history and storytelling, "the meaning to be drawn from an oral account depends on who is telling it, the circumstances in which the account is told, and the interpretation the listener gives to what has been heard" (Canada 1996, 33).

Wanting to create an alternative listening position from which teachers and students would hear the story, the opening address was meant to initiate questions, including who was telling the story, why they were telling "us," and why "we" were being asked to hear. Our hope was that these questions would disrupt the familiar institutional frame and that teachers and students would hear differently. As these lessons demonstrate, the structure of the story was insufficient to disrupt the systems of reasoning that informed the teachers' practice. They used the story to teach about details of culture and the loss of culture. Concerned with covering the content and developing skills, the teachers asked questions that required students to report what they learned about the Beothuk. Students were not required to consider themselves in relationship with the story, to consider who the (re)tellers were, or why we were asking them to hear this story.

During the planning sessions, Diane described a series of language lessons she presented to her students as preparation for the Braiding Histories Stories. During these lessons, completed as part of her language program, students read two short biographies. In response to the biographies, Diane's questions to students were "What events did the author record?" and "Why do you think the author chose those events?" In the move from the language class to the history class, Diane made a discursive change. In the history class, the question was not "What does the author want us to know?" but "What elements of culture can you identify?" Her questions suggested that students listen to the story for details such as "Were the Beothuk hunters or gatherers? Did they live in tipis or longhouses? Did they travel by canoe or dogsled?" Working from the scaffolding that structured her teaching of history, Diane moved away from questions that addressed the context of production. Taking up the social studies discourses offered by their teacher, the students heard the story as a telling about details of Beothuk culture. This approach enabled Diane to maintain her position as the teacher covering the content details in a way that maintained students' attention and their sense of confidence in what they knew. This approach also served to move away from engaging questions that explored the relationship between Canadians and the causes of the violence perpetrated against Shanawdithit, questions that do not have firm answers.

Rather than using the questions asked in the opening address to draw connections between the students and the story, Diane framed it with her own set of queries about culture. Although I recognize the indeterminacy of textual meaning, Diane's use of the opening address was critical in framing students' interpretation of the story. Possibilities for students to learn from the story were determined – and limited – by the terms of attention established by the teacher.[2] Drawing on traditional social studies and multicultural discourses, she set a particular course by asking students to attend to "aspects of culture."

My request that teachers and students attend to Shanawdithit's experience of loss, consider questions of causation, and investigate their own relationship to the story was not heard within the frame legitimated by the teachers. During our fourth planning session, the teachers did discuss whether the stories could be taught as part of a language program or if they had to be taught in a history class. They argued that the stories had to be placed within the historical context and, consequently, would best be taught as part of the history program. In practice, the teachers' attention to the historical context was limited to questions about describing what had occurred. In their teaching of Shanawdithit's story, they did not ask students to attend to why the events had occurred or who was responsible for them; nor did they suggest that students consider Shanawdithit's response to the traumatic events of her life.

Teacher Ignorance

In our (re)telling, Michael and I purposefully refrained from writing the story of Shanawdithit's last days in St. John's. Wanting to tell the story of her response to the events that made her the last-known survivor, we did not want Shanawdithit's position as "the last" to become the focus of her story. Jenna, acting on her limited knowledge of Shanawdithit's story and her understanding of her responsibilities as history teacher, assigned students a research project grounded in the very terms we had wanted to avoid.

In describing the assignment, Jenna remarked that her pupils were frustrated by the limited information that was available. Their response introduces the following key questions:

- What do we know and not know about Shanawdithit and the Beothuk Nation?
- Why do we know so little?
- From whom did we learn what we do know?
- Why are these questions important?

I hear the students' frustration as signs of their learning and recognize the opportunity it opens up. Engaging the students' frustration and the questions their research introduced calls for attention to the relationship between the readers and the story, that is, attention to Shanawdithit's request that listeners bear witness to her testimony. This requires engaging difficult knowledge. Occupied with meeting her responsibilities as history teacher, Jenna was unable/unwilling to engage these questions.

Describing her response to the story, Jenna stated, "it's a depressing kind of story." Although I can understand her response, the story offers more than a depressing litany of loss. It may be that the very limitations Jenna imposed upon it maintained it as "depressing." Unable to hear beyond the pain and suffering, she could not hear the story of Shanawdithit's power, strength, and wisdom. Nor could she hear its call that Canadians (and especially teachers of Canadian history) examine their relationship with colonization. Although this is distressing work, it is not to be done in the absence of hope – hope for a new and better relationship between Aboriginal people and Canadians is exactly what motivates it. To listen and to learn from Shanawdithit's story is what readers are called to do. To consider with respect and to work through a response that honours the existence and experiences of the Beothuk is what it calls for. This means engaging with the traumatic content, investigating the relationship between Aboriginal people and Canadians in the past, and reconsidering what the relationship is today.

From her position as history teacher, Jenna was concerned with students developing their research and presentation skills and with preparing them to learn about the last-known survivor. The significance of their frustration was not visible to her, and the possibility for learning introduced by the students themselves was not taken up but buried within the scaffolding that structures history teaching. Jenna's understanding of what it meant to teach history required her to take care of developing skills and teaching the historical details.

For both Diane and Jenna, the lack of knowledge and their resistance to knowing were a part of the scaffolding that structured their approach to the stories. During the in-class discussions that followed the reading of the story, they continued to rely on their understanding of the function of narrative to structure student engagement with it.

Discussions after Reading the Story and Defining Loss
For the teachers, the follow-up discussion provided the opportunity to evaluate student responses to the story. During the lessons following their reading of the story, the teachers, through their questions, continued to frame students' understanding of the story. Diane and

Jenna both asked questions that required students to focus on the loss of Beothuk culture.

Diane's Class

After Diane posed her introductory questions, students were given a copy of the story and followed along as she read it aloud. Immediately afterward, she asked them a second series of questions:

Diane: All right. What did you enjoy about the story?
Student: Umm, I enjoyed, like, how she went back and relived the memories of her childhood and her family. I thought it was sad because she now had a new language and ah, her culture was dying.
Diane: Okay.
Student: I enjoyed it [....].
Student: How she remembered her memories about her father and stuff ... She remembered her father, she remembered all that.
Diane: She remembered her father. Anyone else in her family? Anyone else? Anyone else? Just her father?
Student: Her mother and her sister.
Diane: Her mother and her sister. Okay. What influenced her most about her people's culture? What were some of the things that influenced her about her people's culture? Let's make a list of some of the things that she talked about.
Student: The way they lived.
Diane: The way they lived.
Student: How they used birchbark a lot.
Diane: Right.
Student: Her fear of the white man.
Student: How they got everything from the land.
Diane: Anyone else, anything else we can add to it? Food that they enjoyed, activities that they took part in? (November 1998)

Considering the content of this story, I found Diane's questions unsettling. For me, it speaks so clearly of loss that I have difficulty hearing or making sense of interpretations that miss this, even when they spring quite reasonably from perspectives other than mine. Given the details of pain and loss, it is incomprehensible to me that students would be asked to talk about what they enjoyed. Although I have difficulty with this question, it made sense for Diane and her students, who recognized it as one commonly posed by teachers when they want to spark discussion. In classrooms (and elsewhere), to speak of what we enjoy in a story is to speak of what makes it good. A story that we appreciate makes us feel something. Thus, students might reasonably respond with, "I enjoyed the story because it made me cry, or laugh," "It reminded me of how much I love my family," "It made me think how sad I'd be if I lost my family," or "It reminds us of all the good things we have in our lives." Diane's question, her students' responses, and my reaction to both of these point to differences between my hope for how the stories would be used and what actually happened in the classrooms.

Drawing on the frame that informed her understanding of how to teach stories, Diane's approach allowed her to maintain control, to put students in the position of supplying answers, and to follow up on the "right" responses. Diane listened to the students' responses, clarified details, then directed students' attention back to the topic of "culture." Conscious of her responsibilities as teacher, she carefully structured student engagement with the story. Defining loss only as it related to the loss of culture, Diane continued with her discussion:

Diane: She also, in reliving and discussing with herself in her memories of her family, her culture, she also talks about some of their losses. What and how, what were some of their losses? Okay. What were some of her losses?

Student: Well, her family members.

Diane: Her family members.

Student: Living outdoors and living off the land.

Diane: Good, living outdoors, living off the land. Anything else?

Student: Living in fear of the white man.

Diane: Living in fear of the white man, that was a loss to her?

Student: Living in fear!

Diane: Having to live in fear. Yes. Okay. Not having a feeling of peace.

Student: Not having any medicine to take care of their sicknesses.

Diane: Okay.

Student: Not being able to live where the white man lived.

Diane: Where the white man lived or seemed to have taken over.

Student: Losing their language and their culture and the ways that they used to live.

Diane: Losing their language and their culture. Yes. Good. Anything else? Go on.

Student: Having to go on with her life without her family.

Diane: Exactly. Having to go on with life without her family.

Student: Knowing you were the last one of your race and there was nothing you could do about it.

Diane: Knowing you were the last one of your race and there was nothing you could do about it. (November 1998)

In asking about loss, Diane began to focus student attention on Shanawdithit's suffering and victimization. Situating the loss as a loss of culture, Diane asked students to make a list. Making a list provides teachers with a means of managing information. Taking up this practice, Diane slipped into a pedagogical approach within which teaching the story is about the transmission of "bits" of information. Completing the list, getting all the details on the list, becomes the focus of the lesson. Thomas Popkewitz (1998, 102) describes this approach: "Knowledge is broken down into its smallest constitutive elements, with the organization of the different bits into a hierarchy whose progression leads to understanding. The learning theory that emerges from this practice is that the sum of the elements 'makes' the whole." As an approach, it allows the teacher to maintain focus on specific details of the narrative and not on having to address the meta-narrative. Managing the story in this way, Diane struggled to maintain a strange kind of separation between the loss of culture and Shanawdithit's experience of loss. In effect, Diane avoided engaging students in a discussion of the connections between the actions of settlers and the eradication of the Beothuk. The consequence was that Shanawdithit and the Beothuk were rendered as victims without a clear sense of how and why the events of victimization occurred.

Drawing on her understanding of the function of the narrative, Diane's approach keeps the difficult knowledge at a distance. Working hard to protect both herself and her students from having to confront the traumatic content of the story, Diane's questions make sense. As the teacher, she is responsible for posing answerable questions, covering the content, checking for comprehension of literal-level details, and avoiding conflict. In the classroom, an approach that accomplishes all of this is both intelligible and permissible.

What Diane's Students Heard   Diane's approach to the story did not erase its trauma, and students asked about and attempted to understand why the Beothuk were victimized and who was responsible. Students heard and reacted to the knowledge that the devastating loss that Shanawdithit experienced was caused by the white settlers. They tried to introduce that knowledge into the discussion. When asked to list Shanawdithit's losses, a student included "living in fear of the white man." This learned fear is specifically detailed in the story, and students refused to ignore it. When this happened, Diane replied, "that was a loss to her?" The student repeated the response, omitting "of the white man," and Diane remarked, "Yes. Okay." She then explained that, expressed as a loss, the experience would constitute the loss of living in peace. Phrasing the answer properly became the point on which she interacted with the student. Doing the job of teacher required that she focus on the complete and correct listing of losses, and thus the opportunity to engage in a discussion of the complex issues of loss and responsibility was missed. Diane did not discuss the presence of the white men or the cause and meaning of the loss of peace. She did not ask who the white men were, why they were there, or what the consequences of these losses were. As she carried on with compiling the list, a student tried to reintroduce the role of the white man, saying, "Not being able to live where the white man lived." Diane rephrased the student's words: "Where the white man lived or *seemed* to have taken over" (emphasis added). She did not altogether dismiss the loss, concerned as she was that students recognize Shanawdithit and the Beothuk as victims.

Although she asked different questions, Jenna's approach accomplished similar results. Shanawdithit and the Beothuk were positioned as victims of loss in the absence of a discussion of the cause. Students in both classrooms attempted to disrupt the teachers' frame by asking questions that drew attention to Shanawdithit's response to loss.

Jenna's Class

Jenna was absent from school on the day that students read the story. Guided by a supply teacher, they took turns reading it aloud. No audio recording was made of this lesson. When they finished reading, students worked on a page of follow-up questions that Jenna had prepared for them. She subsequently devoted two forty-minute classes (spread over two days) to take up the students' responses to her questions.

In dealing with the opening address, Jenna asked students, "Okay, in the opening poem the author tells us indirectly what Shanawdithit lost. What was taken away from her in the course of contact with the new settlers? Who has some answers there?"

Students began by explaining that Shanawdithit lost her family, her land, her clothes. Their comments became increasingly complex as they struggled to voice their understanding of the story:

Nancy [a student]: In a way she kind of lost part of her culture. Like, she probably knew many stories that have been passed on to her,but as she lost her family there were so many more stories to be told and so much more to be learned about the culture which she will never learn because she doesn't have her family there to teach it to her any more.

Jenna: Okay.

Nancy: She only has the knowledge that she knows. She knows it now.

Jenna: Good. Okay, now that isn't in the opening poem but that certainly comes beyond and that's fine. I don't ... It's a good thing to mention that right now in case we don't get to it later on. Sarah?

Sarah: Okay. She lost ... like, they lost their language. They were saying in the poem there they didn't know really whose language it was, like. It could have been the Europeans and not theirs so they're not really sure.

Jenna: Okay, and part of that language then actually ties in to what Nancy was talking about – their stories, you know, all the things that were part of their heritage that was passed on, traditions, everything that was passed on by word of mouth was lost because the language was lost. The language was sort of, um, almost not really, like, disqualified but it was not accepted.

Students: [several voices at once].

Jenna: Well, when they became extinct, that was everything. Exactly. Shane?

Shane: Also, like, how Nancy said, there were many more stories to be passed on to her, well also, she didn't have anyone to pass on the stories that were told to her.

Jenna: Right.

Shane: And um, also, she had to learn English so there was no one for her to teach her old language.

Jenna: Um, hm, okay, good. Nancy?

Nancy: Not only was it through mouth, there probably was, like, literature or sacred statues or stuff that was sacred or very important to her, like, that could have been passed down from her ancestors or whatever, that was probably lost, which was probably taken from them.

Jenna: Um, hm, like artifacts or ...

Nancy: Yeah, like artifacts, like a ring or something. Something sacred or special.

Jenna: Um, hm, good. Yes, okay. Great.

TJ: Like, with what Shane said, um, she didn't know who to pass it on to because people didn't believe her stories or didn't want to hear it or they just ... Because they wouldn't understand it, how she said it.

Jenna: And the Peytons, who were the white family that she was with, they certainly wouldn't have appreciated her stories. Right? (December 1998)

Like Diane, Jenna relied on the structure of the opening address and asked students to list Shanawdithit's losses. Her interaction with students involved clarifying, restating, or correcting their answers. In keeping with the frame that their teacher had established, students began by naming Shanawdithit's losses, but they moved outside of Jenna's frame and started to question the significance of loss and Shanawdithit's response. Nancy recognized a connection between language, stories, and cultural knowledge. She recognized that, for Shanawdithit, the loss of her family and her culture signified that Shanawdithit lost everything that was recognizable as that to which she belonged. Students were edging toward the traumatic character of the story – investigating questions that suggested their understanding that, for Shanawdithit, the complete loss of her social-cultural community signalled a loss of self. A difference was emerging between Jenna's response to the story and the students' responses. Whereas Jenna was concerned with documenting the specifics of what was lost, her students were concerned with investigating what the loss meant and Shanawdithit's response. Nancy shared her insight concerning what was at stake for Shanawdithit. In the loss of her stories, Shanawdithit was losing connection with her culture and her people. Nancy recognized that Shanawdithit was losing the ability to pass on what she knew and the opportunity to learn anything more. The students struggled to understand the implication of Shanawdithit being "the last" and to comprehend the responsibility Shanawdithit was facing. Jenna acknowledged the students' responses, but her follow-up comments and questions suggested that she was not hearing what the students were hearing. Occupied with getting through the content, Jenna did not hear the story of what the loss meant for Shanawdithit; nor did she hear the students' struggle to comprehend the significance of the story.

During the follow-up discussions in both classrooms, the teachers defined loss as a loss of culture; they attended to the details in a way that made the completion of the list the primary focus. Neither teacher engaged students in an investigation of their relationship with the violence perpetrated against the Beothuk; nor did they give consideration to Shanawdithit's response to loss. Rather than disrupting their approach, teachers used the structure of the opening address to frame their follow-up discussion. Students made an effort to engage teachers in questions concerning Shanawdithit's experience of loss, but maintaining their approach, teachers were not able to take up the students' attempts to engage with difficult knowledge.

In Jenna's class, the follow-up discussion continued with the taking up of the homework questions completed by students. I return to this below. Relying on her concept of narrative understanding and empathy, Diane assigned her students the task of writing a poem as a way of responding to Shanawdithit's story. In the following section, I examine how an understanding grounded in empathy repositions Shanawdithit as pitiful victim.

The Written Follow-up and Lessons about Empathy

Overlapping the teachers' desire to teach about Beothuk culture and the loss of culture was a concern with nurturing appropriate responses to the suffering of Aboriginal people. Their approach to the story was informed by an understanding of the power of narrative to, as Martha Nussbaum (1997, 85) explains, "cultivate in ourselves a capacity for sympathetic imagination that will enable us to comprehend the motives and choices of people different from ourselves, seeing them not as forbiddingly alien and other, but as sharing many problems and possibilities with us." The teachers' theory of narrative understanding and pedagogy is an important trajectory in the grid of ideas that structured their approach to teaching the story. Diane's remarks during the planning sessions and interviews revealed her understanding of the use of narrative.[3] Her theory, which is not uncommon, offers important insights into how the story was situated in the concrete practices of classroom teaching.

Diane's Understanding of Narrative, Empathy, and the History Class
When she teaches, Diane uses a variety of activities that encourage students to feel a human commonality with Native people. To achieve this, she asks them, "If you were Native, what would you have done?" or "How would you feel if this happened to you?" During our initial interview, she explained that, as part of her usual approach to teaching the Native peoples unit, she encourages students to empathize with Native people as a way of engaging their attention and teaching about injustice. In our first planning session, I asked the teachers to begin

by talking about their response to the stories. Diane joined the discussion, describing her plan for teaching the stories:

I think what we have to do is maybe start out with where they're [students are] at with those [historical] things and then talk about how do we tell a story and like what you've [Chloe and Jenna] said, how do we tell our story and work with that idea of you tell your story and who are you connected to and with and that will deal with their historical line and their interviewing of Grandma or somebody, whatever, else. Then we'll start to work on, okay, stories have a point of view and define point of view because this definitely is an issue, but it also is their point of view. And then your mother's story, or the Audrey story, is such a personal ... it's not just her point of view as much as it's her personal journey as well. I think you have to take kids ... you have to be careful how you take kids because they connect the subject, and I think you have to take them, sort of, out of that idea of the stories of nature and the environment and then bring them to their story and then teach them about a point of view and to be able to make a choice in that point of view. Given this story here, what are your thoughts; what's fair here; what's unfair and then move into ... And I guess we have to connect literature, and this is what this is going to do and I don't think our textbooks can and even some of the ways we have to teach, especially me, when I teach it on rotary I try to be the storyteller but you're talking a lot too and that's turning a lot of kids sometimes the other way too. (September 1998)

Diane saw the Braiding Histories Stories as useful because they both corrected the curriculum's overemphasis on the pre-contact period and challenged students' ideas that "the study of history is about people and events that happened a long time ago and have nothing to do with us" (June 1998). For her, the stories offered students a window on the perspectives of others and introduced questions of social justice. They called for an examination of events and judgments about fairness.

The stories supplement the curriculum, allowing for a more complete coverage, and in doing so initiate a reworking of what history means. Diane knew the practices of the history class and the practices of the English class. As she pointed out, the stories bring together the discourses of both. Contemplating what this meant for the study of history, she raised an important point – in studying the lives of others, how is one to respond to the issue of justice? For the most part in the

English class, lives and events studied are not real. In the history class, students study the real lives of real people. Additionally, the Braiding Histories Stories engage teachers and students in the study of a history of violence that is their history. Diane recognized the limitations of classroom practice, commenting that "even some of the ways we have to teach" were inadequate. However, though she advocated for the integration of literature and history, she hesitated, perhaps understanding that the Braiding Histories Stories would add complexity to classroom practice. In her experience, a personal story that initiated an empathetic response belonged in the literature class. The story of the broader historical context was the subject material of history. Although Diane recognized the usefulness of teaching the Braiding Histories Stories in her history class, she had not reconciled how to link these personal accounts with the historical context. She had already used stories in her history class and prompted students to empathize with historical characters. Thinking about the demands of the stories, she drew on these discourses in an effort to understand what she was being called upon to teach and how to accomplish it.

Questions of Relationship

During this discussion, Chloe raised the issue of an author's point of view as a critical topic to address in class:

Chloe: And that's why I think, sometimes, the passion and having the storytellers come because there's a spark in someone telling their own story as opposed to you trying to retell my story, so there's power in the retelling, but I think there's even more power in the teller telling it.

Diane: There are so many terms that go along with our history courses that I think that we have to make sure, when we're going through a particular unit, especially about the Native people, and I could teach about the Native people all year round because there are so many terms, there are so many things that I don't think they totally understand.

Chloe: Sorry, I was just going to say that two other things really struck me about the story was the notion about a really strong sense of dignity and self-esteem and that these are two concepts that are really universal in our struggle to maintain the humanity. (September 1998)

In this exchange, Diane agreed with Chloe's observation but made a subtle shift, turning away from a discussion about the consideration of alternative perspectives. Even when Chloe persistently tried to shift back to talk about the inherent power in the telling of a story, Diane remained focused on meeting the practical needs of students. Whereas Chloe made a tentative move toward thinking about the relationship between (re)tellers and listeners, Diane asserted that this relationship is not a part of what it means to read, listen to, or come to understand a story. Diane turned her attention to other responsibilities of teaching. Taking up her concerns with responding to the needs of her students and teaching well, Diane expressed her concern with students' knowledge of vocabulary.

Diane's purpose in teaching history is to engage students' interest, allowing them to learn the lessons from history. The lesson to be absorbed from Shanawdithit's story is that what happened to her was "not fair." This lesson requires empathy for the suffering Other; it does not require empathy for the perpetrator. Taking up a discourse of social care, Diane acted on the understanding that students would arrive at the "right" moral judgment on the basis of their empathetic attachment. Diane's approach to teaching the story, in the context of her history class, is premised on her understanding that empathy initiated in response to the suffering of indigenous Others would lead to action. The narrative offers them an opportunity to feel "what it is like to walk in the other person's shoes," initiating compassion. As Nussbaum (1997, 91) explains, "Compassion requires one thing more: a sense of one's own vulnerability to misfortune. To respond with compassion, I must be willing to entertain the thought that this suffering person might be me." It is the compassion, then, that leads to the judgment regarding fairness and a lesson learned.

Participating in a discussion that focuses on how to nurture the relationship between readers and (re)tellers is not a part of Diane's understanding of how to use narrative. Chloe was suggesting a response to the story premised on the relationship between Aboriginal and non-Aboriginal people – empathy that requires "identification with" and "feeling for" Aboriginal people is safe and even an encouraged response. Recognizing self as Other in relationship with the subject who is suffering is an altogether different investigation. So, though Diane was willing to identify herself and her students as sharing a common humanity with Aboriginal people, thus allowing for the judgment that what had happened was not fair, she moved away from an investigation of the relationship between Aboriginal (re)tellers and non-Aboriginal listeners. Such an investigation might initiate questions concerning

Canada's implication in the acts of violence perpetrated against the Beothuk. The discursive practices that Diane drew from in her approach to teaching history did not provide her with a structure for addressing questions of cause and responsibility. Within a discourse of social care, cause and responsibility are irrelevant. In the follow-up activity, Diane encouraged students to identify with Shanawdithit.

Poetry for Shanawdithit

Diane assigned a two-part written follow-up to Shanawdithit's story. After hearing the narrative, her students wrote a short reply to the question, "How does this story make you feel?" Later, they drew on their responses to write a poem. Although no record exists of the exact directions Diane gave to her pupils, she recalled her presentation of the assignment during our fourth planning session:

> So from there I was able to talk about how a cultural group became extinct, and I talked about extinction and what about your culture. [I asked the students] "How would you feel about your culture being extinct?" I handed them out the story, Shanawdithit's story. And when I gave Shanawdithit's story, I just read it. I just read out loud. The question was, "How does this story make you feel?" and I asked them to just, as soon as I was finished, just write it down, and she [the student] has responded, and then from that response, [I said to the students] I'd like you to take your thoughts and all our discussions and I'd like you to write a poem.[4] (February 1999)

Relying on the scaffolding that structured her approach to teaching, Diane continued to frame the loss as a loss of culture. With this approach, she was able to maintain a distance between Shanawdithit's pain resulting from the loss of her culture and an investigation of the loss of Beothuk lives.

Students' written work in response to the story was a reflection of what they had learned; but more specifically, it was a reflection of what they thought their teacher wanted them to learn. Following their teacher's directions, many students in Diane's class wrote about the loss of culture from the position of Shanawdithit.

Poem, by JC

The white man came over from Europe, they intruded our tribe
The white man spoke a different tongue, we did not comprehend

The white man brought fire water, we drank it like water, it burned
  our throats
The white man stole our food, we felt hunger
The white man introduced powerful weapons, there was death
The white man killed, we lost family
The white man carried diseases, we could not cure
The white man disrupted our spiritual rituals, we suffered greatly from
  this loss
The white man brought newcomers, they started a village, we lost our
  land
The white man discriminated against us, we felt dishonoured
The white man robbed us of everything, we had nothing left
The white man had won, but he had not taken our unforgettable
  memories which will live like the everlasting sun.

Diane awarded JC an A for the poem and wrote, "Very good JC.
General statement toward all Native people not just Beothuk. Images
great."

In many ways, this poem reproduces the list compiled during the
follow-up discussion. Speaking in the voice of an Aboriginal person,
JC affirms Aboriginal people as victims. In her recorded lessons, Diane
did not address who was responsible for the extinction of the Beothuk,
yet, taking up a discourse of blame, JC clearly, and repeatedly, blames
"the white man." This assignment allowed students to express their
empathetic understanding but did not require them to consider the
relationship between themselves, Canadians, and those "white men"
who were to blame. The heroic Shanawdithit and the Beothuk, or, as
Diane puts it, "all Native people," are left with their memories. Framed
by Diane's perception of the function of narrative, the story becomes
complicit in constructing Shanawdithit and the Beothuk as tragic/
heroic figures. The student takes up a discourse of blame but the blame
is on the amorphous "white man" with whom neither JC nor his history are associated.

Commenting on empathy, Peter J. Lee (quoted in Seixas 1996, 774)
writes, "There can be few notions so commonly employed in talking
about what children need to be able to do in history, and so little
examined." Peter Seixas (1996, 774) explains, "Upon examination, the
notion becomes very problematic." Seixas adds that "some have considered empathy as an affective exercise, in which students feel the
human commonality between themselves and historical figures." In

the written assignments, Diane encouraged students to draw on the human commonality between themselves and Shanawdithit, and to express their feelings of sorrow in response to her suffering. Although students are encouraged to empathize with Shanawdithit, Diane nurtures their response to the pain and suffering in isolation from any investigation of its origin or attention to Shanawdithit's response to it.

Diane was equally supportive of a student named LC, who understood the story as speaking of our shared human struggle:

A Poem of Shanawdithit, by LC
Human against Human,
Race against Race,
The feeling of desolate covered her with fear
Disappointment fills the air,
With the past which we can not bare.
In mind she journeys.
Back to her humble home,
With a head packed with worry.
There she'll roam,
Until the frustration drifts off from her fists.

Responding to Diane's invitation to identify with Shanawdithit, who, as the story demonstrates, is a good person and not responsible for her own predicament, LC portrayed her compassionately, as a heroic figure who bears the pain of humanity's struggle. LC received an A for her poem, and Diane wrote, "Good imagery. Well done. Excellent description. You truly interpreted their pain and loss."

The Risks of Empathy

This assignment, meant to elicit empathy for Aboriginal victims, is purposeful. Diane's intention was to initiate a response to the suffering but refrain from engaging in a discussion of the cause of that suffering. Understanding the role of empathy in nurturing a compassionate response, Diane did not require an investigation of cause. From her position, in a discourse of social care, cause was irrelevant. Students were expected to respond to the suffering regardless of the cause.

Peter J. Lee (quoted in Seixas 1996, 774) explains the risks of engagement on the basis of empathy: "This formulation of historical empathy specifies no safeguards against thoroughly ahistorical imaginative reconstructions based on insufficient evidence from traces of the past." For the most part, students have limited data to support their imaginative leaps and do not rely on the data they do have. Lee (ibid.) remarks, "we understand historical agents through the study of evidence." In their written responses, few students looked for evidence, provided in the story or elsewhere, of how Shanawdithit felt. Rather, following their teacher's directions, they projected their own feelings onto Shanawdithit, effectively erasing her historical singularity. Repositioned as "the last of the Beothuk," Shanawdithit became the suffering singular victim.

Diane explained that "I evaluated them for images and the feelings that they felt" (February 1999). Absorbed in feeling sorry for the pitiful victim, students did not hear the story of Shanawdithit's power, her strength, and her wisdom. They learned about culture and to see themselves as compassionate and honourable. They did not learn to investigate their relationship with the perpetrators; nor did they consider the implications of the relationship, including, for example, advantages Canadians have absorbed from the eradication of the Beothuk. Rather, understanding premised on empathy requires Shanawdithit and the Beothuk to occupy the position of victims.

Megan Boler (1999, 159) explains the risks of engagement on such grounds: "The central strategy of [passive empathy] is a faith in the value of 'putting oneself in the other person's shoes.' By imagining my own similar vulnerabilities I claim 'I know what you are feeling because I fear that could happen to me.' The agent of empathy, then, is a fear for oneself. This signals the first risk of empathy: [Passive empathy] is more a story and projection of myself than an understanding of you."

My concern with pedagogy situated within discourses of empathy and social care is not limited to what students do but encompasses what they don't do. Students were not required to empathize with the white settlers; nor were they asked to consider their own implication in the relationship. An emphasis on developing empathetic understanding of "the victims of history" imposes limits on the meaning students make from their reading of the story. Boler (1999, 160) goes on to say, "I wish to point out that the uninterrogated identification assumed by the faith in empathy is founded on a binary of self/other that situates the self/reader unproblematically as judge. This self is not required to identify with the oppressor, and not required to identify her complicity in structures of power relations mirrored by the text."

What happened when English and French fishers invaded the traditional territory of the Beothuk Nation provides for an alternative understanding of Shanawdithit's story, including the role of greed and power. An investigation of the events that went beyond empathy to include a recognition of difference and of the historical context could potentially contribute to students' understanding of Shanawdithit's agentic power, the current conflicts over access to natural resources, and the significance of access. A richness to the story is lost when student engagement is structured by empathy and discourses of social care.

Shanawdithit's Story and Lessons in Citizenship

For both Diane and Jenna, teaching about Aboriginal people in their Canadian history class meant confronting contradictory demands. Whereas teaching history requires developing pride in being Canadian and celebrating the accomplishments of the Canadian nation, as Diane explained, teaching about Aboriginal people includes recognizing that Canada has not always been in the "right place" in its dealings with them.

During the initial interview, Diane remarked, "I think the most important thing that I have [learned] through the teaching of Native people is an appreciation of what they have not been given, as well as possibly, maybe, the unfairness" (August 1998). Diane went on to describe her commitment to teaching about injustice: "Then I get to a part where there is that lack in material, or maybe even make it something that I want to look into and want to look into more. That I can personally interpret what injustice, and there definitely is injustice, and I have even used that tone, and tried to have them [students] then understand that how good they [Native people] were with what they were doing, and how suddenly we became part of their culture and actually destroyed their culture" (ibid.).

For Diane, teaching Aboriginal subject matter included teaching about injustice. Responding to questions of citizenship and injustice, Diane recognized the opportunity to use Shanawdithit's story to teach about the mistakes of the past.

For Jenna, good citizenship included a willingness to question government actions:

> I think my objective is to raise awareness. It's not to give answers and it's not to ... I don't want to close doors. I don't want to tidy it up. That's the exact opposite to what I want to do. I don't ... because I don't think this is a nice tidy issue in Canada's history, and I don't feel that we have to ... I mean, I hear what you're saying about we're trying to raise our, like, you know, let's be proud Canadians. We do that a lot. We do that an awful lot. And I think it doesn't hurt for

them to look at a different perspective and to see that some people don't feel that they have been treated fairly, justly, compassionately. And even if that's all, if that's all they understand. (February 1999)

In the concrete practices of the classroom, teaching about citizenship involves nurturing "habits of empathy and conjecture" that will be conducive to the creation of a certain type of citizenship and a certain type of community – that is, one that cultivates a sympathetic responsiveness to another's needs (Nussbaum 1997, 90). Teaching Shanawdithit's story resulted in an approach with an emphasis on suffering that allows students, as good and caring citizens of the present, to make judgments about what occurred in the past. Teachers take up dominant discourses of "Canadianness" that suggest "although bad things did happen a long time ago, Canada is one of the best places in the world in which to live."

Small-Group Discussion in Diane's Class
A small group of students met to tape-record their previously prepared responses to a series of questions. Diane asked each of the questions and the students replied in turn. There was no discussion:

Diane: How does this story make you feel?
Student: I find this story kind of makes me feel angry 'cause that our nation would actually do that to some other culture.
Student: It makes me pity Shanawdithit and the whole Beothuk race because they were wiped from the face of the earth.
Student: The Europeans coming over, I feel ashamed of our, well, ancestors who came over and destroyed culture and people.
Student: And it all happened just because of the fact that they were different.
Diane: In finding this out, how does this make you feel in terms of being a Canadian and knowing that this occurred to our first Canadians? How does this make you feel as a young Canadian today?
Student: It makes me feel mad that we'd do this to a group of people for no reason.
Students: Yeah [general agreement].
Student: It makes me feel ashamed that people would come over and do this.
Student: I'm very disappointed as how they would do that to such – they never really hurt anyone, we didn't need to do that.

Student: We've actually lost Canadians because of the Europeans and it made us – we can grow stronger because we know what it is and we can act differently towards the Native.

Diane: Okay. Were you surprised to learn about things like this in our Canadian history?

Student: I was 'cause I didn't think that we would actually do that to someone. I thought it was only, like, other people, not us.

Student: You know you don't think that we would actually do that to someone, and when we find out we do, it's kind of shameful.

Student: I wasn't really that shocked when I heard it 'cause nowadays if you ever go look, the Indians only have a little section of a town like a Native reserve and usually they'd have the whole land and now it's only a little section of a city.

Student: Yeah, the white man sure took advantage of the other tribes and the Aboriginal people to Canada and the United States as well.

Student: I found it very disturbing because, like, everyone always thinks, like, we have a great history but when I found this out, it comes out we didn't.

Student: It is sure a low point in our history that I'm not really proud of.

Students: Neither am I, me neither *[general consensus]*.

Student: Yeah, 'cause we don't like bringing it up, we don't want to tell people, "Hey look. We destroyed the Beothuk tribe." We sort of, we would want it to be dark in our history. (November 1998)

In response to their teacher's questions, the students described their emotional response to the story and in the process introduced issues of responsibility and cause. They understood that they had been asked to engage with an account of genocide and wanted to know what motivated the actions of the "Europeans." Diane, taking up the shift the students had initiated, drew their attention to citizenship, asking, "As a 'Canadian' how do you feel?" They answered her question and, pushing past the focus on feelings, continued to engage the topic of responsibility, expressing their disbelief in the actions of their "ancestors." In the absence of an investigation of cause and responsibility, they concluded that the actions of the settlers happened "for no reason." Asking students to express what they "feel for" Shanawdithit and the Beothuk resulted in a repositioning of Aboriginal people as objects; Shanawdithit and the Beothuk are locked into the position of the suffering victims, and students are left with no basis for understanding that settler violence was rooted in self-interest and racism.

Furthermore, they were provided with no basis for interrogating connections between contemporary issues and history. In this pedagogy, the acts of violence are understood to be the result of individual ignorance or prejudice. This allows students and the teacher to create a distance between themselves – who know better – and their ancestors, who perpetrated shameful acts.

Where does the resistance to naming the cause originate? What motivates the move to empathy and compassion? What keeps it in place? Taking up the language of paternalism, Diane said that "*this* occurred to *our* first Canadians." With this statement, Diane used language to both evade naming the act of violence and to erase the status of the Beothuk as an independent nation. June Jordan (1985, 33) explains that when we don't ask the hard questions about "Who did what to whom? and Who's responsible?" we do end up with "a rather foggy mess and not much hope for a democratic state." Jordan argues that the failure to ask is motivated by a desire to avoid further confrontation with the powerful. Rather than asking or even addressing students' questions about who did what to whom and for what reasons, the teachers focus on how the students feel. While the students are invited to express feeling sad, bad, sorry for, or angry, the teachers do not advance engagement with issues of cause and responsibility. Relying on language to avoid confrontation with the oppressive power of the Canadian state, the teachers ask about "our first Canadians." Jordan (ibid.) advises, "If we collaborate with the powerful then our language will lose its currency as a means to tell the truth in order to change the truth." Exploring with students the role of the state in perpetrating violence motivated by the desire for control and ownership of land would allow for the construction of an alternative truth. Jordan (ibid.) writes, "In our own passive ways, we frequently validate the passive voice of a powerful state that seeks to conceal the truth from us, the people." When we use language to get us off the hook, to avoid confrontation, we become implicated in reproducing relationships of oppression.

The stories were written to reflect the impact of colonization on the lives of Aboriginal people and the response of Aboriginal people to the impact. In spite of her resistance to addressing questions of cause and responsibility, Diane did permit her students to articulate their struggle to understand and learn from the story. Seixas (1996, 769, 770) asks, "how does my knowledge of the situation and perspectives of the authors of the account or record lead me to revision, to new interpretations, to new meanings buried in the old stories? ... How should we handle traces in such a way that we can learn about the past? What accounts of the past should we believe? On what grounds? With what reservations?" Diane did not ask whether the story should be believed. The story was written as evidence of the impact of colonization on the lives of Aboriginal people and the response of Aboriginal people to colonization. Comments made during the small-group discussion suggest that students accepted it as evidence and revised their understanding of their country's history. As one student put it, "I found it very disturbing because, like, everyone always thinks, like, we have a great history, but when I found this out, it comes out we didn't" (November 1998). There is a difference here between Diane's use of the story as evidence of hardship and suffering, and the students' use of it as evidence of the need to rethink their understanding of national history.

Although Diane did remark that she enjoyed Shanawdithit's story, she did not elaborate on this point during the planning sessions and interviews. Her approach to teaching the story, structured by both the multicultural and social studies discourses, focused students' attention on learning about the loss of Beothuk culture. Although, for the most part, student responses reflected Diane's approach, there were instances when comments and questions from students disrupted it. They insisted on acknowledging the origin of Shanawdithit's losses and acknowledging the significance of loss. Students expressed their concern with how knowledge of Shanawdithit's story initiated rethinking of their understanding of Canadian history.

Small-Group Discussion in Jenna's Class

Continuing with her questions regarding the opening address, Jenna asked about Beothuk burial practices and whether students understood that this was one more thing denied to Shanawdithit. Jenna then drew their attention to the settlers' response to the eradication of the Beothuk:

Jenna: The Canadians, like, the new settlers, were actually getting a little bit worried as that tribe became extinct. The closer and closer they became to extinction, the more concerned they became, and they actually made an attempt at bringing Shanawdithit from the Peytons' place to another place so that they could record some of this history. Like, all of a sudden they were very interested in what was happening. Erika?

Erika: When we were researching, I read that they made it a national capital crime, or something like that, to kill the Beothuk.

Natalie: And they were offered a thousand dollar reward for someone who brought a live Beothuk to this place.

Jenna: So why do you think they did that?

Tanya: They probably didn't want their culture to get completely wiped out.

Arthur: They'd get in trouble.

Jenna: Or they would get in trouble, like, our new settlers might get in trouble. Like, how would you like to be responsible for a whole race to be wiped out because you were pretty eager to get at their food sources, etc., etc. So they were getting a little bit nervous, I think, as they realized the numbers were dwindling. (December 1998)

Jenna continued to be concerned with listing the loss of specific cultural practices and identifying those responsible. Here, Jenna reflected on the response by the settlers to the events, speculating about what motivated the sudden interest in protecting the surviving Beothuk. Nancy described her understanding of the relationship between race, identity, and culture. Later in the class, when Jenna asked students about Shanawdithit and her stories, Nancy responded to Jenna's comments:

Nancy: Um, she doesn't have children to pass the stories on to, but even if she did find a husband and all, somebody she could have children with to keep the traditions going, since she was the last one of her tribe, the children wouldn't have all of the heritage. Like, they'd have other heritage which they'd probably remember more and kind of be able to get into more because it was still going on. And now she's got this cough that her mother and her sister died of, so she's probably thinking there's not much time. She couldn't write a book or whatever, and even if she did write a book, she doesn't ... I'm not sure, does she speak English?

Jenna: Actually I don't think ... In the research that I was doing, her English was very limited, so who would read it? Good point. Who would read her language?

Nancy: Yeah, and if she wrote the book, it's in her language. No one would be able to understand it anyway.

Jenna: Right, right. Okay.

James: That's why also, in the book, they have a thing where she says maybe she'll make, like, a mamateek for the kids that she worked for, and she was saying that maybe she could show them and stuff, so they'd understand both ways, kind of. (December 1998)

So much is missing for both Jenna and the students in their understanding of the broader context. Through pictures and dialogue, Shanawdithit did share her knowledge. As James noted, by making models of mamateeks and canoes, she was able to communicate details of Beothuk life. Shanawdithit did bear witness to the experiences of her nation. The students were so wrapped up in their struggle to comprehend the details that they had not yet recognized the significance of the detail for her story. The possibility for students to recognize and respond to the call to witness was blocked, in part by Jenna's approach to the narrative.

The discrepancy between what the students heard and struggled to understand and what Jenna heard is reflected in the following exchange regarding Shanawdithit's recognition of her impending death. Jenna asked about the health concerns mentioned in the story and followed it up by discussing the current diagnosis of tuberculosis:

Jenna: Okay. What health concerns were there? What health concerns are mentioned in the first paragraph?

TJ: Well, in the story it said that her mother and sister had suffered from this cough before they died, so she must be ... and if she's starting this cough then she must be kind of worried that she might pass away soon and the traditions would be lost.

Jenna: Um, hm, yeah, but the health concerns are certainly this TB, this tuberculosis, and it's a ... If in the present we get tuberculosis it is very easily ... well, easily, it's probably still a concern. Teachers have to get a TB x-ray on a regular basis. Any new teacher coming to the profession has to have a TB x-ray done to ensure that our lungs are clear, but if they weren't you'd have ... you'd be treated for it with medications and so on, and then you just try your x-ray another time and as soon as your lungs were clear you'd be fine. Back in the 1800s those remedies weren't there, and if they weren't resolved then people died of it. It was just like getting cancer in today's day. (December 1998)

Although TJ wondered how Shanawdithit would cope with confronting her impending death, Jenna did not hear the students' struggle with their questions about how Shanawdithit was coping with this realization or what it means to bear the weight of this realization. Important questions that were not considered included, for example, the actions Shanawdithit took in response to her loss, the knowledge she shared, and what we, as her listeners, are responsible for. Instead, maintaining her control of the lesson, Jenna kept student attention focused on concrete details regarding tuberculosis.

She then carried on with her questions:

Jenna: Okay, in thinking about the prank she played with her sister when she was little, why was her mother fearful of the noise the children were making during play?

Nancy: The Europeans had weapons and ways of hunting not known to them. Like, it was different than how they hunted, so they didn't know what to expect. So, the mom was kind of probably more scared of what she didn't know than what she knew.

Jenna: Yes, possibly and maybe they didn't know. That's a good point actually. They probably didn't understand everything that was going on.

Nancy: They probably didn't understand the firearms because they didn't use the same thing.

Jenna: Right and they didn't know what was going on except that they knew the results of contact with these white people.

Nancy: And they didn't know the reasons why the Europeans wanted to kill off the Beothuk.

Jenna: Um hm, um hm. (December 1998)

Not knowing how to respond to Nancy's comment, Jenna moved on to a question posed by a student named Shane, who asked what access the Beothuk would have had to firearms. Taking up this subject, Jenna explained that, like the Cree in the Mistahimaskwa story, the Beothuk would have known very little about guns.

Paying attention to concrete details helped Jenna organize an intelligible approach to her teaching of this story. In Shanawdithit's narrative, Jenna heard a sad story about genocide. For her, there were no survivors to feel sorry for, and she was left without purpose. In an effort to sustain her interest, she became focused on getting through the content.

The story of Shanawdithit's (re)telling in the classroom reveals the complex ways in which the scaffolding that structured the teachers' understanding of what it meant to teach framed their approach. In the classroom, Shanawdithit's story became a sad story about the loss of a culture. Although, for some students, the story initiated questions about implication and relationship, neither Jenna nor Diane was able to assist students in "learning from" the story, as they were preoccupied with meeting their responsibilities to teach facts and skills and to take care of students.

Reviewing what transpired between the teachers, their students, and Shanawdithit's story reveals the labour of "not knowing." Although my offer of an alternative listening position was refused in favour of the more familiar "learning about," with its acquisition of qualities, attributes, and facts, ignorance, "the active dynamic of negation, the active refusal of information" (Felman 1982, 30), is not easily accomplished or easily maintained. Relying on the scaffolding that structured their approach, the teachers worked at maintaining the familiar, and the students learned about what happened, what was done, to Shanawdithit. Responding to the story and their teacher's direction, Diane's students felt sorry for, angry about, and even ashamed of what was done by the Europeans long ago, but Diane was unable to take them beyond the expression of these emotions.

Students learned about the white European as the subject and observer of history. As learners, they were asked to consume the facts in ways that positioned them as subjects who got to "worry" about and "make judgments" about what happened without ever having to consider their own relationship with, or implication in, history. Teachers must work at accomplishing this approach, yet it is a familiar and comfortable one. It offers a sense of control and satisfaction in lessons well done. This, then, is an offer that, in spite of the effort, is not to be refused. In meeting their responsibilities, the teachers formulated an active refusal of information.

6

"We Wanted to Hear Your Stories": Teaching and Learning from Audrey's Story

Audrey's story presented the teachers with an opportunity to engage students in the study of Canada's recent past and particularly the impact of the forced assimilation policy on the daily lives of Aboriginal people. Reviewing the transcripts of the classroom lessons during which teachers shared Audrey's story with their students, I was confronted with unsettling questions: How did the text that Michael and I had written to honour our mother come to be heard by teachers and students as one of hardship and suffering? How did students, who, in reaction to it, counselled Audrey in the principles of anti-racism education, come to understand this as an appropriate response? Addressing these questions required that I investigate the scaffolding that structured the teachers' understanding of what it means to teach about the relationship between Aboriginal people and Canadians, and that I ask how their understandings of the story coalesced with the grid that structured their approach to teaching. And finally, how did the text itself contribute to the meaning the teachers and students constructed?

Implicating Ourselves

The complexity of my dual commitments to the (re)telling project is manifest in the work with my mother's story. For Michael and me, creating it enabled us to explore our position as Aboriginal people. Listening, writing, and rewriting it, we worked toward understanding something of our mother's experiences as an Aboriginal woman. Forced assimilation demanded that Aboriginal people abandon their language and culture in exchange for a promised acceptance as equal members within Canadian society. In reality, though the assimilation was government policy, the acceptance was not forthcoming. We wanted to pass on to readers how our mother experienced the legacy of colonization, her response to racism, and her commitment to creating a good life for herself and her family. Our intention was to honour her strength and reflect her experiences. Rather than initiating denial, I wanted to (re)tell in a way that would offer teachers and students an alternative listening position. We included the prefatory dialogue to reflect the context of (re)telling, hoping that by portraying our relationship with our mother, we could engage readers in our struggle to understand reasons for not telling stories.

Our personal connection with our mother's story meant that it was interwoven with a lifetime of experiences. Although I knew that I could not control what meaning teachers and students would take from it, the depth of my connections contributed to my expectations for it. I was aware that anti-racism discourses had great currency in the schools but was unprepared for the ways in which the teachers relied on particular themes from them. The consequence of their approach meant that, for me, a kind of violence was done to the story. My efforts to make sense of this required me to read and reread, to write and rewrite about what transpired between the teachers, the text, and the students.

Social Justice and Discourses of Social Care

In Audrey's story, the teachers encountered details of racial discrimination in Canada's recent past. The story addresses the role of Canadian public policy and the actions of individual Canadians in the oppression of Aboriginal people. The teachers framed the story as one of social justice, and their desire to teach well, to take care of the needs of students, and to develop good citizens became focused on Audrey's loss and suffering. Cultivating imaginative empathy in the service of social concern, the lessons to be learned involved developing appropriate attitudes regarding the suffering, arriving at judgments about fairness, and learning the "right" rules of moral behaviour.

The teachers' concerns with taking care of students included the double tasks of "instilling the correct habits and attitudes" and "enhancing subjectivity through making children 'self-motivated,' 'self-disciplined,' and possessed of a 'positive self-image'" (Popkewitz 1998, 64). Defined along these lines, Audrey's story was reformulated: no longer addressing socio-political conditions, it became a homily on personal attributes and overcoming deficiencies. As Jenna explained, "There's those other themes like self-identity, self-esteem, ridicule, all those sorts of things. I'm sort of hoping that I can go to those themes" (October 1998).

When they took Audrey's story into the classrooms, the teachers were confronted with the task of teaching about the history of injustice while still caring for the needs of their students. In keeping with the scaffolding that structured their approach, teachers tied it to a series of lessons aimed at conveying that discrimination is wrong. Relying on a version of the golden rule, they attended to Audrey's suffering. Knowing that students would not like to be treated as Audrey was, they used her narrative to show students how to be "good" and "moral" citizens. They worked from the position that discrimination against Aboriginal people had occurred in the past and that, today, everyone knew it to be wrong. In turn, students framed their understanding of the story within redemptive discourses and, as confident individuals possessed of self-esteem, positioned themselves as responsible for ministering to Aboriginal people.

Responding to the Story and Planning for Teaching
Although Jenna responded to Audrey's story in a more personal manner than Diane, both tended to connect it to their position as educators, speaking in terms of "how I would teach the story" and "why I would teach it." As Sharon Feiman-Nemser and Robert E. Floden suggest, a teacher's knowledge is "actively related to the world of practice" and "functions as an organic whole, orienting her to her situation and allowing her to act" (quoted in Evans 1989, 212). Both Diane and Jenna worked from the understanding that knowledge of one's own history would provide a sense of self-understanding and self-worth. In this section of the chapter, I investigate their responses to Audrey's story as expressed through their ideas for teaching.[1]

The Teachers' Response and Plans for the Story
The teachers' response to the text interlaced with their understanding of their responsibilities as history instructors and became part of the grid that structured their approach to teaching it. During our first planning session, I asked them to begin by sharing their response to it (the list of questions is included in Appendix B). Both phrased their understanding in terms of how and why they would teach the story.

Part of the scaffolding that structures Diane's understanding of what it means to teach history is the idea of history as the story of shared human struggle. With a strong emphasis on content details, she teaches about the ordinary people of Canada's past, intending her pupils to perceive similarities between themselves and the figures under study: "It is about learning how people handled it. History is filled with culture and values, and it provides the opportunity to teach kids about culture and values. I can identify and students can know that there were people who worked hard and struggled and it's only what we're doing. It's humbling, it's not ancient" (June 1999). Diane's understanding of her responsibilities required her to teach in such a way that students would see connections between themselves and events of the past. She believes that if students can relate to what happened in the past, they will want to know more about it.

She also conceives of the history class as acquainting students with their civic duties. She sees the study of history as necessary for self-understanding but also for comprehending the experiences of Others. She teaches her students to be good listeners so that they will be able to consider other points of view and life experiences. She believes that learning about people in the past, the issues they confronted, and how they responded will prepare students to be good citizens. A key element in the teaching of history is for students to learn that, though history is about people just like them, not everyone has had the same experiences that they have had. As good citizens, students have a responsibility for creating a world that would be a good place to live for all people.

During the first planning session, Diane described Audrey's story as "a woman's personal journey." She found its documentation of Audrey's experience of discrimination especially useful. Grounded in anti-racism discourses, Diane's plan was to use the story to teach about discrimination and the resultant hardship encountered by Aboriginal people. The themes of loss and suffering dominated her approach, and students were asked to respond to this. Her objective was for them to develop the proper attitude concerning discrimination, as well as tolerance and respect for Aboriginal people. Concerned with addressing issues of injustice, she concluded that her lessons would help students determine what is fair and what is not fair.

Like Diane, Jenna wanted to open students' eyes to the suffering of Aboriginal people and hoped that empathy would prompt them to take action regarding it. During the first planning session, she started the discussion by expressing a specific interest in Audrey's story:

> The one that touched me the most was the first one I read. The story about your mother, particularly, and it struck me more from the literary ... just the way it was written. I think, how you started with the poem and the need for her to think back to what still had meaning, it seemed ... She touched music, and music is important in my

life so maybe I related to that, I don't know, but it just really grabbed me. And then the ending as I indicated to you on the phone that I just got choked up. So, for whatever reasons, it spoke to me very powerfully, somehow, and her struggle and certainly the name calling and all that was part of it but ... And some of the ... that she lived through it all, it was still positive. Throughout it all, she sounded very positive to me, but it just grabbed me like a piece of literature would. (September 1998)

In this first response, Jenna explained that the feelings elicited by the story engaged and maintained her attention. She felt an emotional connection with Audrey and found the narrative personally significant. An English teacher, Jenna used the language of literary analysis and noted the forceful introduction and conclusion, the elements of style that prompted her response, and the extent to which she identified with the "character" of the story. Jenna described the terms on which she identified with Audrey:

Well, I think it has to do somewhat, again, with Chloe's comment about looking at our own story. I was ten when we came from Holland and part of a large family. The name calling really fits with me because my brothers had some very choice names for me all through my teens, and it was incredibly derogatory but no one seemed to notice. Not that my parents were not loving people but, somehow, with nine kids, who knows, they just weren't aware and my older sister and I were ridiculed a lot. The three adjectives that were used all the time really didn't fit but it didn't matter. It's like this black hair business, you know. You know you have black hair but you know that it doesn't ... someone out there does not approve and so you wish you had something ... and it just stirs up so many emotions, and so that whole notion of name calling I really related to and the whole idea of seeking yourself. My parents were very ... especially my father, did not want to challenge anything in Canada. Like, we came over here. We were going to be Canadian; we weren't going to be Dutch. Canadian is what we were going to be and everything was ... Like, you didn't speak Dutch; you didn't keep the traditions, all of that was gone. This really, it touched me because ... There are certain things, that, you know, fine, I don't care if I do them ever, but we've had family reunions and we've had discussions and all of a sudden my roots became very important to me, and that's partly why I added my name to my married name, and that was done twenty years after

I was married, but that was a really important thing for me. That was part of my identity, so I think we all search for who we really are, and especially around here and in the south where we have a lot of ethnic groups, I think this whole idea of where do I fit in – in this global society, I think could be very important. That's what really reached out ... the ridiculing ... it's something that I hate to hear on the playground, I hate to hear it in my classes. Like, I get very emotional about it because I've experienced that and it just throws self-esteem so much, so that's part of it. (September 1998)

In reading the narrative, Jenna was reminded of her own childhood and was overwhelmed by the ways in which Audrey's story was "just like" hers. Her identification with Audrey was grounded in what she saw as their shared experience of loss. As the child of immigrants who were committed to assimilation, Jenna was denied her cultural identity and subjected to ridicule. This collapsing of differences between the experiences of Aboriginal people and the experiences of immigrants is supported by multicultural discourses that advocate understanding the world from the position that we are all different but we are all the same. Because it operates in this way, multiculturalism complicates a teacher's ability to recognize and respond to differences. During our initial interview (in June 1998), Jenna had questioned multiculturalism, with its emphasis on celebrating cultural difference; in the planning session, she drew upon it not to celebrate difference but to hear a story of mutual loss. In doing so, she took up multicultural and anti-racism discourses, conceiving of the narrative as a way of addressing the significance of claiming one's heritage and respecting difference.

Jenna believed that her recognition of Audrey's pain had initiated her concerned reaction to the story. She added that many of her students endured "pain and suffering" in their own lives and consequently would also be able to identify with Audrey's past. She saw this as the basis on which students would engage with the story:

And I would argue that for some people who have come from, you know, the other side of the Iron Curtain, for instance, who have come from, you know, even, like, Cambodia and Southeast Asia ... They would be different, the pressures and the atrocities and stuff, but I've got a feeling some of them could relate better and more emotionally to some of this than I can, at least. That's what I mean to say ... I have a feeling some of these kids have experienced a lot more than

I have and possibly have seen some things that could come pretty close to being as severe, as atrocious as ... [....] I feel that the more you can, to a degree, identify with a situation, the more sort of global understanding you have of what's going on. I don't ... I mean, I don't know, [....] the ones who have risked, who have tried to understand a little of what it's like to be there or who have tried to even imagine what it would be like to be yanked from your house and plunked into a different foster home. For instance, I've got a boy whose parents, you know; he's been totally abandoned by his parents. Well, you know, he might understand what it's like to live with foster people, dying, wishing like crazy to be with your blood relatives if you can't be there, and obviously he's there for different reasons than in the story but ... And like the connections. I really feel that then the kids can get into the story, can kind of deal with the other emotions of, yes it was unjust, yes, you know, and then the next step, you know, you're talking about responsibility. (October 1998)

Jenna consistently argued that the story would be best comprehended by those who had first-hand experience of suffering – "they will have a more authentic understanding." In teaching it, she planned to take advantage of its power to generate sympathy for Audrey (as emblematic of Aboriginal people). The scaffolding that structured Jenna's understanding of her responsibilities suggested that, once students identified a victim, they would perceive both the associated injustice and their responsibility to correct it.

Drawing on her understanding of the function of narrative and her experiences as an English teacher, Jenna's response to the narrative was structured in part by her understanding of character, theme, and plot. This approach nurtured her identification with Audrey and her hearing the story on the basis of the universal theme of strength in the face of adversity. In her teaching of the story, Jenna planned to elicit a response based on an emotional reaction arising from an identification with the protagonist. Occupied as she was with the narrative, she could draw on what she knew and avoid the less familiar meta-narrative. This approach to literary analysis does not require readers to attend to the time and place of the (re)telling or to the relationship between the (re)teller, the subject, and the reading audience.

Attending to the teachers' responses begins to unravel the ways in which the scaffolding that structures their framework, the texts, and the structures imposed by the context of hearing interact. This interaction has important implications for the meaning the teachers made, for what they could and could not hear, and, consequently, for what they offered students. Diane's understanding of history as the story of "our" shared human struggle and a vehicle to instill civic responsibility is reflected in her emphasis on the study of hardship and suffering, and nourishing appropriate responses to them. Jenna's immediate and lasting reaction to the narrative was established through her identification with Audrey. What she heard was pain caused by the denial of cultural identity, an instance of injustice that became the focus of her work with the story.

The Sequence of Lessons

There were some similarities and some differences between the ways in which Diane and Jenna structured their approach to teaching the stories. In Diane's class, students read a selection from an anthology of life stories titled *Context 2 Anthology* (1982) and answered the questions, "What was the main idea about the character that the author chose to record? Why do you think the author chose to record those details?" In an associated homework assignment, they chose a story from the anthology, read it, and prepared to discuss it. In small groups, they then addressed the following questions: "What events did the author choose to record and why did the author choose to record those?" Next, they completed an assignment titled Five Secrets in a Box, in which they chose five stories about themselves and their family to share with their classmates.

Diane used these lessons to prepare her pupils for the Braiding Histories Stories. She positioned the anthology author as an expert who documented important biographical events, disseminating information about the culture and identity of particular individuals. Reading the anthology informed students that studying history meant acquiring details. Diane believed that they needed to learn details about themselves and their classmates before they could understand the Braiding Histories Stories. Having them research and write their own histories helped them understand that, like the people in their textbooks, they too had a history. Diane reported that the Five Secrets in a Box activity cultivated self-respect as well as concern and appreciation for others. She hoped that, when students read the Braiding Histories Stories, they would display similar appreciation and respect for Aboriginal people.

In Jenna's class, students were encouraged to think about how past events had shaped their own present. Relying on their memories and interviewing parents and other relatives, they completed individual family history projects and reported on incidents such as family separation, the birth of siblings, moving to a new school, and participating in athletic events. Jenna explained that these lessons generated a sense of trust in the class. Students learned to respect differences, and scrutinizing their own history was good preparation for investigating that of others.

Before she taught Audrey's story, Diane completed the section of her Native peoples unit that covered contemporary issues, including residential schools and the reserve system. She believed that the story fit into her unit at this point. She had already taught the Shanawdithit and Mistahimaskwa narratives.[2] Jenna chose to teach Audrey's account as an introduction to the Braiding Histories Stories.

For both Jenna and Diane, teaching history meant presenting the details of course content as well as conveying lessons regarding citizenship education and education for social action. Their approach to Audrey's story made perfect sense within their understanding of what was required of them as teachers.

The Story in the Classroom

My examination of what happened to Audrey's story in the classroom is organized around its opening address, the context of (re)telling, the main story itself and student engagement with it, and, finally, the written work of students (see Table 6.1).

Table 6.1

Lesson sequence for Audrey's story

	Diane Carr	Jenna Marsh
Lesson 1	Opening discussion, reading the story, follow-up discussion	Discussion of the opening address
Lesson 2	Ongoing follow-up discussion	Reading the opening paragraphs and all of the story, follow-up discussion
Lesson 3	Follow-up assignment	Follow-up assignment: students wrote poems and responded to a page of questions
Lesson 4	Small-group discussion	Small-group discussion

The Opening Address

Diane's Class

As with Shanawdithit's story, Diane began Audrey's narrative with a review of the concepts covered in the opening address. During a question-and-answer period, she asked students to define dignity and self-esteem. They provided dictionary-like definitions. For example, when Diane asked, "What is dignity?" they produced comments such as "How much pride you have for yourself; what you deserve; what people give you, like, respect and stuff; your self-respect" (January 1999). Diane, concerned with taking care of the needs of her students, confirmed their mastery of vocabulary.

Turning to the particulars of Audrey's story, Diane asked the class, "What is the value of your history?" Wanting to make the narrative relevant, she drew a comparison between the students' investigation of their history and Audrey's relationship with her own: "What is the value of your history? We did some looking into our family tree. We also, we also did some work dealing with our culture. We asked a few questions, and we created our own presentations of what we wanted to do, but also, along the way some of us know some things about our history, who we are. All right. What is the value of that? What is the value of your history?" (January 1999). Students replied that their histories were a source of pride and that they could pass them on. Responding positively to these remarks, Diane affirmed their understanding of history as a source of pride.

She continued: "Okay, so being proud and hope that it gets carried on. Okay. When we were studying a little bit before and reading some of the things, we found out, and you suggested to me, that some people's history had been denied. Okay, some people's history had been denied at various times in our society. Okay. Today we're going to read a story about a lady, review the story about Audrey, and we know a little bit about Audrey and we're going to talk about how she feels about her history. Okay, let's begin" (January 1999).

Here, Diane was referring to a previous lesson that had included some discussion of "a time when some people's history had been denied." Now, however, she shifted the focus, assigning students the task of "talking about how Audrey feels about her history." Affirming students for what they had learned, she began to nurture empathy for Audrey. As a history teacher responsible for teaching lessons of history and developing good citizens, Diane concentrated on Audrey's feelings to do so.

Jenna's Class

Jenna's approach to the opening address resembled Diane's. She too reviewed student grasp of vocabulary and focused on the question, "What is the value of your history?" Her emphasis was on helping her pupils to recognize injustice while preserving their self-image as good and capable beings. She framed her discussion of the opening address in terms of its themes, metaphors, and similes. After reading it aloud to the class, she posed a series of questions:

Jenna: Now that is a poem to start to focus our attention on what this person's story is going to be all about. Now from this opening can you think of some themes that are hidden in this poem or not hidden in the poem that you think are going to be addressed? Sandy?

Sandy: Um, her mom has something in the past that happened and she is trying not to bring it up again.

Jenna: Okay. What part of the poem?

Sandy: Mom wrestled with her past like a pattern that would not go together.

Jenna: Okay good. Any other ideas? Andy?

Andy: Ah, history, her past, you can't understand, like, people denying [....].

Jenna: Okay. Nancy?

Nancy: [....] remembering the hands that did the stitching.

Jenna: What do you think that meant?

Nancy: Not to remember what was left behind, but the people themselves.

Jenna: So you think the hands represent hope?

Nancy: The mom ...

Jenna: What else, who else?

Nancy: Like, maybe people in her past.

Jenna: Maybe people in her past. Okay, good. Let's go back to the ... Wayne?

Wayne: The second paragraph/stanza, or whatever, it could be telling you not to forget where your roots are from and your history. And, um, maybe in "Mom wrestled with her past," maybe she is remembering it and she is trying to change the past and she shouldn't be doing that.

Jenna: What sort of images do you kind of think about when you hear that word "wrestles"? (October 1998)

Jenna's approach, structured by her understanding of the responsibilities of an English teacher, engaged students in an extended discussion of the opening address. Beginning with a typical reading comprehension question, Jenna in effect asked students to predict the story's content. Responding to her phrase "themes that are hidden," they suggested that it would focus on Audrey's desire not to remember her past. In their efforts to identify her "problem" or "conflict," they were drawn into conceiving of the expected plot as an unveiling of secrets. In this, Jenna began to adjust the lens so that students would see the story as one woman's struggle with her past.

The Study of History as a Source of Self-Worth   Next, Jenna asked her pupils to attend to the "value of history":

Jenna: All right. Let's look at that line, "What is the value of your history?" We've talked about that when you did your timelines. What is the value of your own personal history and some of you reflected on that again in the quiz just the other day. "What happens when that history is denied?" Now let's see what that word, what that line, means to you. Then we'll talk about it a little bit if it were applied to your life history. [Do you have] any thoughts on that? What is the value of your history? So we're going to talk about what is the value of what has gone on in our life and what happens when that is denied.

Wayne: It's, like, um, like, on the timeline, like, you said, um, we have to say how the things, those events shaped, like, who we are today. This time of history goes back way farther so, um, we have to remember it 'cause that could be what we are today also and what a lot of other people are.

Jenna: Okay. What happens if that history is denied? What do you think she is talking about there?

Sandy: Maybe if you deny it, it will come back at you. It's not a good thing to deny history because, um, you have feelings about it.

Jenna: Okay. I think you are on the right track. Okay. You have feelings about it, and if those feelings are denied what happens to the person?

Sandy: Well normally, like, they'll be really upset, like, things might happen, like, they might be in denial or ...

Jenna: Possibly. (October 1998)

Reminding students of their work in creating their own narratives, Jenna prompted them to apply what they had learned to their study of Audrey's narrative. Her questions focused their attention on an individual. They did not support an examination of the wider socio-political implications of historical events, and Wayne's attempt to address this was not taken up. Investigating the significance of colonization for learning about ourselves was not part of Jenna's scaffolding. For her, the story concerned an individual's relationship to the past, and students were engaged in learning about how the painful events in Audrey's past made her ashamed of being Aboriginal.

In her exchange with students, Jenna acknowledged Wayne's response and then prompted students to refocus. Given the structure of Jenna's approach, students were encouraged to understand the question "What happens if that history is denied?" to mean that Audrey was in denial about her personal history. In response to their teacher's question, students explained that if *you* deny history, "you might end up telling the wrong person" and "you need to tell so that you can learn from your mistakes." Students positioned themselves as knowing the value of their history and expressed concern for Audrey, who was in denial about something in her past.

During their years in the intermediate division, students are introduced to the study of history. Like many teachers, Diane and Jenna began this introduction with students' personal histories, devoting a substantive unit of study during which their pupils investigated, reported, and celebrated their personal and family histories. This common approach, suggested in both history textbooks and curriculum documents, is premised on the idea that knowledge of history contributes to a "healthy" sense of self. The value of "knowing" history is that it affirms individual self-worth. Working within this conceptual approach, the study of history is about developing pride in the accomplishments of one's family, community, and nation. Engaging with the (re)telling of Audrey's story within this conceptual framework supports students' understanding of themselves as knowing subjects in opposition to Audrey who is positioned as one who "does not know."

Addressing the Narrative in Isolation from the Meta-narrative   Jenna continued the lesson, asking about metaphors and similes:

Jenna: Let's look at that little line that looks at ... the metaphor, and I think that maybe we talked about metaphors in our literature classes before. It's sort of a symbol of what something is, a figure of speech. Sometimes they talk about this "is like." You know the wind is like rushing water or, um, maybe they flew like lightning through the halls. And we're talking about similes, but metaphors are comparisons that are kind of subtle. They're presented here in poetic form. She didn't come right out and say history is this. She talks about the past being like a pattern that wouldn't go together, not a single garment but a multi-layered gown. What do you think is the significance of those words and that symbolism "Not a single garment but a multi-layered gown"? Alvin?

Alvin: Not something simple but something complicated.

Jenna: Good. I think that's a totally good analogy. Good. (October 1998)

Students offered their understanding of the metaphor, and Jenna continued taking responses until a student named Sandy said,

Um, maybe it has something to do with, 'cause I still think when she says, like, the mom "wrestles with her past" maybe, like, something is upsetting about the past. Like, if someone hits you and it's, like, a loved one you wouldn't forget that and that's something you'd struggle over. So, maybe it's not something ... It's really upsetting and complicated and really you can't forget it kind of thing.

Jenna: Great. Okay. It's not ... you've picked up some really profound themes just from this poem alone. (October 1998)

Jenna accepted Sandy's suggestion that Audrey's struggle was over an individual experience of violence. Through this discussion, students became further invested in understanding the story as one woman's private struggle with a past experience of violence.

In part, Jenna's response was structured by her focus on the narrative in isolation from the meta-narrative. Her ignorance of the relevant socio-political context can be traced to her pedagogical scaffolding. In effect, she was able to teach the story without really knowing – or being required to know – what it was about. At no point did she engage students in an investigation of the socio-political implications of the reserve system or the impact of the forced assimilation policy on the day-to-day lived experiences of Aboriginal people. Nor did they discuss the depth to which racism permeated the relationship between Aboriginal people and Canadians. The suggestion that Audrey's relationship to her past is premised exclusively on an individual experience, which ignores the systemic violence, fulfills Jenna's broader objectives regarding the teaching of history.

Defining Concepts and Making Assumptions   Jenna concluded the lesson by addressing a last detail, key to establishing how students perceive Audrey and how they are positioned to hear her story:

Jenna: Okay. One of the questions that are raised in the very opening of the poem, Andy made a very good insight that something had died or someone had died and perhaps the question that [the story] opens with might help us understand what perhaps had died. Norma [use] big words [speak loudly].

Norma: What is dignity? How do you learn self-esteem? (October 1998)

When the students went on to define dignity and self-esteem, Jenna clarified:

Jenna: How you feel about yourself. And because self-esteem can be good or it can be bad, right?

TJ: If you are constantly putting yourself down, like, that's, like, low self-esteem and it's not good.

Jenna: Right. So when she asks the question "How do you learn self-esteem?" do you think she is talking about negative self-esteem or positive self-esteem?

All: Positive self-esteem.

Jenna: Yeah, she's looking for positive self-esteem in this, I would think, especially when it is tied to dignity because dignity is a positive idea. If you feel dignified about who you are and so on. Okay. Chris?

Chris: [....] how it goes "How do you learn self-esteem?" Maybe it's, like, she's, like, so upset that she doesn't have enough self-esteem to, like, to, like, get herself going.

Jenna: Most likely. Mmhmm. Very good. Nancy?

Nancy: It seems the way she is asking the question, it seems as if she has realized that she is having trouble with self-esteem. So she is asking for help. In her own way.

Jenna: Yes.

TJ: When it says [....] I think that is tied in with her history and why she wrestles with it because somehow she lost it.

Jenna: I think you are right on. That's going right back to what Andy said, that it sounds like something has died, something has gone in her past, in her history, and she is trying to retrieve it. Those are wonderful ideas. All right. Who do you think is talking here? We wanted to hear your stories? Any ideas? Do you think it's this lady here, Audrey Angela Dion? Okay. So, who do you think the "we" is referring to there? Sam?

Sam: The children.

Jenna: Yes there are children. There are others. So the story is taken from sort of a different point of view, and all I'm going to do today is give you that very first excerpt. We'll stop it here. (October 1998)

As the lesson unfolded, Jenna structured student understanding of the concepts introduced. Making connections between student responses, Jenna guided their interpretation, and, perhaps on the basis of their prior work on their own histories, the students collaborated with her. Responding to the teacher's questions, they positioned Audrey as having lost something in her history, as suffering from a lack of self-esteem, and as asking for help. From the point of introduction, then, students were encouraged to feel sorry for Audrey.

Understanding the Teachers' Approach

Asking students to predict what a story is going to be about is a prereading strategy frequently used by teachers to engage students' interest. However, this extended discussion in both Diane's and Jenna's classes, prior to hearing the story, is problematic. Knowing very little about Audrey, and in response to the teachers' questions and comments, the students were called upon to speculate and make judgments about Audrey and her response to the events in her life. In response to the opening address, both teachers and students presumed that its questions about dignity and self-esteem were intended to suggest that Audrey lacked a healthy sense of self because she had denied her past.

In Diane's class, the discussion of vocabulary was not directly linked to Audrey, whereas Jenna made specific connections between Audrey and the concepts of dignity and self-esteem. These differences may have sprung from Jenna's personal response to the story as one regarding the denial of cultural heritage.

The teachers' treatment of the opening address was structured by their understanding of the function of the narrative, their concept of history, and their need to assess student comprehension of the facts of the story. As a result, their pupils arrived at two key conclusions – that Audrey's struggle concerned an individual experience of violence and that she was asking for help because of her poor self-esteem. Without a necessarily conscious effort, the teachers began to establish a dichotomy, as students, having learned to value their own histories, were positioned as knowledgeable in opposition to Audrey, who was positioned as a woman in denial of her history. Due to their understanding of their responsibilities as history teachers and of the function of narrative, Diane and Jenna required students to engage with the story from the position as arbitrators of Audrey's feelings.

The Complicity of the Text

The meaning derived from the opening address is not exclusively the result of the teachers' approach. The text itself is complicit in generating their response. Perhaps the very complexity of the ideas I wanted to introduce shaped the exchange between Jenna and her students. The complex and contradictory position my mother (and many Aboriginal people) occupies in relation to her past cannot be simply represented. Although my mother has always had a sense of pride and dignity in herself, for most of her life she was very much aware that, according to dominant Canadian society, being Indian was considered shameful. The story's opening address invokes questions regarding dignity and self-esteem (see pages 23 and 24). Therefore, the presumption of teachers and students regarding Audrey's poor self-image is reasonable. Nonetheless, it supports an approach that enables a particular way of understanding the narrative as that of the individual, disabling understanding of the broader socio-political context.

Michael and I intended these questions to suggest issues that teachers and students could consider as they read the story. The questions were asked in the hope of initiating a varied discussion. It was through the process of colonization and the assimilationist policies of the Canadian government that Aboriginal people were denied access to knowledge of their history, language, and culture. Students in Canada have been denied knowledge of the history of the relationship between Aboriginal and non-Aboriginal people in Canada. Audrey refused the shame associated with being Aboriginal and made a conscious decision not to share stories of shame with her children. The scaffolding that structured the teachers' approach to the story did not support the investigation of these complexities, and teachers and students were unable to hear these questions. As the (re)telling reflects, Audrey is a woman of dignity and pride, very much aware of her history, yet the assumption that she was in denial about her history dominated the reading of the story in both classrooms.

The Context of (Re)telling

The story's opening conversation is critical to establishing context. Describing our efforts to understand why our mother did not share her stories, it invites readers to hear what we needed to (re)tell. Concerned with "teaching well," the teachers focused their discussion on establishing the facts of the narrative. Whereas Diane attended to the literal-level details, Jenna concentrated on the relationship between mother and daughter.

Diane's Class
After reading the introductory paragraphs aloud, Diane asked,

All right. Who is the conversation between?
Jess: Audrey and Audrey's daughter.
Diane: Good. What is Audrey's daughter suggesting?
Kim: Um, that her mother should tell more stories about her history.
Diane: Her mother should tell more stories about her heritage? Ah, how did her daughter feel? What did her daughter feel about what her mother ... What did she think her mother meant when her mother said, "I'm a Canadian. I'm a Canadian."?
James: There was no pride in her voice when she said it. She wasn't very proud of it.
Diane: Okay, you're saying what? Say it again James.
James: When she was saying "I'm a Canadian," there was no pride in her voice when she said it. She wasn't very proud of it.
Diane: Okay, her daughter noticed that there was no pride in her voice. Okay. All right. Anything else? Anybody else want to contribute anything?
Kim: Her daughter noticed that Audrey was denying her history, like.
Diane: That Audrey appeared to be denying her history. Good. Okay. Someone else, anything else?
Kevin: A little embarrassed maybe that she was Indian because her rights were taken away. The whites were more high class than the Indians were.
Diane: Okay. In this setting, in this part that we've read of the story, um, how, what age differences do you think – is the daughter a young daughter, a young daughter? Is Audrey the young mother? Or what's happening? (January 1999)

Attempting to understand Audrey's actions, and adhering to the terms of reference set up by their teacher, students assumed that the story was about "having pride in your heritage." The opening dialogue, which Michael and I wrote to reflect our desire to hear our mother's stories, was interpreted by students to mean "our mother should tell more stories." Listening from within a frame that makes the story about us telling our mother that she should have told more stories, they could not hear it as an expression of love in which we expressed our desire to share the stories of her childhood. Listening within the frame established by their teacher, students were unable to hear the significance of my request or of my mother's telling of her story. Rather than asking why they were being asked to hear it and what they were meant to learn from it, they listened from a position of knowing and judgment. In this approach, the following critical questions remain unexamined:

- Whose history was denied?
- Why was it denied?
- What were the consequences of the denial for Audrey, her children, and Canadians?

When these questions are ignored, the historical specificity of Audrey's experience is erased.

Diane asked students to acknowledge the lack of pride in Audrey's voice and to identify that this was a problem for Audrey and her daughter. Situating the "problem" as one specific to Aboriginal people excludes Canadians from the relationship. Diane addressed neither the role of Canadian government policy nor the social practices of the Canadian people. Kevin interrupted her approach when he said, "A little embarrassed maybe that she was Indian because her rights were taken away. The whites were more high class than the Indians were." Attempting to take up a discussion of what caused Audrey's lack of pride, Kevin presented it as a response to racial discrimination. Although Diane's question initiated his comment, she herself was unable to respond and redirected the dialogue to literal-level details.

Concerned with her responsibility for teaching well, Diane's questions focused on what she had determined to be the facts of the story. Asking about "what happened to whom," Diane was able to confirm student understanding of content details. Identifying and reporting the facts, students gained a sense of mastering the story. Occupied with responding to their teachers' questions, they were unable to hear the story of my struggle or to understand my mother's experiences. Asking questions that had, in her mind, firm answers, Diane was able to maintain a position of control. With this approach to the story, she addressed what she knew and avoided content that she was unfamiliar with. Audrey's relationship to her history and the implications of Canadians in the story might introduce conflict and would require Diane to confront questions that she was unprepared to address. The scaffolding that structured her approach did not support such an investigation.

Next, Diane returned to the question of why Audrey did not share her stories with her children:

Diane: "I felt like you didn't want us to be Indian," who is making that statement?

Jay: Audrey's daughter.

Diane: Audrey's daughter. Why is Audrey's daughter making the statement to her mother?

Sam: Maybe she feels that her mother isn't telling her everything about her life and she wants to know.

Diane: Okay, but at what point did Audrey not share with her children?

Bob: When she was growing up.

Diane: When the children were growing up. Why did she not want, why did she feel, what made her feel that she couldn't share this with her children?

Jessie: Probably because they were too young to understand.

Diane: I don't know whether it's their being too young to understand. What did she not want to have happen for them?

Leslie: She was afraid that they might feel ashamed of themselves.

Diane: She was afraid that they might feel ashamed of themselves. I'm having to repeat your answers for the tape purposes only.

Sam: Maybe she didn't want them to live through the same pain that she had lived through.

Diane: She didn't want them to live through the same pain that she had lived through. Interesting huh. Interesting! (January 1999)

Doing the work of teaching, Diane established that students had a stable comprehension of the facts of the story and then asked an interpretive question – why Audrey's daughter "felt like you didn't want us to be Indian." Diane had her own interpretation of why I made the statement, "I felt like you didn't want us to be Indian." Maintaining her position as teacher, Diane continued to call on students until she got the interpretation that she was looking for. As the teacher in the position of knowing, Diane was not required to investigate alternative understandings or to justify the authority of her understanding.

In asking why Audrey did not tell, Diane was not looking for a recognition of the cause of Audrey's complex relationship with her past. Rather, she was looking for an answer that focused on the product of telling. Diane rejected Jessie's suggestion that, in part, Audrey was acting on an informed conscious decision to protect her children. Diane waited for and marked as interesting Sam's comment that Audrey did not share because she did not want her children to feel ashamed or to experience the same pain that she had experienced.

In this exchange, Audrey was positioned as one who was made to feel shame and pain. Without recognition or explanation as to the cause of those feelings, the implication was that the pain and shame came from being Aboriginal. Diane did not discuss with her students what stories were left untold, what the children might have been too young to understand. Nor did she turn to the point in the text where Audrey explained why she did not tell her stories. Rather than taking up Audrey's words, Diane asked students for their judgments about why she did not speak. Although Diane's rejection of Jessie's comment in favour of Sam's did not eliminate Audrey's agentic power, it nonetheless eroded agency. Diane's lesson, structured by professional discourses of mastery and control, ignored the complexity of Audrey's relationship with her past in favour of a familiar frame of understanding.

Writing about historical agency, Peter Seixas (1996, 776) explains that it "is one aspect of the problem of historical causation. The concept of agency, however, focuses the historian on relationships of power. Who makes historical change and how (Mahoney and Yngvesson, 1992)? Central to the historiography of the past 30 years has been the project of bringing previously marginalized peoples into the purview of the discipline, not as victims or textbook 'sidebars,' but as active participants." In the investigation of the relationship between Aboriginal people and Canadians, Seixas' question, "Who makes historical change and how?" is critical. Audrey's story is about how Canadian government policy affected her life; it is also about her response to the hardship that resulted from that policy. What Diane heard and passed on was the story of hardship in isolation from the causes of hardship and Audrey's response to it, leaving students with a distorted understanding that repositions Aboriginal people as heroic victims.

Drawing on the scaffolding that structured her approach, Diane was concerned with teaching students the lessons from history. As Diane explained, one of the lessons to be learned from this story had to do with developing proper attitudes about racial discrimination. Diane relied on the recognition of pain and hardship resulting from discrimination to teach her lessons. This approach is aimed at nurturing good citizens, who have proper attitudes regarding discrimination and who recognize their responsibility to respond to the pain and suffering of Others. Diane structured her discussion of these opening paragraphs around mastery of the facts and making truth claims that leave no room for ambiguity in meaning.

Jenna's Class
Jenna began with the mother-daughter relationship in Audrey's story. After reminding students of their previous discussion, she read the opening paragraphs and asked, "How old is the daughter?" The students offered suggestions and agreed that the daughter was grown-up. Jenna continued with her questions:

Jenna: Okay. And she is reminiscing with mom, and the daughter has some disturbing questions about her own history about her past. And she wants to know and she wants to kind of dig into it a little bit.
Mark: My two sisters who are Indian don't have black hair, and my mom does and she's nowhere, she's not Indian.
Jenna: [....] it's possible.
Mark: [....] so it's kind of implied that just because you have black hair you're part Indian.
Jenna: No, I don't think that that is what is being said here, but the fact was that these people do have black hair. This person who is writing these stories has black hair and is Aboriginal. But at the time she didn't – whenever [it] was said that it was black hair – she said no, that it was brown hair. What does that tell you? Brad?
Brad: She's kind of denying any kind of connection to Aboriginal history.
Jenna: It seems like that doesn't it? And it's the mom, like, it's not the person, the I – it's the mother who is denying no that's the black hair. Yes.
TJ: She seems kind of afraid or ashamed to be Indian.
Jenna: The mother does, mmhmm. (October 1998)

What Jenna heard and passed on to students is a story of struggle and conflict between the mother and the daughter and the mother and her past. Jenna drew the students' attention to particular details: The daughter, an adult, asks her mother disturbing questions. The mother's refusal to acknowledge the hair colour is taken as proof that she was ashamed of being Aboriginal. In effect, Jenna positioned me in opposition to my mother and, in doing so, created an imaginary parallel between my experience and her own. Although Jenna valued her Dutch identity, her access to her language and culture had been denied by her parents' commitment to assimilation.

Jenna did not hear the story of the bond between me and my mother, my desire to understand her silence, my realization that she chose not to tell stories because they were not pleasant stories to tell, or the significance of her claim for Canadian identity. These elements of the (re)telling were missed in Jenna's hearing of the story. In her approach to teaching the story, Jenna struggled to make the (re)telling fit the story that both she and her students were expecting to hear. I had used the word "disturbing" to describe my memory of my mother's remark, "I'm a Canadian, I'm a Canadian." Through the process of writing the story, I realized that her words were a claim for Canadian identity, that is, for acceptance – acceptance that Canadian society refused to grant, no matter how successfully she adopted its ways. In Jenna's interpretation, the disturbing aspect was not the shameful actions of Canadians but her understanding that Audrey was in denial of her ancestry.

Like the story as a whole, the introductory paragraphs are subtle, complicated, and controversial. The scaffolding that structured the teachers' approach to the story supported conditions in which the complexities were not taken up. In different ways, both Diane and Jenna approached these introductory paragraphs in ways that established a frame for understanding the story as one woman's struggle in the face of adversity.

Diane's emphasis on mastering facts erased the need to examine the relationship between Michael and me as (re)tellers and our mother, the subject of our (re)telling. Jenna's experiences as the child of an immigrant family that embraced assimilation became a part of the scaffolding that structured her approach to teaching the story. Drawing on her personal experiences, she framed student understanding of the relationship between the mother and daughter. Thus, students were unable to hear what motivated our desire to hear our mother's story and the significance of our mother's not telling and her telling.

As a result, they were unable to examine the role of Canadian public policy and Canadian society in producing shame. The true source of shame was the way in which Aboriginal people were treated by Canadian society, but this was never touched upon. Although Audrey was not ashamed of being Aboriginal or of her childhood, students were nonetheless given to understand that she was. The failure to investigate these issues left them with the idea that the shame originated in Audrey herself or in "Indianness," and they never understood that she was ashamed of Canadian society's treatment of Aboriginal people.

In Jenna's class, the story of conflict and struggle between the characters provided a frame familiar to both Jenna and her students. It allowed Jenna to accomplish her objective of focusing students' attention on the story of the individual's pain and suffering, avoiding the difficult issues of responsibility, implication, and an investigation of the historical context. Preoccupied with reporting the facts of the story, Diane's students were unable to hear the story of relationship. In both classrooms, questions regarding the time and place of (re)telling, including why I was (re)telling now, why I was (re)telling to them, and why I was (re)telling the story in the context of their Canadian history class, were never considered.

Reading Audrey's Story and Nurturing Empathy

Wanting to instill the "right" attitudes regarding discrimination, the teachers relied on imaginative empathy to develop social concern. Their initial questions focused on a repetition of the details of hardship and suffering. Cultivating sympathetic understanding in an effort to address an ethic of social care and justice, they asked about causation and consequence. Although this approach enabled them to fulfill their professional responsibilities, it reproduced ways of knowing that position Aboriginal people as pitiful victims.

Diane's Class

Continuing with her concern for students' understanding of the facts of the story, Diane read Audrey's story in sections, pausing to ask questions that tested student comprehension of literal-level details:

Diane: What's the most interesting fact you may have heard about in what I've just read? What's the most interesting fact to you?

Kevin: It's interesting but sad the way the minister made the children feel like they, they were nothing ... [tape unclear].

Diane: Interesting but sad, maybe I could reword that to the way Kevin did, maybe it's a sad fact. An interesting fact can be a revelation of something that is good, but it can also be a revelation or reveal something very sad or, ah, sad in the fact for someone else or sad in that you didn't recognize it this way.

Parul: I thought it was interesting how they used newspaper to fill up the walls for insulation.

Diane: Why did you find that using that for insulation was interesting?

Leslie: It was a good idea!

Diane: Good idea. Okay. They were very resourceful. What do you think about having to live that way? What do you think about them living that way? Kevin?

Kevin: I think it would be terrible to live that way, like, eating that sticky mush stuff made of flour and water. That'd be, like, would be, like, really hard and stuff.

Diane: John, what do you think?

John: Uh, I found it also sad because they had to learn the ways of the white community and pretend like they're something they're not.

Diane: Pretend they're someone they're not. Where abouts did Audrey grow up? Up to this point in the story, where has Audrey been living? Yes?

Jamie: On the reserve.

Diane: On the reserve. What do you think of the kind of housing on a reserve? What do you think about the fact that the family didn't have very much money? Why did they not have much money on the reserve? Living on the reserve. What are some of the startling facts here? That you're finding out?

Cam: That there were no jobs, that they didn't have a lot of money, we take for granted the way that we live. When we read stories about people who are less fortunate, it makes us think.

Diane: Because there were no jobs on the reserve and, therefore, there was no large income. Okay. All right. It makes you think a little bit about that. Okay.

CJ: Native people, if they want to get jobs, they would get lower-class jobs because, like, there were some jobs, there were signs in the windows, like, "No Indians Allowed."

Diane: All right. So the jobs they had to take were lower class because of the discrimination. "No Indians Allowed" you're suggesting, right. Okay. Also any other reasons why they would have to take just seasonal jobs? All right. Um, so any other reason why they might have to take just seasonal jobs? Why her dad would only work a few months of the year. Why would her dad work only a few months of the year?

John: Because they only needed them at certain times of the year.

Diane: Where are most of our reserves? Remember we've looked at the map of Ontario, at our map, the recent map we were able to obtain. Where are most of the reserves located?

John: Further up north, where there is not much ...

Diane: Urban centres.

John: Yeah.
Diane: So, what are your job prospects, um, the further away you are
    from an urban centre?
Kevin: Very rare, I would think. (January 1999)

Asking students to catalogue "interesting facts," Diane's question
elicited details of hardship and suffering that served to create empathy
for Audrey. The question also enabled her to evaluate student comprehension and to nurture their concern for the experiences of Aboriginal people. With her question, "Why did they not have much money
on the reserve?" Diane took up discourses of historical causation and
consequence, requesting that students advance plausible reasons for
why these conditions exist. When CJ suggested racial discrimination
as a contributing factor, Diane acknowledged him and offered geo-
graphic isolation as a further cause of unemployment and poverty.
Within this analysis, neither the cause nor the perpetuation of discrimination are grounded in human society. Rather, they take on what
amounts to an independent life of their own: like "geography," they
exist outside of human interaction. Decisions about the location of
reserves were made in the distant past; anchoring the causes of discrimination in the past serves Diane's purpose and ensures that students will learn about Audrey's suffering without having to investigate
the role of Canadians and government policy in creating it.

By teaching about the hardship and misery caused by discrimination, Diane sought to address the goals of anti-racism education. Reading aloud, she covered Audrey's experiences on and off the reserve
and posed more questions regarding causes and consequences:

Diane: Let's talk about who forced, who forced these things to have
    to happen to Audrey and possibly her family, who was behind this?
Student: The day-to-day white people that she came across.
Diane: The day-to-day white people that she came across. What are
    [your] thoughts about that?
Student: It was sad how people judged people by just their background.
Diane: People could be judged by their cultural background and maybe
    what they physically looked like.
Students: [It must have been very hard for her, to deal with people.]
Diane: So you're saying it may have taken a lot of ...?
Student: A lot of bravery, courage ...
Diane: A lot of bravery, courage ... Should that have been the case?
    How many times a week does your father or your mother or you or

anyone of your family members have difficulty going out of your home worrying about (you might worry about the homework not done) but worrying about whether you are going to be accepted by the people on your street, think about that, worried about the fact that at your job that you are not considered equal and maybe you're even treated that way. Okay. Interesting huh! Let's continue on. (January 1999.)

Guided by Diane, most students' responses remained within a framework of racism and discrimination, which they were able to see at work in the story. Diane acknowledged their comments, but, seeming not to know where to take them, retreated to the familiar territory of empathy by imagining what enduring prejudice must feel like. Students were asked to recite the details of Audrey's life, to make judgments about how she lived, and were expected to conclude that no one should have to live as she did. This approach to teaching history, grounded in empathy, requires that Audrey's suffering be explicitly described. In order for students to determine that it was wrong, they have to "feel what it was like for her." In this exchange, Audrey is positioned as the sad but brave and courageous Aboriginal subject.

Jenna's Class
After discussing the opening paragraphs, Jenna read Audrey's story straight through. Clearly engaged with it, her pupils listened attentively. By this point in the lesson sequence, they were curious to know what had caused Audrey such feelings of shame. When Jenna finished reading, students quietly said, "It's good," and others quietly clapped. Jenna said, "You may clap," and the students applauded. At this point, she showed them an enlarged photocopy of Audrey's picture and told them where it would be displayed.
　　She then asked,

Was there anything in the story that surprised you? Just think about her story, about her mother's story. Was there anything in it that surprised you? Keith?
Keith: How she had to eat poor food and stuff and, like, how she had to starve because, like, it's sad [....].
Jenna: Mmhmm, I think so, and that was while she was living on the reserve.
Sandy: When she was looking for a job or, and, like, if she went shopping there would be signs saying "No Natives Allowed."

Jenna: Allowed. Okay.

Sandy: That must have been really hard.

Jenna: I would think so.

Joe: Well, it must have been hard to feel, like, all left out, like, an outcast because everybody hated you and there were two different groups and they just wouldn't let you do anything.

Jenna: Carol?

Carol: But I think it was horrible how people outcasted them just because of their culture and their background.

Jenna: Okay. Anything else? Brad?

Brad: I was sort of surprised that she kept so much contact with her religion 'cause I thought she completely left it alone. I didn't know she went home every night and listened to the Indian music. I didn't know she kept in touch as much as she did. When I thought she just forgot about it.

Jenna: Mmhmm, that might be a question that we might raise as to when that happened. She starts her story like that, doesn't she, then she ends the story like, "I listen to the flute music and I know who I am." What surprised you about the story?

Norma: That people could be so mean to people that, like, are different cultures and stuff and don't celebrate the same things as them. They wouldn't let them go in the stores and stuff. (October 1998)

When Jenna asked her pupils which story elements surprised them, most focused on the details of hardship. She did not ask them to explain why they found these details surprising, suggesting that they had understood the purpose of her question. Like Diane's students, who were told to list "interesting facts," Jenna's students reported the facts of the story. In Jenna's class, the emphasis was on Audrey as the subject of the story, and student responses derived from identification with Audrey and an imaginative understanding of her experiences of hardship.

Jenna's approach was structured, in part, by her understanding of how to teach a story. Focused as she was on nurturing student identification with Audrey, she was unable to see the ways in which her question contributed to reproducing a discourse of pity. Students positioned Audrey as a victim of discrimination who had endured a horribly difficult and sad life, and, in their litany of details, Audrey's historical singularity was lost.

The comments of Joe, Carol, and Norma opened the possibility of investigating why Audrey experienced such hardship. These students paid attention to the issue of race and culture as determining factors. The depth of discrimination experienced by Aboriginal people in Canada goes against what these students had been taught. They heard the story of Audrey's pain but also heard and asked why racial discrimination was acceptable. In the absence of any discussion, students relied on both the multicultural and anti-racism discourses, concluding that racism is wrong and that Audrey should have been proud of her identity. Consequently, their reading of the story was limited to "It was sad. It was wrong. Poor Audrey."

Brad deviated from the emphasis on hardship by remarking on the role of music and religion in Audrey's life. In highlighting this, he recognized that Audrey's relationship to music signified a change but was unclear about its significance. In the 1940s, music produced by Aboriginal artists was not generally available. During the 1990s, this changed significantly: art, music, and literature produced by Aboriginal artists became much more accessible. Brad's observation introduced an opportunity to investigate changes that have occurred in the broader sociopolitical context as well as in Audrey's personal life – changes that are reflected in her relationship to music. Although Jenna acknowledged his comment, she could not respond to its significance, due to her lack of knowledge and the stress she placed on suffering.

Because Jenna's personal reaction to the story was so strong, she relied heavily on instigating engagement on these grounds. For her, the success of her lesson depended on student identification with Audrey's pain. Through her questions, Jenna drew student attention to the details of hardship, considering them in isolation from the rest of the (re)telling. Expanding the focus to include the mother-daughter relationship and that between students and Aboriginal people could potentially draw students into the story and support "learning from." Audrey's decision not to share her stories with her children, critical to the narrative, constitutes her response to discrimination and reveals her agentic power. Lack of attention to this results in its erasure and weakens the representation of her humanity.

Jenna concluded her lesson by describing an upcoming assignment:

> Okay. We'll stop the discussion right here. We'll pick it up next history class, and I'll have a copy of the story for you with a more specific assignment about, um, like, looking at the story for some particular details to the things she had to give up. You know there is the whole question of when she starts talking about when she entered the residential school and what was she taught, like, that sort of life didn't

start here in Canada until the European settlers came. And for people who were already living here, that must have been an incredible insult to them, to their dignity and to their just total being. Okay. Thanks a lot. (October 1998)

Jenna's closing statement to students secures Audrey's position as victim. Telling students that the follow-up assignment will emphasize "the things [Audrey] had to give up" and the way in which Audrey's "dignity was insulted" informs them regarding what is important to know about Audrey. Focusing exclusively on what was done to Audrey, Jenna did not address the role of the Canadian government and the Canadian people. Students were not asked to examine either their motivation or what it meant to them as Canadians that Audrey's history was part of their own. Nor were they told to consider why the (re)tellers had asked them to listen or to reflect on the mother-daughter relationship.

The Follow-up Activity

In both classes, the pupils completed follow-up assignments in response to Audrey's story. Diane's students wrote letters to Audrey, and Jenna's were offered a variety of choices, including writing a poem or a journal entry or drawing a picture.

Diane's Class

I have no record of the directions Diane gave to her students when she first presented the assignment. However, in a subsequent session, she offered them the following guidelines: "All right, you have your thoughts now ready for your letter to Audrey – of what you would like to say to Audrey. Is there someone who would like to share what they would like to say to Audrey and explain that ... How you know that today as you sit here that ... How you know that, umm, that was not an acceptable way to be treated as you know the Canadian society or as you know our Canadian story" (October 1998).

In this class, structured by a discourse of social care, learning about Audrey's story was reconstructed as a study of personal attributes. In "By Virtue of Being White: Racialized Identity Formation and the Implications for Anti-racist Pedagogy," Carol Ann Schick (1998) found that teacher candidates reproduce this pattern in negotiating the Aboriginal curriculum. This positioning, she argues, enables them to deny complicity with racism while supporting a sense of self as good and moral. Schick (ibid., 180) writes that "Relegating racism and intolerance to the past is the action of the redeeming of history (Benjamin, 1955), an act in which the subjects [teacher candidates] regularly engage. For Canadians generally, and for white Canadian subjects in this research, the psychic effect of their identification as the good and tolerant person is that intolerance is not a possibility. Instances of it must be rationalized, denied, or repressed so that the subject and her national identity can remain. These negative qualities are not generally available for examination and can be acknowledged only at peril."

Diane's directions reaffirm for students that they should write as good citizens who have learned from the mistakes of the past. Wanting students to explain to Audrey that Canadians know that discrimination is wrong, Diane asks them to inhabit a discourse of social care and to perform it in their letters. Schick (1998) remarks, "tolerance and selflessness become an identification of who teachers are; and as indicated in the voices of this research, teachers in Canada are the ones who do countless good deeds for children in their charge. Their professional obligation of showing others 'how to live' is also a technology by which teachers are produced as citizens able to participate in governance."

In response to the story and to their teacher's directions, the students wrote letters that reflected their particular understanding of antiracism. They asserted that the problem of racism had been solved and that, as good and caring Canadian citizens, they themselves were in a position to provide Audrey with helpful advice.[3]

Student Letters to Audrey

> Dear Audrey
> You should be proud to be an Aborigine and continue to share your stories. Through the people the Aboriginal culture will live forever.
> p.s. I'm glad you finally built up the courage to tell your daughter about what it was like for you to grow up as an Indian.

> Dear Audrey
> I hope people have stopped making fun of you where you live now. All people are equal and not many people believe in it, but it is true. People are people no matter what colour their faces are. We are all alike in a way. I guess it will take a while for people to understand that.

Dear Audrey

If some people had only taken the time to look past what others thought they may have seen what only a few others did, that everybody should be treated equally regardless of any stereotypical assumptions people may make. I do believe that Canada is making progress in the battle against racism and that we are learning from the mistakes we have made in the past. I also think that soon everybody will be treated with brotherhood and equality.

In different ways, the students framed their responses within the discursive practices that structured their hearing of the story. Responding primarily from within a discourse of social care, they demonstrated the extent to which they saw Audrey's story as a lesson about themselves as good citizens. Telling Audrey that she simply needed to be proud of her heritage, that racism is wrong, that Canadians have learned from past mistakes, and that things are improving, the letters instruct both Audrey and their own authors in the principles of anti-racism and multicultural education.

In their letters, the students reproduce dominant ways of knowing about the relationship between Canadians and Aboriginal peoples. The latter are positioned as needing care, the former as knowing what Aboriginal people "should" do and what is "best" for them. The letters display a range of consequences, all of which enact their own forgettings while, especially in the first case, reproducing power relations. In spite of Diane's intentions, and yet structured by her approach, they are condescending: the students adopt a discourse of blame while simultaneously consoling Audrey by assuring her that things are "all better now."

Diane's approach to the story allows her to construct a frame that obstructs "learning from" the story. Neither she nor her students are required to confront questions of responsibility. They do not, for example, examine the inequitable distribution of power as a root cause of hardship and suffering, or the ongoing denial of Aboriginal rights, or the implications of the limited representation of Aboriginal topics in schools. Grounded in imaginative empathy, engagement with Audrey's story is limited to learning about the miseries of Aboriginal people without having to confront either their implication or the incommensurability of understanding. Diane's approach enables her to meet her professional responsibilities. She was pleased with the success of her lessons, in which she was able to cover the content and teach vocabulary. In their follow-up assignment, students demonstrated what they had learned from history. Focusing on their letters as reflections of their feelings for Audrey, Diane remarked, "Some of them were handwritten. Some of them had the poems dyed on tea paper so they really did a good job. I have some wonderful, wonderful letters to Audrey, very personal, extremely ... They're wonderful. Some are better than others but we know what they're feeling" (February 1999).

Megan Boler (1999, 156) asks, "But who and what, I wonder, benefits from the production of empathy? What kinds of fantasy spaces do students come to occupy through the construction of particular types of emotions produced by certain readings?" In the letters, Diane heard that students valued cultural diversity and supported the reduction of cultural antagonism. She did not hear the reproduction of dominant ways of understanding the relationship between Aboriginal and non-Aboriginal people. Student perception of the relationship centred on suffering as caused by individual acts of discrimination. Students put themselves in the position of being able to teach Audrey something about racism and discrimination. Their involvement was limited to feeling sorry for Aboriginal people and recognizing that discrimination is wrong. In effect, they did not learn about Audrey – they learned about themselves. Yet, what they learned, very limited in itself, confirmed their sense of self as good and responsible. They did not learn to confront unsettling truths about themselves or to discuss their implication in perpetuating racism and domination. Indeed, as Boler argues, identification, empathy, and pity do not in themselves lead to action or even necessarily to the recognition of injustice. Nor do they support the self-interrogation necessary to address racism. Boler (ibid., 160, 161) points out that "the uninterrogated identification assumed by the faith in empathy is founded on a binary of self/other that situates the self/reader unproblematically as judge. This self is not required to identify with the oppressor, and not required to identify her complicity in structures of power relations mirrored by the text ... The Aristotelian definition of pity can indeed be produced through reading literature. Passive empathy produces no action towards justice but situates the powerful Western eye/I as the judging subject, never called upon to cast her gaze at her own reflection."

Jenna's Class

In Jenna's class, students were presented with the assignment and then given time to work independently. In explaining the assignment, Jenna asked them to consider specific questions from a particular standpoint:

Jenna: What I would like you to do today is think about a personal
response. So, we heard, we shared a lot of our ideas. We talked about
what surprised you, what kind of disgusted you, um. I'm going to
put some other questions on the board, things like, umm, what,
what about, like, how did you relate to what you heard in her story?
And in particular, I just want you to focus on an emotional response,
an emotional reaction to what she told you in the story and you
have a copy in front of you now so if you need to kind of reread
it, refresh your memory, um, maybe kind of zoom in on some
specific things, you can actually do that. The other thing that I
would like you to think about is the fact that Canada is sort of
known to be sort of a great place to live all over the world. If you
hear, if you listen to some radio responses or radio reports will say,
you know, the latest Gallup poll came in and when they asked
people in general in, you know, what makes your country a great
place to live Canada always comes out on top. And my question
today would be, for Audrey, would that be so? Would Audrey think
it was or did she think at the time when she was growing up, when
she was your age, was Canada a great place for her to live? So think
about that a little bit. And as we go through this unit I want you
to keep another question in mind because we have our picture up
there and a banner at the top is "History Our Proud Heritage." And
do you think you can be proud of the story that she is telling us?
And how are we involved in all of that. How are our forefathers
involved in all of this story? Those are some difficult questions that
we want to try [to] address. Andy?

Andy: Some of our forefathers weren't here when her story took place.

Jenna: No. I'm sort of thinking sort of, um, like, my forefathers weren't
here either because they were in Holland. But, in general, those of
us who are not of Aboriginal descent have perhaps some responsibility, and throughout the unit we're [going to] start talking a little
bit about ... Okay. Brad's family wasn't here and Jane's family wasn't
here. Lots of us weren't here. But we have this sort of image of Canada as a great place to live and we like to promote that and we certainly want to be proud of our Canadian heritage. But at the same
time there were some Canadian citizens who perhaps didn't experience, you know, what the masses out there figure what Canada is
all about. So these are some questions to keep in your mind. But,
for this morning, you are going to get an opportunity to make sort
of a personal response, and these responses will be shared with Susan
[Dion]. You can do it in a variety of ways. (October 1998)

In this exchange, Jenna asked students to write about how the story made them feel, shaping their responses with two queries: Would Audrey agree that Canada is a great place to live? Given Audrey's treatment, can we continue to claim that ours is a "proud heritage"? Posed in this way, Jenna's questions provoked shame and apology. Jenna was calling for responses that reflected students' understanding that discrimination is wrong and an acknowledgment that, as good citizens, they knew that Aboriginal people deserved an apology. Having previously positioned me as an "authentic" First Nations representative, Jenna cued her class regarding the need for appropriate responses, explaining that they would be shared with me.

Jenna's attempt to establish this frame was interrupted by Andy, who resisted her suggestion that Canadians have "some responsibility" for addressing the relationship between themselves and Aboriginal people. In reply, Jenna repeated that she wanted a "personal" response. Her reiteration gave students permission to focus on what they had learned about themselves in isolation from a consideration of the indigenous Other.

Given the nature of Jenna's lessons to this point, her assignment directions make sense within the grid of ideas that shaped her approach to the story. Jenna's concerns with taking care of the needs of her students and teaching well operated in tandem with anti-racism and multicultural discourses, as well as those of the intermediate history class, with its emphasis on the study of history as a vehicle for self-knowledge. Informed in part by Jenna's own history, her teaching emphasized the psychological well-being of her students. Thus, she accorded priority to developing their self-understanding and self-esteem. She and her students drew on a limited interpretation of anti-racism/multicultural discourses calling for tolerance and the celebration of difference.

Students' Written Work   Jenna felt that the majority of students put a lot of effort into the assignment and produced thoughtful written responses. I asked her to choose three samples of what she considered to be exemplary work and to describe for me what made them so. The samples – three poems – appear below, followed by Jenna's written comments to the students and her remarks to me.[4] This work is important for understanding how students' responses are structured in significant ways by their teachers' approach to teaching the story. Although I understand the students' responses to be a significant representation of the meaning students make from the (re)telling, I also

responses that could have been a starting point for discussing students' understanding of the story shut down rather than initiate discussion.

Audrey [by Nell]
Being an outcast just because of your Race.
Stores with signs saying no Indians allowed,
How cruel can human beings be?
It was hard to find work bad looks, sign, why?
What did Indians ever do?
Feeling like you have to hide from people!
Life was hard.
Wanting to become Canadian because
Indians were nothing to white people.
Outside trying to hold all the pain in
But on the inside screaming was being done.
Trying to make it through life was tough,
But if you're strong you will make it.
And Audrey made it.

To the student, Jenna wrote, "Nell, you hit on a theme of the poem that we hadn't really talked much about. Great insight on your part – 'trying to hold all the pain in, but on the inside screaming was being done.' You have grasped the picture of her pain." To me, she commented,

> I remembered this piece and chose it because this child has a learning disability and this was the first piece of written work she produced. She was able to express her ideas. She was able to focus on the fundamental ideas I was hoping I was presenting through the stories. And she doesn't talk about "we." She recognizes cruelty. Asking of questions, my students question and look deeper. There are significant concepts it speaks powerfully towards. I don't recall that was stated as such but she picked up on it. Maybe she has identified with it, given her disability. How do kids relate to the pain? Some of these kids have experienced their own difficulties and can identify with someone else's. (February 1999)

Here, Jenna articulated her expectation that the story would cultivate empathy on the basis of identification with pain. Nell duly produced an account of suffering in which Audrey, as heroic victim, demonstrated strength in the face of adversity. In keeping with Jenna's structure,

Nell's message to Audrey is really at root a message to herself for herself. Here, as in Erika's work, the narrative of suffering on the basis of difference turns away from a history lesson into a lesson in the formation of the self, specifically, the rejection of the control of one's life by others.

Nell provided a repetition of pain and suffering, positioning Audrey as a heroic victim who demonstrated strength in the face of adversity. She described the significance of knowing the past but added that one must put the past in its place and get beyond it. The theme of "rugged individualism" that runs through each of the students' responses reflects Nell's understanding of the lesson that she learned from the story. If "we" are strong and proud of our history, "we" can accomplish anything.

Audrey Angela DION [by Joe]
Audrey Angela DION,
It pains her to remember what went on.
She tries to hide it and put it aside,
But it keeps coming back to haunt her.
When she was young, she was denied,
She felt she had to run, she had to hide.
She looked different and wrong, thought others,
But she had a heart of gold, and at that they couldn't scold.
She tried to fit in, she's right within,
But they thought she was wrong, because of her skin.
She wasn't wrong because of her race,
She wasn't wrong because of her face.
Not putting the past, behind, you pain from it,
But if you do, you will surely make it.
It's a dog eat dog world,
But no matter who you are, you can make it,
And the light will shine on you!

Jenna's comments to the student read, "Some great, deep thoughts, here Joe. Excellent. (my eyes feel a little moist ...)." To me, she remarked,

Here the student talks about Audrey's pain. He does not claim to know it but recognizes it was a painful experience for Audrey to remember her past. And this had a profound affect on some of my students. It does not go away. The concept of identity [is] an interesting point.

The type of person, your mom was a great legacy ... He has learned about a First Nations person who was caring, loving and responsible. He wasn't there [but] at least he recognizes the hurt and the wrong. He recognized in your mother's coming to terms with her past she was better for it. That to me is a profound observation. I think it is a reflection on how he thinks her life is closing in a positive way. It reflects peace. I think Joe in his poem [is saying], if we can come to terms with our own identity and who we are we will be the better for it. How difficult it is to have your history denied, and it is great that he could express it in this form. (February 1999)

To the repetition of pain and suffering called for by the assignment, Joe added the fundamental idea structuring Jenna's approach to the story – recognizing the significance of coming to terms with one's past as a necessary step in the formation of a healthy sense of self.

What the Teachers Heard in Student Responses
In response to Jenna's approach to teaching the story, students expressed what they learned about Audrey:

• she had a horrible life
• what she experienced was wrong and should not have occurred
• she deserved pity.

Considering themselves in a position to help Audrey learn that her feelings of shame are misplaced, the students in both classes instruct Audrey in the lessons of multicultural and anti-racism education, telling her that everything will be alright if only she takes pride in her difference. They affirm their knowledge that racial discrimination is wrong. Jenna was not only pleased but overwhelmed with her students' responses. Her reaction to the students' work indicates the extent to which she was successful in accomplishing her objectives. Students express their sympathy for Audrey, identify the pain and hardship that was inflicted, and express compassion and respect for Aboriginal people.

Both teachers were able to structure student engagement with the story in ways that were framed by their pedagogical scaffolding. In their classes, a text that was meant to disrupt was used to reproduce existing ways of knowing. Although I agree with Jenna and Diane that their pupils did learn important lessons from it, these had little to do with Audrey or the relationship between Aboriginal people and Canadians.

7

Disrupting Moulded Images

> By exploring the denied past, we might push back the
> blacked-out, repressed areas and in so doing understand our
> nonsynchronous identity as Americans. One place to begin
> in this labor of self-understanding is remembering where our
> national identity became repressed.
>
> – William Pinar, "Notes on Understanding
> Curriculum as a Racial Text"

This "labor of self-understanding" is complex, contradictory, and not easily accomplished. When I began my project of investigating a denied past, I was cognizant of my dual commitments: I wanted to (re)member and (re)tell in a way that would honour the strength and humanity of Aboriginal people. Additionally, I wanted to (re)tell in a way that would engage teachers and students in rethinking their understanding of the relationship between Aboriginal people and Canadians. Observing from my position as parent, teacher, and researcher, I saw the classroom as a significant site for the reproduction of dominant ways of knowing and asked what it would take for things to be otherwise. In our writing of the Braiding Histories Stories, Michael and I created a project that enabled us to investigate and "learn from" the lived experiences of Aboriginal people. (Re)membering and (re)telling the stories of our ancestors, the project became for us a labour of self-understanding. Through our research and writing, we came to recognize ourselves in relationship with Aboriginal people, and we shared our narratives with teachers and students in the hope of contributing to a new and just relationship between Aboriginal people and Canadians. In spite of the always complicated and often frustrating interactions between the teachers, the students, and the stories, I continue to locate hope and possibility within education.

The project draws attention to the structures of teaching and how those structures work on and through teachers, enabling an approach that, rather than disrupting, supports the reproduction of dominant ways of knowing. What I hear in the teachers' work is the way in which their approach to teaching the stories is structured by a complex grid of ideas about what was required of them as professionals and what they, in wanting to be good teachers, are invested in. In this book, I have identified three discourses of professionalism that are key components of this grid that structures the teachers' practice: teaching well, pastoral care, and citizenship education. These discourses speak to the teachers' legitimate concept of their responsibilities as teachers, and doing the work of teaching requires that they attend to their responsibilities. Although their work is structured by "rules of reason," it is also necessary to pay attention to the agency of teachers. Even as discourses and knowledge shape their thoughts, they are not without purpose and accountability. As agents, teachers premise their interpretations and actions on their experiences, investments, and understanding of their place in the socio-political world of teaching. In some ways, their understanding of their relationship with Aboriginal people permeates their practice. In some ways, it is hidden in the scaffolding that structures their approach.

The work of the Braiding Histories Project points to the significance of teachers' need to investigate their prior investments and commitments. In this final chapter, I draw on my current work with teachers to explore the complexities of their relationship with Aboriginal people. I offer a method for initiating a critical pedagogy of remembrance that allows teachers to attend to and learn from what I term the biography of their relationship with Aboriginal people. Employing Roger Simon's (1992) concept of "remembrance as a source of radical renewal," I ask teachers to work with their memories. Drawing together images from their pasts and holding their images up against the work of Aboriginal artists, they begin to recognize not only their investments and commitments but also how they came to be so inscribed by dominant discourses. This recognition opens the possibility for teachers to take up alternative ways of knowing and to imagine new relationships.

Confronting the Perfect Stranger Relationship and Responsibility

Writing about identity and difference, Stuart Hall (1989, 18) explains, "There is no way, it seems to me, in which people of the world can act, can speak, can create, can come in from the margins and talk, can begin to reflect on their own experience unless they come from some place, they come from some history, they inherit certain cultural traditions." Engaging previously hidden histories in an effort to honour the lived experiences of Aboriginal people, I came to understand not only the position from which I speak but also that the stories of my ancestors are a resource for what I have to say. If knowing the past was useful to Michael and me in understanding the present, perhaps it is necessary to engage teachers in a more specific investigation of their relationship with Aboriginal people. If our project of (re)telling contributed to our understanding of the need to continue listening and learning from and with Aboriginal people, what of the teachers? What place were they coming from, what was their history, what cultural traditions did they inherit, and what would it take to uncover those traditions?

When I asked Diane and Jenna about their relationship with Aboriginal people, both initially denied its existence. Like those of many teachers and teacher candidates with whom I work, their responses went something like "Oh I know nothing, I have no friends who are Aboriginal, I didn't grow up near a reserve, I didn't learn anything in school, I know very little, or I know nothing at all about Native people." One way or another, teachers, like many Canadians, claim the position of "perfect stranger" to Aboriginal people. There is an ease with which they claim this position. But, what does it offer them? Where does it come from? What is its appeal? In what ways is it problematic? And, perhaps most critical, how can it be disrupted? I argue that it is not an uncomplicated position. It is informed simultaneously by what teachers know, what they do not know, and what they refuse to know. For many, it is grounded in the recognition that what they know is premised on a range of experiences with stereotypical representations.

With the advent of multicultural and anti-racism education, teachers have been inundated with demands that they discuss "difference" in their classrooms, yet many are unsure of how to proceed. They do know that ways of teaching that reproduce stereotypical representations are inadequate. Thus, there is a fear and a silence involved in addressing this content. The fear of offending, of introducing controversial topics, and of introducing content that challenges student understanding of the dominant version of Canadian history all support the claim for the position of perfect stranger. Dominant stories that position Aboriginal people as, for example, romanticized, mythical, victimized, or militant Others enable non-Aboriginal people to position themselves as respectful admirers, moral helpers, or protectors of law and order. In classrooms and elsewhere, there is a dialectical relationship between these discursive practices. While dominant discourses structure their engagement with post-contact history, teachers and students take them up as a form of protection against having to recognize their own attachment to and implication in the history of the relationship between Aboriginal people and Canadians.

Although teachers typically claim to be perfect strangers, a closer examination reveals that a range of experiences with Aboriginal people informs both their understanding and their pedagogy. For example, when I ask them what they learned in school concerning the First Nations and what books they have read, courses they have taken, and subjects they have taught on the subject, I uncover a biography of relationship that fits within the grid that structures their teaching of Aboriginal topics. Thus, I ask, what would it mean to engage them in an examination of their experiences, to invite them to uncover, write, and interrogate this biography?

Remembrance as a Source of Radical Renewal

Currently, my work with teachers occurs during a graduate course I teach called Teaching and Learning from Indigenous Ways of Knowing. To satisfy part of the course requirements, students construct a File of (Un)certainties. The assignment requires students to collect and write about a series of "cultural artifacts" that reflect their relationship with Aboriginal peoples and their learning of and from "indigenous knowledge."[1] Key to the working of the assignment is the coursework that happens prior to and alongside the compilation of the file. The reading list for the course comprises articles by Aboriginal scholars who address issues of art, culture, identity, and representation. Students are also required to engage with stories, poetry, visual art, film, and video written, and, for the most part, produced, by Aboriginal artists. These texts allow students access to a range of Aboriginal perspectives, and students are immersed in the work of a community of artists who ask readers to reconsider questions of knowing, identity, and representation. These readings, along with in-class discussions, allow students to interrogate their own and each other's understanding and expectations of Aboriginal people and Aboriginal knowledge.

In this course, my intention is to construct a teaching practice that enables the students to "call into question existing 'truths' and imposed limits on what they know, while simultaneously envisioning new possibilities for both themselves" and their ways of teaching (Simon 1992, 141). Making use of the relationship between personal and public memory, I ask students to draw together stories and images from their past with contemporary work by Aboriginal artists and, through juxtaposition, speak to their understanding of themselves in relationship with Aboriginal people. This practice calls on the students not to live in the past but in relation with the past, acknowledging the claim that the past has on the present.

My intention follows on the work of Walter Benjamin (1969), whose strategy was, as Simon (1992, 140) explains, "not to obliterate the past but to radically reconfigure the relationship between the past and present. This meant challenging the existing modes of inheritance of our views of our selves, others and our environment with new patterns and forms of presentation, representation and association." I engage the students in a sustained conversation with contemporary texts created by Aboriginal artists, scholars, storytellers, and visual artists, while simultaneously asking that they begin to think about and to tell stories about their experiences with and memories of Aboriginal people. Students work at remembering and begin to hold their own experiences up against what they are engaging with in class. This process creates conditions whereby the students can begin to recognize their investments in relationships structured by particular ways of knowing Aboriginal people. They then consider what they are learning in relation to their practice.

Learning from a Community of Artists

My turn toward the work of contemporary artists is informed by my understanding of the relationship between community and indigenous knowledge, the healing and transformative role of artists, and the possibilities offered through a critical pedagogy of remembrance. When confronted with the challenge of teaching a course titled Indigenous Ways of Knowing, I struggled with how to structure the course in the absence of community participation. Indigenous knowledge is attached to community and is accessed through experiencing the day-to-day work and play of the community (Cajete 1999; Smith 1999; Semali and Kincheloe 1999). I understand that engaging with, and immersing myself and my students in, the work of a community of artists provides an opportunity for students in a university classroom to learn from, and with, the work of Aboriginal artists. I focus primarily on the work of visual artists Jane Ash Poitras (Plains Cree) and Gerald McMaster (Plains Cree) and storytellers Daniel David Moses (Lenape), Beth Brant (Mohawk), Paula Gunn Allen (Laguna-Sioux-Pueblo), Kimberly M. Blaeser (Anishinaabe), and Thomas King (Cherokee).[2] These artists draw on Aboriginal ways of knowing and experiences of colonization, history, and culture to create works that reflect on their understandings of what it means to be "Indian" in the twenty-first century.

Jane Ash Poitras recognizes the transformative potential of the artistic vision. She understands "the sacred red art path" as offering the means to honour the spirit, to validate and acknowledge identity and cultural existence, and to transmit teachings from generation to generation. In the catalogue that accompanied her exhibition Who Discovered the Americas, Poitras (quoted in Clark 1992, 10) writes that the "creative production of an artist can be a *regeneration* of his or her spirit that enables the artist to live an enlightened life and to enlighten others." In their work, the artists offer an address to both Aboriginal and non-Aboriginal audiences; it raises questions of difference and identity and initiates dialogue. A critical component of my course is the creative response required of the students. The course is not about simply consuming the work of the artists. Students are called upon to engage with and position themselves in relationship to the work. Engaging the work of Aboriginal artists provides a decolonizing practice – challenging the ahistorical memories of Canada's colonial past, it offers a way to challenge the hegemony of Western regimes of knowledge and representation.

The File of (Un)certainties as a Critical Pedagogy of Remembrance

Wanting to offer students a structure to begin investigating the biography of their relationship, I ask them to identify and collect "cultural artifacts," that is, objects of cultural interest that are reflective of their relationship with Aboriginal people or Aboriginal knowledge. In the past, students have included family photographs, pictures from school textbooks, and pictures from their summer camp. This collecting of artifacts requires students to attend to their own experience and draws attention to the ways through which their participation in particular cultural practices inscribe ways of knowing. My objective is to engage students in a process that will provide the possibility for the individual to, "as Gramsci says, 'know thyself' as a product of the historical process to date" (Sarris 1993, 153). This is possible only when one's history and assumptions about it are challenged.

In the file, students position images (either in visual, aural, or written form) from their past alongside content from the course readings or work by Aboriginal artists, creating stereoscopic images – that is, images that are three-dimensional, works created not from one image but from two. This process allows the students to see the positions they occupy in relation to, and with, Aboriginal people and, importantly, how it is they came to occupy those positions. The assignment offers students a means of "speaking to themselves," a speaking that, though instigated by the image, is premised on what they know in and of the present. Often, it is a text we have taken up in class that initiates a connection with memory. The two held together provide an opportunity to speak to what the students have been marked by, the construction of their frames of reference. In the construction of their file, students are required to put themselves in the centre, to make themselves present; it is not about others out there – it is about them, their very selves. The students are, in a sense, bearing witness to their own inscription. It is a process that supports a reworking of the normalized frames of understanding themselves as perfect strangers to Aboriginal people. Whereas the classroom and school context encompass fear of confrontation, of saying the wrong things, of exposing ignorance, of contradicting parents, faith communities, and the official curriculum, within the file, teachers are invited to be less fearful, and a space is created for them to explore their ways of knowing.

Learning from Student Work

As a critical practice of remembrance, the assignment does not require students to accumulate knowledge about the past. My concern is not with what students learn about historical or cultural events. I am concerned with what the students are learning of, and within, the disturbances and disruptions created in the construction of their files. Different from multicultural education, with its focus on the celebration of cultural difference, and anti-racism education, which teachers have in practice understood to require tolerance and respect for difference, as a critical pedagogy of remembrance, the File of (Un)certainties assignment cultivates a recognition of difference and a consideration of the implications of difference.

Whereas learning *about* an event or experience focuses upon the acquisition of qualities, attributes, and facts, so that it presupposes a distance (or, one might even say, a detachment) between the learner and what is to be learned, learning *from* an event or experience is of a different order, that of insight. Both of these learning moves are made more fragile in difficult knowledge. But precisely because insight concerns the acknowledgment of discontinuity from the persistence of the status quo, and hence asks something intimate from the learner, learning from requires the learner's attachment to and implication in knowledge (Britzman 1998, 117).

Working in support of attachment to and implication in knowledge, the assignment focuses students' attention on themselves in relationship with Aboriginal people. In the construction of their files, students encounter moments of recognition that initiate thinking about implication and, importantly, what purposes their attachments to particular ways of knowing serve. They investigate the history of colonization and its consequences for both Aboriginal people and for themselves. In their files, students reflect on how engagement with certain texts instigates their own learning and speak of that which they have learned.

With permission from students and following on the work of Celia Haig-Brown (1997a), A. Berlak (2004), and Leeno Karumanchery (2005), who also write in response to their students' work, I am drawing on samples of student work to learn from them.[3] Students do not come away from the assignment with a sense of having answers or having figured out their relationship. Rather, students are overwhelmed by what they have learned, what they are beginning to learn, and what they cannot learn; they express a desire to act on that which they are learning/unlearning. In my analysis of their work, my objective is to understand what it means for them, when given time and support, to investigate their relationships. What is important for the students, and what do they learn?

Recognizing Humanity

Jessica, an elementary school teacher with approximately five years teaching experience, considers herself a teacher who works at incorporating multicultural and anti-racism education in her teaching practice.[4] She is a white woman who teaches in an affluent suburban community where the majority of her students are also white. Jessica teaches Aboriginal subject material as part of her social studies curriculum; she took the course in the interest of improving her approach to teaching.

In her file, Jessica registers surprise. She is surprised by the extent to which she was accustomed to the dehumanized representations of Aboriginal people and shocked by what she learns about herself. She describes the moments in which she recognizes the humanity of Aboriginal people and how that recognition brings to her attention the extent to which she was implicated in accepting and reproducing a dehumanized representation of Aboriginal people. Jessica begins with an expression of her emotional response, suggesting that it is both a consequence of learning and an instigation of learning:

> Humility, uninformed, embarrassment, ignorance [....]. These are feelings that I experienced after having viewed the film, "Rabbit Proof Fence," and having observed a collection in the McMichael Art Gallery. I recognized that they were/are humans. In other words, prior to this experience, I still carried false images and perceptions of

Indigenous peoples, their culture and history. As I viewed the film, I was shocked by what I learned of myself. I thought that I regarded all races nationalities, and religions equally, and that I respected their differences. However, as I viewed the movie, I realized that I was acknowledging Indigenous peoples as human beings for the first time.

These revelations resurfaced when I visited the McMichael Art Gallery. During my visit to this museum, I came across a series of pictures that were photographed by the artist Richard Harrington. These photographs were taken in Puvirnituq, Nunavik – an area in Arctic Quebec. Harrington's black and white images capture various daily activities carried out by Inuit families. While observing the photographs, I recognized individuals hanging clothes to dry, men and women cutting and carving stone, children playing and dogs sleeping. Furthermore, as I observed these pictures I realized that the daily tasks that the Inuit carried out compared to chores that my own family carried out. In other words, their day-to-day activities resembled my own. Coincidentally, I was surprised by these images, in the same manner that I was moved by the events that I observed in the film.

I realized that I had preconceived notions of what I expected to see on Indigenous reservations, and in their communities. My education experiences instilled stereotypic images of Aboriginal life, within me. His work moved me, aided me in identifying with Indigenous humanity.

Drawing together scenes from the film and the Harrington photographs with images of her own family participating in day-to-day household chores, Jessica demonstrates how attention to detail allows her to see what she had not seen before. The images resist assimilation, exposing contradictions in her already articulated discourses, creating disruption and the possibility of recognition. Jessica becomes conscious of how prior engagements with stereotypical representations set her up to perceive and to expect a certain "exotic" Other. Her stereoscopic image challenges that expectation, opening a space to see humanity. Although Jessica understood herself as an individual who considered all people as equals, her stereoscopic image disrupts her understanding. Once disrupted, Jessica is opened to recognizing the depth to which her understanding of Aboriginal people was premised on the stereotypical images with which she was so familiar. Within the disruption, Jessica recognizes the humanity of Aboriginal people, and in that moment of recognition, she is confronted with her own ignorance. There is nothing simple about this articulation; it is not an easy acknowledgment. The encounter moves Jessica outside of her existing ways of knowing and understanding. Learning from the construction of her image, Jessica comes to know herself differently.

What are the implications of this recognition of humanity? How might Jessica hear voices of Aboriginal people differently? How might she engage and teach differently? Although Jessica recognizes a shared humanity with Aboriginal people, she does not collapse the differences. She acknowledges the significance of her recognition in relation to her understanding of herself and the implications for her teaching and learning.

Implication and Responsibility

A student in the Communication and Culture graduate program, Kat was a cultural worker. Thus, her interest in the course did not stem from her work as a teacher in a formal school setting. As one who crossed various borders in both her practical and academic work, Kat was particularly concerned with understanding relationships of difference and how to work across difference in respectful ways. Kat, a white woman whose family had lived in Canada for generations, came to the class with a conscious recognition of the race and class privilege that came with her position as a white upper-middle-class woman.

In her File of (Un)certainties, Kat built on that consciousness, engaging with questions of privilege, relationality, and what it meant in terms of her own understanding of ethical responsibility. Looking at photographs from her days as a camper and a camp counsellor at Camp Onondaga, Kat wrote,

When I look at these photographs now however, the word "Onondaga" is imbued with more than simply "camp." I ask myself who these people [the Onondaga] were and what does it mean that the place where I spent my summers is called "Onondaga"? I have included a photograph of some campers making bannock and recall doing so myself, however I do not recall ever being told why we were making bannock. This lack of acknowledgement for me, parallels a larger historical erasure of the Aboriginal people which is still very much a part of the contemporary Western reality. Genocide, land removals, forced assimilation, "breeding out," and legislation which "essentially legalizes the Aboriginal out of existence" (King 2003: 132) have all been part of a long and violent process of rendering the Aboriginal "invisible."

My heightened awareness of the systemic erasure of the Aboriginal through various means raises some important concerns. This "erasure" allowed my ancestors and continues to allow many to essentially "forget" their role in the brutal oppression of a people who were the first to live on a land that we now enjoy and call our "Canada." In not forgetting, I attempt to take on the responsibility of acknowledging this history, of not erasing but rather allowing myself to work through the uncomfortable awareness that the land I have the luxury to live on, attend summer camp on, and call my country was founded upon the attempted and violent erasure of Aboriginal peoples.

Looking at her immediate experience and what came before it, Kat is able to use remembrance as a means of ethical learning, that is, "learning that impels us into a confrontation and 'reckoning' not only with stories of the past but also with 'ourselves' as we 'are' (historically, existentially, ethically) in the present" (Simon, Rosenberg, and Eppert 2000, 8). Remembering her experience on the land, and holding that experience up against what she has learned about Aboriginal presence and erasure, Kat recognizes her implication in the story.[5] Prior to her participation in the course, she enjoyed memories of being at Camp Onondaga, "forgetting" the actions that led to the land being made available for her to enjoy. Kat's images assert a truth that disrupts the dominant story of the building of a nation on a vacant land. Kat challenges Canadian innocence and challenges herself to reconsider her own innocence, and, in this regard, she asks herself, "enjoy at whose expense?" Kat is responding to, and being responsible for, what she recognizes as an injustice. Whereas remembering camp experiences offers her affirmation of who she is and what she knows, constructing her stereoscopic image calls for a redefinition of her self. She recognizes that she is not innocent. Kat's (re)membering has been of consequence. In speaking to the erasure, she names her structure of knowing and takes up the challenge to articulate what she has heard, how it challenges her way of knowing, and her effort to make sense of this new knowledge. Kat acknowledges implication and makes a conscious articulated commitment to "not forget" and to explore what that might mean, what it might look like, knowing full well that it will involve "discomfort." For, to know her implication is "discomforting." It requires an acknowledgement of the previous state of luxury that is being let go of in exchange for a state of "uncomfortable awareness" accepting an obligation. It is not what she already knew, but what she was allowed not to know that Kat finds discomforting. It is her recognition of the luxury of enjoyment in contrast to the experiences of the Onondaga, who didn't/don't have that luxury. Calling what she knows – and how she knows it – into question, Kat is involved in a reworking of the politics of her relationship. The work of the course and the work of the assignment calls what she knows, how she knows, and the consequence of knowing/not knowing into question. Kat is moved by her image to scrutinize her own identity.

Roger Simon (1992, 144) explains that stereoscopic images are meant to make apparent "those rough and jagged places at which the continuity of tradition breaks down [revealing] 'cracks' [that provide] a hold for anyone wishing to get beyond these points." Kat takes hold, learns from her experience, and gestures toward new possibilities. She engages with and makes use of the course texts to think differently about her experiences, to examine her investment, and to seriously consider the implications both for herself and her relationship with Aboriginal people.

Resisting the Desire to Collapse Difference

Britt came with her family to Canada from India when she was four years old. Throughout the four weeks that the course ran, Britt was comfortable in her position in relationship with Aboriginal people. As a woman of colour, she identified with Aboriginal women and spoke about a shared experience of colonialism.[6] In class, she spoke about her relationship with her grandmother, about loss of language, and loss of home. Britt drew on the course texts to affirm her understanding of the experience of colonialism and her understanding of herself. Although I appreciated Britt's own learning and her contribution to the class, I was anxious for her to recognize difference and the singularity of experiences. I continually asked questions drawing her attention to what the Aboriginal artists were telling us about their experiences as Aboriginal people in Canada. During the in-class presentation of her file, Britt suddenly began to explore her recognition that the Aboriginal experience of colonialism in Canada was, and is, different from her own. Britt completed her assignment in the days that followed the final class. It seems that this entry provided a safe starting point for speaking to her emerging recognition of implication in reproducing dominant discourses – a recognition that brought with it the potential for disrupting those discourses.

No Two Tipis Are Ever Pitched The Same [a painting by Gerald McMaster] made me really question what I knew about Native history. I found this piece of art engaged me in a manner that allowed me to admit that all through my education I have never really questioned what happened to all the Nations that once existed on this land.

I had a difficult time coming to terms with how as educators we teach our curriculum without really questioning why. Why am I telling students about the different tribes without understanding that this term "tribes" was really a cover up for the fact that this land and its people were once part of great Nations. A people, who had (and still have) a history, culture and developed political systems that worked well for them. The objective of the colonizers is well achieved when even a hundred years later we still see the world through their eyes.

McMaster's painting, which depicts tipis of varying colours and shapes, is both simple and complex. The name of a First Nation is printed on the side of each tipi. The simplicity has a profound impact on Britt. Naming all Aboriginal people "Indians," Columbus erased our nationhood and our differences. This erasure was key in positioning Aboriginal people as primitive. In drawing attention to nationhood, McMaster disrupts the erasure and the discourse that positions Aboriginal people as a primitive people of the past.

Like Kat and Jessica, Britt was concerned with what she knew, what she didn't know, and why she didn't question. In response to her thinking about the McMaster painting, she encounters a special reflection – a reflection that causes her to observe, "I never questioned." Deborah Britzman (1998, 7) writes that "A special reflection is necessary if we are to move to the fragility of understanding others and disrupt the wish for a continuity and sameness that attributes to others the same state of mind." It is as if, while looking at the painting, Britt "catches herself in the act" of participating in the colonial project.

As one whose family survived colonization on another continent, and motivated in part by a need to position herself and her family in a good light, in solidarity with colonized people on this continent, Britt had difficulty recognizing the complexity of the position she occupies in relationship with Aboriginal people in Canada. Although Britt was comfortable identifying with Aboriginal people, she was challenged by the position she occupied as one whose family gained benefits from the colonization of the Americas. In her talk to the class, Britt described the burden of history she became implicated in when she and her family made their home on this land. In the process of speaking, Britt was suddenly confronted by the need to do something other than legitimize her own claims. Following up on her in-class experience of working through in her file, Britt spoke to her understanding of the shared challenge confronting educators. What instigated learning for Britt – what was important for her to explore – was the implication and responsibility that she had as an educator. Britt asked, "What didn't I know, why didn't I question, and what are the implications for my teaching?" In the discomfort, she located comfort in knowing that it is a responsibility that she shared with other educators.

In Closing

The File of (Un)certainties assignment provides students with a forum to investigate the biography of their relationship with Aboriginal people; it provides a means of investigating their own investments in dominant discourses and supports the possibility of affecting a change in their ways of knowing and their ways of teaching. Through this work, students come to recognize themselves as something other than perfect strangers to Aboriginal people and begin to recognize how their own engagements with dominant discourses have informed their understanding, contributing to a reproduction of dominant ways of knowing about Aboriginal people. In the class and in the assignment, I use the act of remembrance to raise awareness of the ways in which the identities of both Aboriginal and non-Aboriginal people in Canada have been shaped by the colonial encounter and its aftermath. The construction of this ethical awareness among teachers is a promising way to progressively transform relationships between Aboriginal and non-Aboriginal people in the Canadian educational system.

The work of the Braiding Histories Project supports the ongoing call for increased attention to Aboriginal subject material at all levels of schooling. Teachers, like most Canadians, require increased opportunities to learn about and to "learn from" the history of the relationship between themselves and Aboriginal people.

Reference Matter

Appendix A
The Braiding Histories Stories as Distributed for Classroom Use

The three Braiding Histories stories are reproduced on the following pages in the format in which they were distributed to teachers (reduced from their original 8½ × 11 size).

Image Credits

The publisher gratefully acknowledges the following for permission to reproduce photographs from their collections in the facsimiles of the Braiding Histories stories.

Her Solitary Place
Shawnadithit (also appears on p. 33): The Rooms Provincial Museum, St. John's, Newfoundland. Beothuk Comb: copyright © Dennis Minty, used by permission of Dennis Minty, The Human Nature Company. Beothuk Canoe: The Rooms Provincial Museum, St. John's, Newfoundland. Mamateek: Newfoundland Museum.

I Share Their Anger
Mistahimaskwa 1825-1888 (also appears on p. 40): National Archives of Canada. Cree Camp 1871: National Archives of Canada. Treaty Negotiations, 1876: A.C. McIntyre, after a sketch by M. Bastien in Canadian Illustrated News, 16 Dec. 1876, National Archives of Canada. Mistahimaskwa in prison, 1886: Hall and Lowe and Public Archives of Manitoba, used by permission of Glenbow Archives.

BRAIDING HISTORIES
Learning From The Life Stories Of First Nations People

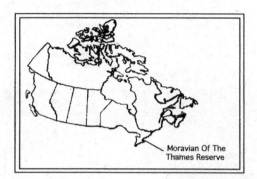

Moravian Of The
Thames Reserve

What is dignity?
How do you learn self-esteem?

What is the value of your history,
and what happens when that history is denied?

Mom wrestles with her past
Like a pattern that would not go together

Stitching and ripping and stitching again
Not a single garment but a multi-layered gown
that becomes a baby's frock and a son's shirt.

The comfort comes not from wearing the garment
but from remembering
the hands that did the stitching.

Audrey Angela Dion

The blinds were open and I could feel the heat from the sun as it cast shadows on the kitchen table. Standing on the inside I had a deceptive impression of warmth on a cold February afternoon. I had just finished lunch with Mom and as I cleared the dishes I found myself thinking back to family meal times when I was growing up. Including Mom and Dad there were seven of us gathered around the table and when supper was finished we would stay at the table talking, listening and telling stories. Many nights we would ask Mom and Dad to tell us about what it was like when they were little.

"How about some tea" Mom asked bringing me back to the present. She started to fill the kettle. I noticed that she was leaning against the sink — for support. As if she knew my thoughts, she asked, "do you remember when you were little how we would sit around the table after supper drinking tea and talking. Sometimes we would still be sitting there at 11:00 o'clock"?

"I was just thinking the same thing" I said, struck by the mystery of our connectedness. "You would tell stories about driving the coffee truck and dad would talk about people at his office. The news of the day was always a good topic to keep the conversation going longer. But, the stories we liked best were the ones about what life was like when you were little. Dad was always telling us stories about his mother and growing up in Quebec. I paused for a moment to see if she would again continue my thought for me, and then with a bit of hesitation, "Mom, you rarely told us about your life".

"I didn't know what to tell you kids so I let your father do most of the talking".

I could tell from the sound of my mother's voice that this was a sensitive subject. These were not easy questions for her to answer. Feeling a need to go on I asked, "Was it because you were so poor"?

"No, it wasn't that. Your father's family was poor too. But your father's family was white and I was Indian. When I was growing up being Indian meant being poor, being called nasty names and being made to feel as if we were worthless. What kind of after dinner stories would those have made. Remember I always said, 'I'm Canadian'. I didn't want to be Indian".

I paused for a moment to think back. I could hear those words again. It was a disturbing memory "I'm a Canadian! I'm a Canadian!" There was no pride in her voice in fact it was almost the opposite feeling I was getting. I struggled with a word to suit the feeling. Her words were not an assertion of pride but a claim for self-respect.

I have lived with these words all my life and only now am I beginning to understand what motivated my mother to make this claim. Mom always argued, "My father joined the army during World War II and we gave up our Indian status—that meant that we were Canadians." I began to understand the contradiction. Being Canadian meant denying her Aboriginal identity. Other details started to come back to me. "I felt like you didn't want us to be Indian. Whenever anybody said something about our black hair you insisted that our hair wasn't black it was dark brown. I always wondered what was wrong with having black hair. It was so confusing because we knew we were 'part' Indian but we didn't know what that meant. The Indians we learned about at school, and on TV were noble chiefs and pretty princesses who lived in tipis, rode on horses and carried bows and arrows."

"Those were not my stories".

"But Mom we wanted to know, we wanted to know you. We wanted to hear your stories". As I spoke these words I could hear a longing in my voice and recognized my desire to hear her story. I spoke again. "I remember you telling me a few stories about growing up on the reserve and I remember that you took us to the reserve a couple of times. What was it like for you Mom when you were growing up?"

Audrey's Story

At the end of my day I like listening to Aboriginal flute music. I turn out the electric lights, light a few candles and sink into my favourite blue chair. It is an old but sturdy chair, re-covered more than once. I can feel the new, soft, velvety material as my hands stroke the arms. I remember, when you children were young, walking into the living room and one of you would immediately jump out of the chair shouting, "Mom's chair, Mom's chair". I

give the arm another soft caress and listen to the relaxing, even soothing sounds, of the flutes. The music evokes feelings of connection and I remember.

Audrey's Mother

I was born on March 28, 1930 to Effie and Victor Tobias on the Moravian Town Indian reserve and was named Audrey Angela. I never could figure out why my mother couldn't have put it the other way around. I always hated my odd sounding name. I thought Angela would have been a much better choice. It sounded pretty.

Our house was set back from the dirt road, past a dried out, scruffy lawn. It was a very small, two story, wood frame house. The ground floor was one big open room. There was a table and a wood stove on one side and a bed for my parents and baby sister Elizabeth on the other side. I slept upstairs with my four brothers and sister.

There was a curtain dividing the girls' side from the boys' side. In the summer it was stuffy and hot but the winters were cold. Lying in bed with my sister, I would try to ignore the cold but the flimsy shingles rattling in the wind made it hard to sleep. The closest we came to insulation was the newspaper my brothers and I stuffed into the space between the walls and the roof. In the morning we would struggle, pushing the rickety old beds from one side of the room to the other. Stretching with all our might with fists full of newspaper, we tried to remember where the gusts of wind from the night before had blown in. The floor was just as bad. In the fall the whole family would work at collecting dirt to pack around the bottom of the house. This banking was supposed to stop the wind from gusting below the floor boards on cold winter days. But no matter how much newspaper and mud we packed in, it was impossible to keep the cold out of that house.

We grew most of our own food in a large vegetable lot out behind the house. In the spring the ground had to be prepared and the seeds planted. One of my happy childhood memories is playing "Peter Cotton Tail" in the garden during the late summer. When the garden was in full growth my sister Joan, who always played the part of Mr. MacGregor, would try to catch me and my brother Ken sneaking food out of the garden. If she caught us she would scare us and we would run away. In the fall the garden was a lot of hard work. We had to pick the vegetables and store them in the 'dug out'. We would be eating the potatoes, carrots, onions, squash and turnips until just after Christmas when the vegetables would run out and there was not much to eat. January and February were hungry months. For supper Mom would cook a pot of macaroni and mix it with a can of tomatoes. At breakfast we would sit around the table watching her mix flour and water in a big bowl. She would take a wad of the gooey mixture in her hands, roll it into little strings and drop them into a pot of boiling water. I called this stuff "slippery mush". With canned milk and sugar it was good, but most of the time we had to eat it plain.

There were no jobs on the reserve. My father worked a few months of the year at a sawmill in town and during the spring he fished, but there were many months when there was no work. During the winter I remember Mom was always busy weaving baskets. Dad would go into the bush and cut down a certain kind of tree. Then came the work of preparing the wood for weaving. I remember them cutting and pounding the strips of wood. The strips had to be soaked in the wash tub for a couple of days and then there was more cutting and splitting. When the strips were the right thickness Mom and Dad would smooth the edges with sandpaper. Sometimes they would dye the slats to make fancy patterns in the baskets. Grandma taught Mom how to weave when she was little and Mom taught us. We made laundry baskets, waste paper baskets, and baby cradles. When we had a stack of baskets ready, Mom and Dad would go into town and sell them.

I knew that my family were members of the Delaware Nation. What I did not know then is that Delaware is the English name given to my father's people. The

**Traditional Territory Of
The Lenape First Nation**

original name of my father's nation is Lenni Lenape. My mother's family belong to the Potawatami Nation and she was from the nearby reserve on Walpole Island. I can picture my father and his friends sitting by the wood stove singing in the Lenape language but I never learned to speak Lenape. My father went to residential school and when he became a parent he believed that it was best for his children not to know their own language and culture. He said that we needed to know the ways of the white community. My two older brothers went to the residential school at Muncey Town. Thankfully by the time I was ready for school the residential school had been closed down. We went to a small school on the reserve where the Anglican minister was the teacher. He was very strict and did not hesitate to use the strap. He taught us about the Europeans who discovered and conquered the Americas. We read stories about the white settlers who came and built a country out of nothing. The teacher and the lessons made us feel like nothing, as though we were nothing until the settlers arrived. It wasn't true. We had our own good way of living before the Europeans arrived. We knew how to take care of ourselves.

I was nine years old when I first moved off the reserve. Just after WW II began, my father and brother joined the army and were stationed in Petawawa. My mother took the rest of us kids and moved to a small town near Hamilton so that we would be closer to Dad and my brother Albert. There was work for Aboriginal people doing manual labour on the farms in the area. Mom went to work on one of the farms and we kids went to a school in the town of Aldershot. The teachers at this school were not quite as bad as the minister on the reserve but still we were made to feel that because we were Indians we were not as good as the white children. The white families owned the farms our parents worked on and the tone of the teachers' voices let us know where we belonged on the social ladder.

When my father and brother joined the army, our whole family became enfranchised. This meant that legally we became Canadian citizens. Mom and Dad were eligible to vote but we lost our Indian status and all treaty rights. At one point before the war had ended we moved back to the reserve but stayed less than a year. As non-status Indians we were not entitled to a house. We lived with Grandma for a while but we really needed a house of our own. We moved back to Aldershot and when I was nineteen years old, I left home and moved to Hamilton where I looked for work as a waitress.

After my family was enfranchised I believed that I was no longer Indian. But being Indian was not something I could put on and off like a pair of shoes. Even if the government of Canada no longer considered me Indian, the people I met in my day-to-day life were not willing to let me forget that I was. In those days there were places I could look for a job and other places I could not even consider applying. There were stores and restaurants I could go into but there were many where I would not even think of going. Signs in store front windows read, "No Indians Allowed", and in other places a look of disgust from the clerks was enough to send me back out onto the street. I finally found a job as a waitress at a restaurant owned by a Chinese family and I worked very hard. I was determined to make something of my life. I wanted to be a part of Canadian society, I wanted to fit in.

Audrey and Lindy, 1952

I needed to prove that I was just as good or better than the other people I worked with.

I met your father at the restaurant where I was working. Lindy was a regular customer. He was kind, attractive and he was white. The waitresses were scheming, trying to match Lindy up with one of their pretty friends. But Lindy often sat in my section and we would talk and laugh together while I served his food. I thought he was just being friendly. He was not Indian and I never really believed that he would be interested in me. One night as I approached his table Lindy stood up and said, "I have something to give you." When I asked "What?" he kissed me. I think that our fate was sealed with that kiss. We started seeing each other regularly and before too long we were married. I remember the Catholic priest who rather reluctantly agreed to marry us. When the brief ceremony was over he mumbled just loud enough for us to hear, "It'll never last."

But the priest was wrong. It did last. Life was not easy but Lindy and I loved and supported each other for over fifty years. We lived in Hamilton until 1965 when your dad was offered a better job in a smaller city. We thought the move to a smaller town would be good for us so in 1965 we moved to Sarnia. In some ways life in Sarnia was better but in some ways it was harder. We were the only family of mixed race living in an all white middle-class neighbourhood. Some people were very friendly. Remember the couple who lived across the street? You kids always thought they were grouchy but they always waved and said hello to us. Not like the family who lived up the street. They had two little girls about the same age as you but those girls were never allowed to play with you.

Looking for a job in Sarnia was horrible. When I went to apply, lots of people just told me to get out. But I needed a job and I kept on looking. Finally I got a job driving a coffee truck. It was hard. I felt like I was always working, and always tired but we had a home and a good life. I

Audrey and her brother, George 1998

worked at that job for twelve years and drove a taxi for eight years before I retired.

I grew up at a time when Indians were considered savages who had no culture and nothing of value to offer me or anyone else. I was made to feel that to be successful I had to become a non-Indian. At home, at school or at church I had no opportunity to learn about Aboriginal culture. I knew nothing about Lenape language, history and ceremonies. When you and your brothers and sister asked, "What was it like when you were little?" I did not know what to tell you. But you wouldn't be discouraged. You and your brother kept asking questions. On Sunday afternoons while I was in the kitchen baking with you kids at my elbows wanting to stir, pour and lick the spoon, you two would start again with the questions. My hands were busy stirring, measuring, and pouring but my mind was free to think. Maybe it was the warmth and security in that kitchen, maybe it was the civil rights movement of the sixties and the rise of the National Indian Brotherhood. Whatever it was, while I prepared the cakes, cookies, and pies that you kids would devour I began to realize that maybe there was something I could tell, that maybe it was important for you to know a little bit about what it was like for me when I was growing up.

It was hard for me, but that was when I began to tell you a few of the stories. When I look at you today I see a commitment to family, a joy in the telling and hearing of stories and a deep sense of responsibility to our ancestors. This is a part of our Aboriginal culture that was not lost.

Today, I am a widow and live in Toronto close to some of my family. Each night I listen to the music of the flutes and I know who I am.

A (Re)telling By
Michael Dion And
Susan Dion

BRAIDING HISTORIES
Learning From The Life Stories Of First Nations People

Traditional Territory of the
Beothuk

HER SOLITARY PLACE

For the last five years of her life

Shawnadithit lived with a family.
Was it her family?

Shawnadithit wore clothes.
Were they her clothes?

Shawnadithit learned a new language.
Whose language was it?

Shawnadithit was buried.
Was her body painted with red ochre,
was she wrapped in birch bark?

Shawnadithit's Story

Shawnadithit spent the whole afternoon cleaning the Peyton's house. A couple of times she walked out the front door and sat on the steps, resting. Her energy was not what it used to be, and now there was this annoying cough that just would not go away. Shawnadithit had heard this kind of cough many times before; both her mother and sister had suffered with

Shawnadithit 1801 - 1828

it until they died. Shawnadithit looked up to the sun, there was not a cloud in sight. She stared directly into the shining ball of fire and was momentarily blinded, but she found some pleasure in this forced darkness. *She could see herself in a canoe, paddling up river, with her father in front. The banks of the river were lined with beautiful trees, only interrupted by grassy meadows. It was in one of these grassy meadows that Shawnadithit once lived with her family.* The vision disappeared as quickly as it came. As Shawnadithit stood up, maybe too quickly, she felt a little unsteady. Her unfinished chores waited for her inside.

Shawnadithit used all her strength to squeeze the rag dry; she watched closely as the dirty water slowly dripped into the rusted basin. The lye soap she used to scrub the floor made her hands burn and turned her skin to an ugly, blotchy mess. It was not the same colour as the beautiful red ochre that had once been used deliberately to coat her skin.

When she had finished cleaning, Shawnadithit took one more long look around the house to be certain everything was in its proper place. She noticed the wood she had put beside the fireplace had been toppled. Probably a mouse had disturbed the delicately balanced stack. It was a trick she had learned from her father, when she was a little girl. He taught her how to pile the wood awkwardly and if the wrong piece was chosen first the entire pile would fall. This way you would know if some animal had been to your campsite while you were gone. It was a game she enjoyed playing with the children of the house. As Shawnadithit bent over to straighten the stack, the comb from her hair fell to the floor. She stared at it for a moment, remembering her mother, Doodebewshet, who had

 given the comb to her the first time she had braided Shawnadithit's hair. She picked it up and tenderly pushed it back into place.

Feeling satisfied that her chores were complete, she left once again, out the front door, down the steps, not stopping to rest. She walked around the house to the back. The clearing behind the house stretched back at least thirty feet. Shawnadithit walked to the edge and began to gently spread the bushes apart as she stepped into the woods.

Shawnadithit did not know the names of the months, however, she did know that it was late in the summer. The cranberry bush that she knelt beside was full and ripe. Some of the berries had already fallen from its branches. Picking a few, she rolled them in the palm of her hand. She could feel their plumpness. She popped them into her mouth one by one, savouring the flavour. As Shawnadithit felt the burst of fresh juice she remembered a life from which she had been separated. *She was picking berries with her mother, little sister, aunt, and small cousins. They were searching for the ripe blueberries, partridge berries, and marsh berries that grew in the fields. Together they worked to fill their birch bark containers to the brim. As they worked, Shawnadithit grabbed a handful of berries and as quietly and carefully as possible placed her full container down. She sneaked through the brush and quiet like a fox, pounced on her little sister, squishing the berries into her hair. Shawnadithit looked to her mother expecting a scolding for playing when she was supposed to be working and although she got the scolding, she also caught a glimpse of a smile.*

Doodebewshet had enjoyed watching the childish prank but her protective spirit was constantly on guard. Shawnadithit listened to the scolding and recognized fear in her mother's voice. Doodebewshet was fearful the noise of children playing might attract the attention of a white hunter. An encounter with the whites could mean capture or even death. Doodebewshet spoke to the children of the need to complete their work. Others in the village were depending on them to bring back an abundant collection of berries. While Doodebewshet spoke she slyly took a single berry from her container. Turning back to her work, with a smile she tossed the berry to Shawnadithit, who caught it, rolled it around the palm of her hand and tossed it into her mouth. Startled out of the day dream by the loud snap of a branch breaking under her foot, Shawnadithit had to think for a moment about where she was. The time of berry picking with her family was gone and she was alone.

This pleasant memory of her childhood brought a small smile to Shawnadithit's lips, it also came with an ache in her heart. Who would listen to her story of berry picking with her mother? Who would remember? This story, with the many other stories that she had heard from her mother and father, would soon be lost, remembered by no one. Shawnadithit looked back at the Peyton house and decided to move on in search of her special place. The sun was beginning to set but Shawnadithit didn't feel fear, she began to feel more at ease.

Shawnadithit reached the clearing, and could see the fallen tree with its huge trunk, covered in a blanket of moss. Moving closer to the tree she sat down, relieved to be in her favourite place. She felt the damp coolness of the moss and then pulled the moss away to reveal the tree's bark. In Shawnadithit's mind everything still seemed so clear. She missed collecting the bark from the trees and the work of moulding the bark into utensils and containers. Her hands were always busy. She had especially enjoyed watching her

father use the bark to build canoes. Shawnadithit had an eye for detail and her father would smile as she stood watching as the canoes took shape. Shawnadithit felt tired. Maybe tomorrow she would collect some bark and make a small canoe for the Peyton children to play with.

It was almost completely dark now. On a previous visit to this place Shawnadithit had dug a deep trench beside the trunk. With the light of the moon guiding her, Shawnadithit began to remove the leaves and branches to reveal her precious sleeping spot. It was a space just big enough for her to lie down in. She curled up and pulled a blanket of leaves over her body to keep her warm. The coughing started again and Shawnadithit could not sleep but lay thinking, her eyes grew heavy and closed *and Shawnadithit felt the squirming of her little sister asleep beside her. She could hear the soft breathing of her parents and the buzzing of insects. She opened her eyes and saw the mamateek where her family slept. It was big and round, with long wooden poles bound together, covered with birch bark and deerskin. There was a fire pit in the centre. She shivered again and watched the curl of smoke from the fire rise to the opening at the top.* Shawnadithit heard the branches creak and felt the gust of wind blow through the trees, she closed her eyes again and waited a little anxiously for the voice of her mother to come back to her.

When Shawnadithit woke with the morning sun she was hungry. Wearily she raised herself and found the spot on the tree where she had been peeling the bark the night before. This time she dug a little deeper, to get at the inner bark; she tore a piece, put it in her mouth and started to chew. The flavour of the bark was familiar to Shawnadithit. As she sat there quietly, Shawnadithit thought about the painful nightmares that had disrupted her dreaming. *Her father, her uncle, there were no men asleep in the mamateek. There was no food. She saw herself with her mother and sister, weak from hunger. They had left their camp and were walking toward the coast in search of food. Shawnadithit saw the terror in her mother's eyes. What was the price of survival? They had resisted with nearly every ounce of their energy but sensing it was their last hope for survival, they gave themselves over to the white hunters.*

Shawnadithit could not escape her memories. She saw the faces of her aunts, uncles and cousins. She recognized the face of hunger and disease and death. The newcomers had made these faces familiar to Shawnadithit. The stories that Shawnadithit heard around the fire changed from stories about her people to stories about the newcomers and the grief, hardship and revenge they had brought. The men spoke about being robbed of their ability to move freely around their land in search of food. They talked about how the newcomers used their powerful weapons and hunted for more than was needed, stealing food from the Beothuk. The newcomers even used their weapons to kill the Beothuk. Shawnadithit remembered the blast of gun fire and rubbed her leg. She could sometimes still feel the pain from her own wound.

Shawnadithit dug for another piece of bark and remembered that *when she was a little girl, there had*

always been food to eat. During the summer they had spent time on the seacoast. In a canoe her father had built, Shawnadithit and her mother would paddle to nearby islands to collect eggs from the wild birds that nested there. Her father and uncle fished for salmon that would be dried on racks in the hot summer sun. In the fall after the caribou hunt, its meat was hung to cure. She remembered visiting the storage mamateeks that stood along the banks of the rivers. Everyone worked together all summer long, filling them with food

for the long winter season. There was even time for playing in the river.

The heat from the sun was beginning to get intense. Shawnadithit got up and began to cover her dugout with leaves. It was these trips to the woods, to her special place, that helped Shawnadithit live in a world that was not her own. Shawnadithit knew that she would go back to the Peyton's frame house. She understood that it was not hers. She would return to the family that was not hers, to a language that was not hers.

A (Re)Telling by
Michael Dion And
Susan Dion

Primary Source For This (Re)telling

Marshall, Ingbord. (1996). A History and Ethnography Of The Beothuk. Montreal: McGill-Queen's University Press

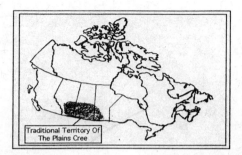
Traditional Territory Of
The Plains Cree

I SHARE THEIR ANGER

The charge was treason-felony and the verdict was guilty.

Mistahimaskwa, chief of the Plains Cree was sentenced to three years in the Stoney Mountain Penitentiary.

Mistahimaskwa spoke in his own defence:

"I always believed that by being the friend of the Whiteman, I and my people would be helped by those of them who had wealth. I always thought it paid to do all the good I could.

Now my heart is on the ground."

Mistahimaskwa fought for the rights of his people
Why was he sent to prison?

Mistahimaskwa was not in my history book.
Why did I not hear his story?

On the morning of April 2, 1885, members of Mistahimaskwa's band went into the white settlement at Frog Lake and killed nine people. They then travelled to Fort Pitt and, after evacuating the fort, burned it to the ground. At his trial Mistahimaskwa accepted responsibility for the actions of his warriors saying: "Even as they rallied I called to them Tesqua! Tesqua! (Stop! Stop!). But they would not be stopped. They were angry and although I did not share their desire to shed the blood of the intruders on our land I share their anger".

When Mistahimaskwa spoke at his trial he was not able to tell his story but now speaking to you, to Canadians who have come to inherit the land that once gave life to the Cree Nation, I will pass on to you his story. It is the story about his life and the events that led up to the attack at Frog Lake, Alberta in 1885.

Mistahimaskwa 1825-1888

Mistahimaskwa's Story
Before going out on a hunt Mistahimaskwa would go with his spiritual leaders to make an offering at the Iron Stone. At this sacred monument he would pray for a successful hunt, a hunt that would give life to his people. The Iron Stone was a protector of the buffalo and a guardian of the Cree because as long as there were buffalo there would be food, clothing and shelter for people. But in 1866 the Iron Stone was taken away. Christian missionaries, who had no respect for Cree spiritual practices, loaded the Iron Stone on a cart and moved it 160 kilometres north to Victoria mission. When Mistahimaskwa saw that the stone was taken away he was angry. He heeded the words of his Holy Men who recognized the removal of the stone as a sign of impending danger. Without the protection of the stone the Holy Men warned that disease, starvation and war would overtake the people. The prophecy of the Holy Men came true. Each year more and more white people came to Cree territory and their presence became a threat to the lifeways of the Cree Nation.

Cree Camp 1871

The Cree were a hunting people and their lives were tied to the buffalo. The buffalo was a gift from Manitou to the Cree and they praised its spirit. They made use of every part of the buffalo: the hides became their clothing, the stomachs were used as bags, the bones and horns were made into tools and the meat fed the people. When he was a young chief Mistahimaskwa had many lodges and people looked to him for leadership. He spoke with Head Chief Wihaskokiseyin about the prophecy and the declining buffalo herds. They talked about the white hunters with their automatic rifles who killed hundreds of buffalo, taking only the hides and leaving the carcasses to rot. Without the buffalo the Cree could not survive but for many of the white hunters killing was nothing more than a sport.

Four years after the Iron Stone was taken smallpox erupted in the Cree camps and spread like a prairie fire across the plains. Hundreds of their people died and those that survived were too weak to hunt. Mistahimaskwa had been afflicted with smallpox when he was a child and this time he did not get sick but many people in his band died. When the worst was over he sent scouts out in search of buffalo. When the scouts returned they described what they had witnessed. "Our land was desolate, entire families have been eliminated. We saw abandoned camps where the only signs of life were the wolves gnawing on the corpses of men, women and children." Mistahimaskwa listened in horror to the stories of his scouts and remembered the prophecy that echoed in their words.

When fall came Mistahimaskwa thought the worst was over but because there had been so little hunting through the summer he could not move his band north to the protection of the woods. They was forced to spend the winter on the prairies in search of food. That winter the herds did not come north and Mistahimaskwa had to take his band far to the south. There were a few scattered herds around the Hand Hills and a large gathering of Cree had assembled there. Many council fires were held and the Cree bands talked

about their conditions. "We heard reports that the Hudson Bay Company had sold Cree land to the Canadian government and there was a lot of talk about what we would do." Mistahimaskwa met with Chiefs Little Pine, Wihaskokiseyin and Kehiwin. "We did not know who or what the Canadian government was but they must have heard about our meetings. They sent Missionary John McDougall with a message of friendship and goodwill." Wihaskokiseyin, Head Chief of the Cree Nation expressed their response saying: "We heard our lands were sold and we did not like it, we don't want to sell our lands; it is our property and no one has the right to sell them." Wihaskokiseyin asked McDougall to tell the Canadians to come and meet with the Cree. The Canadians refused and Cree concern turned to anger. They were being ignored and their land was stolen from them.

In the fall of 1872 the buffalo disappeared and the Cree were once again forced to spend the winter on the plains enduring harsh conditions with insufficient food to sustain the people. Some members of Mistahimaskwa's band left in search of buffalo, hoping to kill a stray. Others returned to hunt and fish in the lakes north of the North Saskatchewan River. Mistahimaskwa moved the remaining members of his band into the South Saskatchewan River Valley where they found some protection from the winter and a few buffalo. That year there was a frantic search for food. "I can still see the thin wasted bodies of my people who were forced to eat their horses and dogs. There were times when we were so hungry we tore our tipis and boiled the bits of hide to make a watery soup. I thought again about the prophecy of our Holy Men. We had known starvation before the white people came to our territory but the buffalo had never before been so scarce."

The Cree had lived side by side with the missionaries and the Hudson Bay Company men for many years. But this thing called the Canadian government was a mystery to them. Some of the younger Cree warriors wanted to fight. Many times Mistahimaskwa had to speak to his warriors. "I told them that we would not win against the white soldiers with their automatic weapons and that fighting with the newcomers would not solve our problems. Each year more settlers were moving west, occupying our lands, killing our game and burning the woods and prairies. We needed an agreement with the newcomers that would protect our land and the remaining herds of buffalo for our people." Again, George McDougall was sent to speak with the Cree and this time he had gifts to distribute. He told Mistahimaskwa that the government would meet with the Cree the following summer and in the meantime they wanted the Cree to accept gifts of food, blankets and ammunition. Mistahimaskwa's people were starving but he told McDougall, "We want none of the government's presents! When we set a fox trap we scatter pieces of meat all around but when the fox gets into the trap we knock him on the head. We want no baits! Let your Chiefs come like men and talk to us." It was not easy for Mistahimaskwa to walk away from food when his people were starving but he would not be bought off with a few pounds of meat when his land and freedom were at stake.

The following year agents representing the Canadian government came to meet with the Cree. But the agents had no intention of listening to their demands. They came with promises of food and medicine to those of who would sign away their land and agree to live on what they called an Indian Reserve. The agents said that the buffalo were disappearing and that Indians would have to give up hunting and make the change to an agricultural way of life. Cree Head Chief Wihaskokiseyin had come under the influence of the missionaries and he agreed to sign a treaty, but Chief Poundmaker was unmoved by the offers. He spoke for those who would not sign. He told the government agents "The government mentions how much land is to be given to us. He says 640 acres, one square mile for each family, he will give us. This is our land! It isn't a piece of pemmican to be cut off and given in little pieces back to us. It is ours and we will take what we want." Conditions were desperate but Mistahimaskwa was not prepared to accept the government's deal. He wanted a treaty that would protect the land and the remaining buffalo for the Cree. The treaty that the Canadians were offering was no more than a rope around their necks. It would be the end of their freedom and turn the Cree into prisoners in their own land.

Mistahimaskwa's band was growing. He had 65 lodges, more than 500 men, women and children. Wihaskokiseyin was still considered the Head Chief and even though he had a larger following, Mistahimaskwa deferred to the elder. They were close friends and often consulted one another. Wihaskokiseyin would say that Mistahimaskwa was a dynamic and effective leader and that his band was destined to do great things. But the white newcomers had a different impression of him. The missionaries saw Mistahimaskwa as a pagan because he would not convert to Christianity. Government officials saw him as a troublemaker because he would not accept their gifts and sign a treaty. They were angry when he spoke to the Cree and warned them not to sign their treaties but Mistahimaskwa was not afraid to voice his opposition to the Canadian treaty system. The treaties did not provide a fair exchange for surrendering their land and freedom. They had no guarantees that they would escape starvation if they could not adjust to farming. Mistahimaskwa wanted something better. The buffalo were almost gone and he knew that eventually he would have to deal with the Canadians but as long as there were buffalo on the plains Mistahimaskwa would not sign away their freedom. At the summer gathering Mistahimaskwa told the government agents that he would wait four years and during that time, "I would

Treaty Negotiations - 1876

watch to see whether the government would faithfully carry out its promises to the Indians who had signed their treaties".

Mistahimaskwa met with the leaders in his band and told them that they would travel south in search of the remaining herds. They would wait four years and watch what happened with those bands that had signed treaties. Mistahimaskwa was not willing to give up their land until he had assurances that their conditions would improve. Again he had to argue for peace. His war chief, Wandering Spirit, was anxious to fight. Mistahimaskwa had gained the reputation as a leader who would not give in to the whites and had attracted many young rebels to his band. His son Imasees was one of the most rebellious. He, like Wandering Spirit, was anxious to show the Canadians that the Cree would not give up easily. Mistahimaskwa managed to persuade his followers to hold back. He told them about a battle in his younger days when the Cree were at war with their traditional enemies the Blackfoot and the Peigans. Their enemies had been armed with automatic rifles given to them by white traders. And again the prophecy came back to him. War was the third element of the prophecy. It had been a warning. They had suffered great losses in their last battle with the Blackfoot and he did not want to go up against the rifles of the Canadians. His warriors listened and they moved south.

Four years later when the last of the buffalo were gone, pressure to sign a treaty was great. The people in Mistahimaskwa's band were starving and many families had left his band and signed a treaty under other chiefs. Mistahimaskwa travelled north to see for himself what the conditions were like for the Treaty Indians and what he saw sickened him. "Two thousand Treaty Indians were camped near Cypress Lake, their skin teepees rotting and falling apart; families were living in makeshift shelters of cotton cloth and tree branches. Many people were emaciated and in rags, their moccasins worn out, their horses sold and even their dogs gone to make stew." The transition from hunting to farming was not made easily and the Canadian government had not kept its promises. As chief, he had to make a decision. Those bands that had signed a treaty received some support but because he had refused to sign his band received nothing. Tensions were rising and still the consequences of signing weighed heavily. Mistahimaskwa was haunted by the words of the prophecy. He had taken the warning seriously and worked to prevent the loss of freedom but his people were dying and his first priority was to them. Mistahimaskwa signed his adhesion to Treaty Six on December 8, 1882.

Signing the treaty increased the tension within his band. Many of his warriors were angry. They were angry at him for not signing earlier and for not arranging a better deal. They wanted to know why they were still starving. Again many of his young followers wanted to fight. Mistahimaskwa knew that they could never win a war against the newcomers and believed that the only way to pressure the Canadians into honouring their promises was to unite. Mistahimaskwa believed it would take the power of a united Aboriginal assembly to force the Canadians to keep their promises. He travelled to other reserves, met with their chiefs and organized a Grand Council at Poundmaker's reserve near Battleford. During this council, the leaders of twelve bands sent a message to the Canadian Government protesting its failure to keep its promises. But the government continued to ignore them. The Cree had agreed to sign treaties and live on the reserves but they were not willing to sit by and watch their people die from starvation. After the failure of the gathering at Battleford many of Mistahimaskwa's followers dispersed. He was left with a hostile core of young warriors and their resentment smoldered through the winter.

In the spring of 1885, his people rebelled. Mistahimaskwa was away from the reserve on a hunting trip and returned late on April 1, 1885. Word had arrived only that day that Louis Riel and the Métis had been successful in a battle at Duck Lake.

Misthimaskwa in prison - 1886

Mistahimaskwa knew nothing about the attack until after the first shots were fired at Frog Lake and although he counseled for peace his war chief was in command and he was unable to stop his warriors.

After his trial Mistahimaskwa said "Even after the Iron Stone was taken I always hoped that we could live in peace. We were not put here by the Great Spirit to shed each other's blood nor were we meant to control each other's lives. I believed that one day Canadians would recognize our rights to the land and respect our traditional lifeways. Did my faith in the newcomers cost me the trust of my people?"

A (RE)TELLING BY MICHAEL DION AND SUSAN DION

Primary Resources Used For This (Re)telling Include:

Cameron, William Bleasdell. (1926). The War Trail of Big Bear. Toronto: Ryerson.

Dempsey, Hugh (1984). Big Bear The End Of Freedom. Lincoln: University of Nebraska Press.

Fraser, William, Bernard. (1966). "Big Bear, Indian Patriot", Alberta Historical Review. Spring 1966. Calgary: Historical Society of Alberta.

Appendix B
Initial Teacher Interview Questions

1. Why do you think it is important for your students to learn about Aboriginal people?

2. How is what you teach determined by school/ministry guidelines or available resources?

3. What are your concerns with how you teach about Aboriginal people?

4. What do you want to do differently?

5. What has contributed to your desire to teach differently?

Appendix C
Planning-Session Agendas and Discussion Questions

Planning Session One
September 1, 1998

Questions for consideration:
1. Which of the stories were of most interest to you and which the least?
2. What specifically engaged you about the stories?
3. What would you say you learned from your engagement with the stories?
4. In what way would you say the stories are difficult?
5. Did the stories initiate questions for you? If so what kinds of questions?
   I'm thinking here about questions at two levels
      a. Information that you require to understand the story clearly.
      b. Questions like "Why did the subject do what he or she did?"
6. What surprised or disturbed about the stories?
7. Did you talk about the stories to others? Who did you talk with? What did you tell them about the stories?

Planning Session Two
October 1, 1998

Agenda
1. Petition
2. Distribute transcripts of session one
3. Request from the transcriber to speak up
4. Board approval
5. Focused discussion

6. Comments on formatting
7. Next meeting
8. Other?

Questions for consideration:
1. How do you feel about working with these stories? Do you have any concerns?
2. What do you want students to learn from working with the stories?
3. Is there additional information that you need before proceeding?
4. What are your thoughts about teaching the stories?
   a. How will they be introduced?
   b. How will students encounter the stories?
      Will you read them aloud, students read alone, in a small group?
      What kind of work will you ask students to do?

Planning Session Three
October 21, 1998

Agenda
1. The issue of "not wanting to offend"
2. Your "lesson plans"
3. Focused discussion
3. Letters of permission
4. Scheduling, logistics of taping, etc.
5. Visiting each others' classrooms
6. Other?

Planning Session Four
February 18, 1999

Agenda
1. Presentations from teachers
   a. Chloe
   b. Diane
   c. Jenna

Questions for consideration:
1. What do you think you and your students learned from working with these stories?

2. Did anything surprise you about your work with the stories?
3. Was there anything hard about your work with the stories?
4. What did you tell other teachers/parents/administrators about the work you were doing with the stories?
5. Pseudonyms
6. Concluding remarks

Notes

Chapter 1: Historical Amnesia and the Discourse of the Romantic, Mythical Other

1 Various proper names have been applied to the original people of Turtle Island (the Americas), some of which are considered incorrect or demeaning. If possible, I use the names of individual nations. The terms "Aboriginal" and "First Nations" describe the people. "Indian" is used in its legally defined sense or when referencing another author's work. "Native" is used when referring to another author's work.

2 Premier Harris, during an interview on CBC news the day following the shooting. At the time, I was struck by the premier's response. Calls for a provincial inquiry were ignored by successive Conservative governments. Shortly after taking office, Premier Dalton McGuinty called for an inquiry that began in August 2004. For a detailed discussion of the events at Ipperwash, see Peter Edwards (2001).

3 The prevailing classroom discourse, including recent changes introduced as a result of multicultural and anti-racism education, will be reviewed in Chapter 3.

4 This discourse has also portrayed Aboriginal people as "savage" Others. In recent years, this image has declined but has not been completely eliminated. Although attempts have been made to alter this representation, it is difficult to say what kind of impact this is having on non-Aboriginal peoples' understandings and perceptions of Aboriginal people, history, and culture. In speaking with students, I have not observed significant changes in how Aboriginal people are positioned by non-Aboriginal people.

5 I insert parentheses in "(re)member" as a way of acknowledging a particular kind of remembering. This practice moves against the grain of dominant stories of remembrance. As Gail Guthrie Valaskakis (1993, 164) puts it, "It is the collective memory about which Homi Bhabha writes: 'Remembering is never a quiet act of introspection. It is a painful remembering, a putting together of the dismembered past to make sense of the trauma of the present.'" I distinguish between Aboriginal people and Canadians not because I do not consider the former to be Canadians but to draw attention to the fact that the two groups occupy different positions in Canada.

6 I recognize that not all Canadians occupy the same subject position. In using the term "Canadian," I refer to the dominant sense of national identity that has real implications for how people understand themselves and their relations with "Others."

7 The *People of Native Ancestry* documents were produced by the Ontario Ministry of Education in 1975 and 1977.

8 Here, the term "subject material" includes content addressing Aboriginal people, culture, history, and issues.
9 For an in-depth review of events at Kanesatake, see Geoffrey York and Loreen Pindera (1992).
10 His reading comprehension book was Donald Anderson, Clarence Stone, and Anne Eliasberg (1978).
11 Sacagawea was the young Shoshone woman who accompanied Lewis and Clark on their expedition from St. Louis, Missouri, to the Pacific Ocean and back. Her role on the expedition has been both idealized and disregarded. Although she is considered an "American heroine," we know very little about her. The travel journals of Lewis and Clark portray Sacagawea as resourceful and strong, an excellent guide with diplomatic skill.
12 For a detailed description of the representation of Aboriginal people in the school curriculum, see Susan Dion (2000).
13 Employing the term "our ancestors" references a concept familiar to many Aboriginal peoples of the Americas. It reminds us of the extended relationship we share specifically with all Aboriginal peoples and more generally with all living beings. It is a way of acknowledging the responsibilities we have to live our lives in a harmonious and moral manner.
14 I insert parentheses in "(re)tellings" to signify that our process represents more than simply repeating the story of someone's life.

Chapter 2: Listen Again and I'll Re(tell) You a Story

1 Here, "alter," as opposed to "Other," signals incommensurability. By contrast, "Other" is based on comparisons involving deviation from a certain normative standard.
2 Ingeborg Marshall (1996) served as the primary source for the following (re)telling.
3 We incorporated actual speeches from various Aboriginal people into this story, which are enclosed in quotation marks. The following texts served as primary sources for this (re)telling: William Bleasdell Cameron (1926); Hugh Dempsey (1984); William Bernard Fraser (1966); and J.R. Miller (1996).
4 See Appendix A for the stories as they were formatted for classroom use.

Chapter 3: Listening – But What Is Being Heard?

1 Piper (1993, 25) differentiates between cognitive discrimination and political discrimination. She defines the former as "a manifest capacity to distinguish veridically between one property and another, and to respond appropriately to each." Political discrimination is "a manifest attitude in which a particular property of a person which is irrelevant to judgments of that person's intrinsic value or competence, for example his race, gender, class, sexual orientation, or religious or ethnic affiliation, is seen as a source of disvalue or incompetence; in general, as a source of inferiority."
2 This approach fails to acknowledge the existence of Aboriginal governance prior to contact.
3 For an in-depth review of various approaches to curriculum studies, see Elliot W. Eisner (1979) or Henry A. Giroux, Anthony N. Penna, and William Pinar (1981).
4 See Chapter 2 of Jo-anne Dillabough (1996) for a comprehensive review of the place of cultural representation in the politics of schooling literature.
5 The *People of Native Ancestry* resource guide for the primary and junior Divisions was published in 1975. The *People of Native Ancestry* resource guide for the intermediate division was published in 1977.
6 For an examination of the challenges of engaging student teacher candidates in

discussions about racism and its implications for teaching and learning, see, for example, C. Schick and V. St. Denis (2005).
7 These comments were made during formal workshops I conducted with teachers as part of a research study and during more informal conversations with colleagues.
8 Scully et al. (1992) is one example of a textbook with expanded chapters.
9 Relevant studies include Himmani Bannerji (2000); Deborah Britzman et al. (1993); Agnes Calliste and George J. Sefa Dei (2000); George J. Sefa Dei and Agnes Calliste (2000); Eva Mackey (2002); and Sherene Razack (1998).

Chapter 4: The Braiding Histories Project
1 The names of the teachers, their students, schools, and communities are pseudonyms.
2 These presentations were made in a series of pre-service and graduate classes in the Faculty of Education at York University.
3 Jenna is referring to gas sniffing by Aboriginal youth in northern communities, including Davis Inlet. The desperate conditions confronting Aboriginal youth had received intense media scrutiny before the study began.
4 Her concern predated her participation in the Braiding Histories Project but intensified as a result of teaching the stories.

Chapter 5: "Her Solitary Place"
1 The intermediate students in these classes were young adolescents. Early adolescence is a period of change in which students develop the ability to reason regarding abstract concepts, to derive conclusions from hypothetical premises, to process information faster, to use processing resources more efficiently, and to better understand their own memory processes. Their improved language skills and increased ability to recognize multiple perspectives help them to explore complex issues through dialogue with their teachers and peers. Socially, adolescents search for personal identity and a sense of belonging. They are immersed in developing a sense of themselves as independent beings, questioning belief systems, and exploring personal philosophy and moral standards. Peer group relationships are increasingly important to them. They enjoy discussions of controversial topics and moral issues. Participation in such discussions seems to advance their moral reasoning and increased perspective taking.
2 The relation between texts and students as readers is highly mediated by, among other things, the context of schooling, classroom relations, curriculum expectations, and the work of teachers.
3 Jenna's approach to teaching the stories showed that she shared Diane's theory of narrative understanding and pedagogy. Jenna relied most heavily on empathetic understanding in her discussion of Audrey's story. Her treatment of it will be considered in Chapter 6.
4 Students wrote their initial responses to the story on 24 November; the poems date from 1 December.

Chapter 6: "We Wanted to Hear Your Stories"
1 Diane devoted more time to the Shanawdithit narrative than to Audrey's. Thus, her work is examined more fully in Chapter 5. Because Jenna concentrated on Audrey's story rather than Shanawdithit's, her work figures more prominently in this chapter.
2 Diane did not tape-record her Mistahimaskwa lessons or assign written follow-up work regarding the story.
3 The letters were written in January 1999.
4 The poems were written in November 1998.

Chapter 7: Disrupting Moulded Images

1 The majority of students who take this course are practising teachers.

2 See References for specific works by these artists.

3 In the year following their participation in the class and well after I had submitted their grades, I asked students for permission to use their work. I provided them with a copy of what I had written regarding it and asked for feedback. None requested changes.

4 Student names are pseudonyms.

5 Course texts addressing questions of presence and erasure include Thomas King (2003), Jonathan Bordo (1993), and Lenore Keeshig-Tobias (1992a).

6 I have no record of what occurred during classes and thus cannot comment specifically about what was said during them. Nonetheless, it is useful to think about how, in speaking of her collection of artifacts, Britt encountered a moment in which she saw herself differently.

References

Acoose, Janice. 1993. "Post Halfbreed: Indigenous Writers as Authors of Their Own Realities." In Jeannette Armstrong, ed., *Looking at the Words of Our People: First Nations Analysis of Literature,* 27-44. Penticton: Theytus Books.

Allen, Paula Gunn. 1986. *The Sacred Hoop: Recovering the Feminine in American Indian Traditions.* Boston: Beacon Press.

–. 1989. "Introduction." In Paula Gunn Allen, ed., *Spider Woman's Granddaughters: Traditional Tales and Contemporary Writing by Native American Women,* 1-25. New York: Fawcett Columbine.

Anderson, Donald, Clarence Stone, and Anne Eliasberg. 1978. *New Practice Readers.* 2nd ed. New York: McGraw-Hill.

Apple, Michael. 1979. *Ideology and Curriculum.* London: Routledge.

Archibald, Jo-ann. 1997. "Coyote Learns to Make a Storybasket: The Place of First Nations Stories in Education." PhD diss., Simon Fraser University, Vancouver, BC.

Baker, Marie Annharte. 1994. "Medicine Lines: The Doctoring of Story and Self." *Canadian Woman Studies* 14, 2: 114-18.

Bannerji, Himmani. 2000. *The Dark Side of the Nation: Essays on Multiculturalism, Nationalism and Gender.* Toronto: Canadian Scholars' Press.

Battiste, Marie. 1998. "Enabling the Autumn Seed: Toward a Decolonized Approach to Aboriginal Knowledge, Language, and Education." *Canadian Journal of Native Education* 22, 1: 16-27.

Benjamin, Walter. 1969. *Illuminations.* Trans. Harry Zohn; ed. Hannah Arendt. New York: Schocken Books. (Orig. pub. 1955.)

Berlak, Ann 2004. "Confrontation and Pedagogy: Cultural Secrets, Trauma, and Emotion in Antioppressive Pedagogies." In Megan Boler, ed., *Democratic Dialogue in Education: Troubling Speech, Disturbing Silence,* 123-44. New York: Peter Lang.

Blaeser, Kimberley 1999. "Writing Voices Speaking: Native Voices and an Oral Aesthetic." In Laura J. Murray and Keren Rice, eds., *Talking on the Page,* 53-68. Toronto: University of Toronto Press.

Boler, Megan. 1999. *Feeling Power: Emotions and Education.* New York: Routledge.

Bordo, Jonathan. 1993. "Jack Pine – Wilderness Sublime or the Erasure of the Aboriginal Presence from the Landscape." *Journal of Canadian Studies* 27, 4: 98-128.

Brant, Beth. 1990. "Turtle Gal." In Thomas King, ed., *All My Relations,* 107-22. Toronto: McClelland and Stewart.

–. 1994. *Writing as Witness: Essay and Talk.* Toronto: Women's Press.

Britzman, Deborah. 1998. *Lost Subjects, Contested Objects.* Albany: State University of New York Press.

Britzman, Deborah, Kelvin Santiago-Válles, Gladys Jiménez-Múñoz, and Laura M.

Lamash. 1993. "Slips that Show and Tell: Fashioning Multiculture as a Problem of Representation." In Cameron McCarthy and Warren Crichlow, eds., *Race, Identity and Representation in Education,* 188-200. New York: Routledge.

Brownlie, Robin, and Mary-Ellen Kelm. 1996. "Desperately Seeking Absolution: Native Agency as Colonialist Alibi?" In Ken Coates and Robin Fisher, eds., *Out of the Background,* 2nd ed., 210-22. Toronto: Copp Clark.

Cajete, Gregory, ed. 1999. *A People's Ecology: Explorations in Sustainable Living.* Santa Fe, NM: Clear Light.

Calliste, Agnes, and George J. Sefa Dei, eds. 2000. *Anti-racist Feminism: Critical Race and Gender Studies.* Halifax: Fernwood.

Cameron, William Bleasdell. 1926. *The War Trial of Big Bear.* Toronto: Ryerson.

Canada. Royal Commission on Aboriginal Peoples. 1996. *Report of the Royal Commission on Aboriginal Peoples.* Vol. 1, *Looking Forward, Looking Back.* Ottawa: Canada Communication Group.

Chambers, Iain. 1996. "Signs of Silence, Lines of Listening." In Iain Chambers and Lidia Curti, eds., *The Post-colonial Question,* 47-62. New York: Routledge.

Cherryholmes, Cleo. 1988. *Power and Criticism: Poststructural Investigations in Education.* New York: Teachers College.

Clark, Janet. 1992. *Who Discovered the Americas: Recent Work by Jane Ash Poitras.* Thunder Bay, ON: Thunder Bay Art Gallery.

Clark, Penney, and Roberta McCay. 1992. *Canada Revisited.* Edmonton: Arnold.

Clifford, James. 1986. "Introduction: Partial Truths." In James Clifford and George E. Marcus, eds., *Writing Culture: The Poetics and Politics of Ethnography,* 1-26. Berkeley: University of California Press.

Context 2 Anthology. 1982. Scarborough, ON: Nelson Canada.

Couser, G. Thomas. 1996. "Oppression and Repression: Personal and Collective Memory in Paule Marshall's *Praisesong for the Widow* and Leslie Marmon Silko's *Ceremony.*" In Amritjit Singh, Joseph T. Skerrett Jr., and Robert E. Hogan, eds., *Memory and Cultural Politics,* 106-20. Boston: Northeastern University Press.

Cruikshank, Julie. 1990. *Life Lived Like a Story.* Vancouver: UBC Press.

Davies, Bronwyn. 1993. *Shards of Glass: Children Reading and Writing beyond Gendered Identities.* Cresskill, NJ: Hampton Press.

Dei, George. 1996. *Anti-racism Education: Theory and Practice.* Halifax: Fernwood.

Dei, George J. Sefa, and Agnes Calliste, eds. 2000. *Power, Knowledge and Anti-racism Education: A Critical Reader.* Halifax: Fernwood.

Deloria, Vine, Jr. 1994. *God Is Red: A Native View of Religion.* 2nd ed. Golden: Fulcrum.

Dempsey, Hugh. 1984. *Big Bear: The End of Freedom.* Lincoln: University of Nebraska Press.

Dillabough, Jo-anne. 1996. *The Deconstruction and "Re-representation" of First Nations People in Social Studies Education: The Dialectic of "Voice" as an Epistemological Tool for Change.* Montreal: McGill University.

Dion, Susan. 2000. "Molded Images: First Nations People, Representation, and the Ontario School Curriculum." In Tara Goldstein and David Selby, eds., *Weaving Connections: Education for Peace, Social and Environmental Justice,* 342-64. Toronto: Sumach Press.

Dion, Susan, and Michael Dion. 2004. "The Braiding Histories Stories." *Journal of the Canadian Association for Curriculum Studies* 2, 1: 77-100.

Dyck, Noel. 1991. *What Is the Indian Problem?* St. John's: Institute of Social and Economic Research, Memorial University.

Edwards, Peter. 2001. *One Dead Indian.* Toronto: Stoddart.

Eisner, Elliot W. 1979. *The Educational Imagination on the Design and Evaluation of School Programs.* New York: Macmillan.

Erasmus, Georges. 1996. *Address for the Launch of the Report of the Royal Commission on Aboriginal Peoples.* Indian and Northern Affairs Canada. http://www.ainc-inac.gc.ca/ch/rcap/spch_e.html.

Evans, Ronald. 1989. "Teacher Conceptions of History." *Theory and Research in Social Education* 18, 3: 210-40.

Felman, Shoshana. 1982. "Psychoanalysis and Education: Teaching Terminable and Interminable." *Yale French Studies* 63: 21-44.

–. 1992. "Education and Crisis, or the Vicissitudes of Teaching." In *Testimony: Crises of Witnessing in Literature, Psychoanalysis, and History,* by Shoshana Felman and Dori Laub, 1-56. New York and London: Routledge.

Felman, Shoshana, and Dori Laub. 1992. *Testimony: Crises of Witnessing in Literature, Psychoanalysis, and History.* New York and London: Routledge.

Francis, Daniel. 1992. *The Imaginary Indian.* Vancouver: Arsenal Pulp Press.

Fraser, William Bernard. 1966. "Big Bear, Indian Patriot." *Alberta Historical Review* 14: 1-13.

Friedlander, Saul. 1992. "Trauma, Transference and Working through in the Writing of the History of the Shoah." *History and Memory* 4, 1: 39-59.

Geertz, Clifford. 1973. *The Interpretation of Cultures.* New York: Basic Books.

Giroux, Henry. 1992. *Border Crossings: Cultural Workers and the Politics of Education.* London: Routledge, Chapman and Hall.

Giroux, Henry A., Anthony N. Penna, and William Pinar, eds. 1981. *Curriculum and Instruction: Alternatives in Education.* Berkeley, CA: McCutchan.

Godard, Barbara. 1990. "The Politics of Representation: Some Native Canadian Women Writers." In W.H. New, ed., *Native Writers and Canadian Writing,* 183-225. Vancouver: UBC Press.

Grant, Agnes. 1990. "Contemporary Native Women's Voices in Literature." In W.H. New, ed., *Native Writers and Canadian Writing,* 124-32. Vancouver: UBC Press.

Haig-Brown, Celia. 1997a. "Gender Equity, Policy and Praxis." In L. Roman and L. Eyre, eds., *Dangerous Territories: Struggles for Difference and Equality in Education,* 233-54. New York: Routledge.

–. 1997b. "Healing a Fractured Circle." In Celia Haig-Brown, Kathy Hodgson-Smith, Robert Regnier, and Jo-ann Archibald, eds., *Making the Spirit Dance Within: Joe Duquette High School and an Aboriginal Community,* 15-32. Toronto: James Lorimer and Sons.

Hall, Stuart. 1989. "Ethnicity: Identity and Difference." *Radical America* 23, 4: 9-21.

Jordan, June. 1985. *On Call: Political Essays.* Boston: South End Press.

Josephy, J.R., and M. Alvin. 1994. *500 Nations.* New York: Alfred A. Knopf.

Karumanchery, Leeno. 2005. "Implications for Anti-racist Education: A Pedagogical Needs Assessment." In Leeno Karumanchery, ed., *Engaging Equity,* 179-99. Calgary: Detselig.

Keeshig-Tobias, Lenore. 1992a. "After Oka – How Has Canada Changed?" In D.D. Moses and T. Goldie, eds., *An Anthology of Native Canadian Literature in English,* 234-35. Toronto: Oxford University Press.

–. 1992b. "Stories Are Not Just Entertainment." In B. Slapin and D. Seale, eds., *Through Indian Eyes,* 98-101. Gabriola Island, BC: New Society.

Kincheloe, Joe. 1997. "Introduction." In I. Goodson, *The Changing Curriculum: Studies in Social Construction,* ix-xi. New York: Peter Lang.

King, Thomas 2003. *The Truth about Stories: A Native Narrative.* Toronto: House of Anansi Press.

Kirkness, Verna, and Sheena Bowman. 1992. *First Nations and Schools: Triumphs and Struggles.* Toronto: Canadian Education Association.

LaForme, Harry S. 1997. "Foreword." In Stephen B. Smart and Michael Coyle, eds., *Aboriginal Issues Today: A Legal and Business Guide,* vii-xiv. North Vancouver: Self-Counsel Press.

Laub, Dori. 1992a. "Bearing Witness, or the Vicissitudes of Listening." In *Testimony: Crises of Witnessing in Literature, Psychoanalysis, and History*, by Shoshana Felman and Dori Laub, 57-74. New York and London: Routledge.

–. 1992b. "An Event without a Witness: Truth, Testimony and Survival." In *Testimony: Crises of Witnessing in Literature, Psychoanalysis, and History*, by Shoshana Felman and Dori Laub, 75-92. New York and London: Routledge.

Lusted, David. 1986. "Why Pedagogy?" *Screen* 27, 5: 2-14.

Mackey, Eva. 2002. *The House of Difference: Cultural Politics and National Identity in Canada*. Toronto: University of Toronto Press.

Marshall, Ingeborg. 1996. *A History and Ethnography of the Beothuk*. Montreal and Kingston: McGill-Queen's University Press.

McCarthy, Cameron. 1993. "After the Canon: Knowledge and Ideological Representation in the Multicultural Discourse on Curriculum Reform." In Cameron McCarthy and Warren Crichlow, eds., *Race, Identity and Representation in Education*, 289-305. New York: Routledge.

McMaster, Gerald. 1991. "Hunter/Hunted." In A. Ryan, ed., *The Cowboy/Indian Show*, 36-37. Kleinburg, ON: McMichael Canadian Art Collection.

McMaster, Gerald, and Lee-Ann Martin. 1992. *Indigena*. Toronto: Douglas and McIntyre.

Miller, J.R. 1996. *Big Bear (Mistahimusqua)*. Toronto: ECW Press.

Moses, Daniel David. 1992. "King of the Raft." In D.D. Moses and T. Goldie, eds., *An Anthology of Canadian Native Literature in English*, 300-302. Toronto: Oxford University Press.

National Indian Brotherhood. 1972. *Indian Control of Indian Education*. Policy Paper. Ottawa: National Indian Brotherhood.

Neel, David. 1992. *Our Chiefs and Elders: Words and Photographs of Native Leaders*. Vancouver: UBC Press.

Nussbaum, Martha C. 1997. *Cultivating Humanity: A Classical Defence of Reform in Liberal Education*. Cambridge, MA: Harvard University Press.

OME (Ontario Ministry of Education). 1975a. *Multiculturalism in Action*. Toronto: Ontario Ministry of Education.

–. 1975b. *People of Native Ancestry: A Resource Guide for the Primary and Junior Divisions*. Toronto: Ontario Ministry of Education.

–. 1977. *People of Native Ancestry: A Resource Guide for the Intermediate Division*. Toronto: Ontario Ministry of Education.

–. 1991. *Curriculum Guideline: Native Studies Intermediate Division*. Toronto: Ontario Ministry of Education.

–. 1993. *Antiracism and Ethnocultural Equity in School Boards*. Toronto: Ontario Ministry of Education.

Peshkin, Alan. 1988. "In Search of Subjectivity: One's Own." *Educational Researcher* 14, 198: 17-22.

Pinar, William, ed. 1975. *Curriculum Theorizing: The Reconceptualists*. Berkeley, CA: McCutchan.

–. 1993. "Notes on Understanding Curriculum as a Racial Text." In Cameron McCarthy and Warren Crichlow, eds., *Race, Identity and Representation in Education*, 60-70. New York: Routledge.

Piper, Adrian M.S. 1993. "Two Kinds of Discrimination." *Yale Journal of Criticism* 6: 25-74.

Popkewitz, Thomas S. 1998. *Struggling for the Soul: The Politics of Schooling and the Construction of the Teacher*. New York: Teachers College Press.

Razack, Sherene. 1998. *Looking White People in the Eye: Gender, Race and Culture in Courtrooms and Classrooms*. Toronto: University of Toronto Press.

Ross, Rupert. 1992. *Dancing with a Ghost: Exploring Indian Reality*. Markham, ON: Octopus.

Said, Edward. 1994. *Culture and Imperialism*. New York: Vintage Books.

Sarris, Greg. 1993. *Keeping Slug Woman Alive: A Holistic Approach to American Indian Texts*. Berkeley: University of California Press.

Schick, Carol Ann. 1998. "By Virtue of Being White: Racialized Identity Formation and the Implications for Anti-racist Pedagogy." PhD diss., Ontario Institute for Studies in Education, University of Toronto.

Schick, Carol Ann, and Verna St. Denis. 2005. "Troubling National Discourses in Anti-racist Curricular Planning." *Canadian Journal of Education* 28, 3: 295-317.

Scully, Angus, John Bebbington, Rosemary Evans, and Carol Wilson. 1992. *Canada through Time: Book One*. Scarborough: Prentice Hall.

Seixas, Peter. 1996. "Conceptualizing the Growth of Historical Understanding." In David R. Olson and Nancy Torrance, eds., *The Handbook of Education and Human Development*, 765-83. Oxford: Blackwell.

Semali, Ladislaus M., and Joe L. Kincheloe, eds. 1999. *What Is Indigenous Knowledge? Voices from the Academy*. New York: Falmer Press.

Simon, Roger I. 1992. *Teaching against the Grain*. Toronto: OISE Press.

–. 1993. "Forms of Insurgency in the Production of Popular Memories: The Columbus Quincentenary and the Pedagogy of Counter-Commemoration." *Cultural Studies* 7, 1: 73-88.

Simon, Roger I., Claudia Eppert, Mark Clamen, and Laura Beres. 2000. "Witness as Study: The Difficult Inheritance of Testimony." *Review of Education Pedagogy and Cultural Studies* 22, 4: 285-322.

Simon, Roger I., and Donald Dippo. 1986. "On Critical Ethnographic Work." *Anthropology and Education Quarterly* 17: 195-202.

Simon, Roger I., Sharon Rosenberg, and Claudia Eppert. 2000. "Between Hope and Despair: The Pedagogical Encounter of Historical Remembrance." In Roger I. Simon, Sharon Rosenberg, and Claudia Eppert, eds., *Between Hope and Despair*, 1-8. Lanham, MD: Rowman and Littlefield.

Singh, Amritjit, Joseph T. Skerrett Jr., and Robert E. Hogan. 1996. "Introduction." In Amritjit Singh, Joseph T. Skerrett Jr., and Robert E. Hogan, eds., *Memory and Cultural Politics*, 3-18. Boston: Northeastern University Press.

Smart, Stephen B., and Michael Coyle. 1997. "Preface." In Stephen B. Smart and Michael Coyle, eds., *Aboriginal Issues Today: A Legal and Business Guide*, xv-xvi. North Vancouver: Self-Counsel Press.

Smith, Linda Tuhiwai. 1999. *Decolonizing Methodologies: Research and Indigenous Peoples*. New York: St. Martin's Press.

Spivak, Gayatri. 1993. *Outside in the Teaching Machine*. New York: Routledge.

Thomas, Barbara. 1984. "Principles of Anti-racist Education." *Currents* 2, 3: 20-24.

Valaskakis, Gail Guthrie. 1988. "The Chippewa and the Other: Living the Heritage of Lac Du Flambeau." *Cultural Studies* 2, 3: 267-93.

–. 1993. "Postcards of My Past: The Indian as Artefact." In Valda Blundell, John Shepherd, and Ian Taylor, eds., *Relocating Cultural Studies: Developments in Theory and Research*, 155-70. London: Routledge.

Weedon, Chris. 1997. *Feminist Practice and Poststructuralist Theory*. 2nd ed. Oxford: Blackwell.

York, Geoffrey, and Loreen Pindera. 1992. *People of the Pines*. Toronto: Little Brown.

Index

Aboriginal–non-Aboriginal relations, 177-90; collapsing differences, 188-90; cultural artifacts, 182-83; dominant understanding of, 168-69, 209n4; historical amnesia, 5-8, 51, 55, 56-57, 67, 153; implication and responsibility, 186-88; learning from artists, 181-82; missed opportunities, 131, 155-56, 176; pedagogy of remembrance, 182-90; perfect stranger relationship, 178-81, 183; polarization, 9; positionality, 168-69, 179, 209nn4-6; remembrance and radical renewal, 180-83; school curriculum, 5-8, 65-66, 99-100; self-experience, 91-92, 97-99, 182-90; transforming of, 67-68, 113. *See also* post-contact history; racism

Aboriginal people: Aboriginal identity, 21, 24-25, 28-29, 51, 209n1; agency, 9, 13, 52, 109, 181; artists, 19, 48-49, 181-82, 188; conceptions of history, 14-17; cultural production, 20; dehumanization, 4, 6-8, 12, 56, 61, 184; heritage, 18; heroic contexts, 94, 125-26, 157, 174-75; as Other, 3-8, 12, 64-66, 71, 73, 78, 86, 209n4; perfect stranger relationship, 178-81; pre-contact history, 73, 210n2(ch3); "sacred red art path," 181-82; systemic erasure, 186-87, 189-90, 212n5; as victims, 127, 157, 166, 173-76. *See also* First Nations; Aboriginal–non-Aboriginal relations; land claims; stereotypes

Aboriginal rights, 168
Acoose, Janice, 47
adolescents, 211n1(ch5)
affirmation: collective, 14-17, 19-20; personal, 17-18, 19, 22, 83-84, 137-38, 167, 177, 187-88

African Americans, 69
agency: Aboriginal, 9, 13, 52, 109, 181; artists, 181-82, 188; historical, 157; teachers, 85, 178
Aldershot, 28
Alexander, Theresa, 10-12
Algonquin Park, 102
alienation, 69
Allen, Paula Gunn, 48, 50, 110, 181
alterity, 19, 20, 53-54, 210n1(ch2). *See also* the Other
Alvin, M., 48
ancestors, 6-7, 15, 20, 30, 210n13
Anderson, Donald, 210n10
Anglican church, 28
anti-racism discourse: *Antiracism and Ethnocultural Equity in School Boards*, 71; Braiding Histories project, 97-98, 162-63, 165, 167-69, 171; emphasis on, 71-73, 90, 97-98, 138, 140, 142, 183; missed opportunities, 131, 155-56, 176; Native Studies Guide, 71-73; *People of Native Ancestry* (PONA) guidelines, 68-71, 74-75, 209n7, 210n5; zero-tolerance policy, 72, 90. *See also* racism
Anyon, Jean, 70
apology, 171, 173
Apple, Michael, 69
approaches to teaching: conflict avoidance, 98-102; defining concepts/making assumptions, 151-53; engaging emotions, 170-71, 184-85; limitations to, 166-69, 174-76; nurturing empathy, 120-28, 160-69, 211n3(ch5); reasoning systems, 80-86; teacher ignorance, 102-4, 112-13, 119-20, 136; understanding of, 152-53; use of storytelling and narrative, 15-17, 110-14, 116, 120-24,

Printed and bound in Canada by Friesens

Set in Stone by Robert Kroeger, Kroeger Enterprises

Copyedited by Deborah Kerr

Proofread by Lesley Erickson

Indexed by Lillian Ashworth

FSC

Mixed Sources
Cert no. SW-COC-001271
© 1996 FSC

ENVIRONMENTAL BENEFITS STATEMENT

UBC Press saved the following resources by printing the pages of this book on chlorine free paper made with 100% post-consumer waste.

TREES	WATER	ENERGY	SOLID WASTE	GREENHOUSE GASES
9	3,281	6	421	791
FULLY GROWN	GALLONS	MILLION BTUs	POUNDS	POUNDS

Calculations based on research by Environmental Defense and the Paper Task Force.
Manufactured at Friesens Corporation